CAIRO PAPERS IN SOCIAL SCIENCE

Volume 24, Numbers 1/2, Spring/Summer 2001

THE NEW ARAB FAMILY

Edited by

Nicholas S. Hopkins

THE AMERICAN UNIVERSITY IN CAIRO PRESS

Cairo   New York

Copyright © 2003 by the American University in Cairo Press
113, Sharia Kasr el Aini, Cairo, Egypt
420 Fifth Avenue, New York, NY 10018
www.aucpress.com

All rights reserved. No part of this publication may be reproduced, stored in a retrieval system, or transmitted in any form or by any means, electronic, mechanical, photocopying, recording or otherwise, without prior written permission of the copyright owner.

Dar el Kutub No. 11671/02
ISBN 977 424 763 9

Printed in Egypt

CONTENTS

INTRODUCTION: THE NEW ARAB FAMILY
Nicholas S. Hopkins -- 1

FRAMEWORKS FOR STUDYING FAMILIES IN
THE 21st CENTURY
Carol B. Stack -- 5

NUPTIALITY IN ARAB COUNTRIES: CHANGES AND
IMPLICATIONS
Hoda Rashad and Magued Osman ------------------------------- 20

AGE-DISCREPANT MARRIAGES IN EGYPT
Magued I. Osman and Laila S. Shahd ---------------------------- 51

RATIONALES FOR KIN MARRIAGES IN RURAL UPPER EGYPT
Hania Sholkamy -- 62

THE COSTS OF MARRIAGE IN EGYPT: A HIDDEN
DIMENSION IN THE NEW ARAB DEMOGRAPHY
Diane Singerman and Barbara Ibrahim -------------------------- 80

FROM SEXUAL SUBMISSION TO VOLUNTARY
COMMITMENT: THE TRANSFORMATION OF
FAMILYTIES IN CONTEMPORARY TUNISIA
Lilia Labidi -- 117

FAMILIES AND HOUSEHOLDS: HEADSHIP
AND CO-RESIDENCE
Zeinab Khedr and Laila El Zeini ----------------------------- 140

AMONG BROTHERS: PATRIARCHAL CONNECTIVITY AND
BROTHERLY DEFERENCE IN LEBANON
Suad Joseph -- 165

SISTERHOOD AND STEWARDSHIP IN SISTER-BROTHER
RELATIONS IN SAUDI ARABIA
Soraya Altorki --- 180

THE ABSENT FATHER
Josette Abdalla -- 201

SOCIAL CHANGE AND PARENT-ADOLESCENT
DYNAMICS IN EGYPT
Sahar El Tawila, Barbara Ibrahim, and Hind Wassef ---------------------- 214

TERMINATING MARRIAGE
Philippe Fargues --- 247

ABOUT THE CONTRIBUTORS --- 274

LIST OF TABLES AND FIGURES

Proportion Ever Married in a Specified Base Year
for Women Aged 15-49, 20-49 and 40-49
in Different Arab Countries -- 23

Proportion Ever Married in a Specified Recent
Year, for Women Aged 15-49 and 40-49
in Different Countries --- 24

Indicators of Delays in Marriage and Increase
in Celibacy for Different Countries and Years ------------------------------ 25

Distribution of Arab Countries by their Current Stage in the Nuptiality
Transition --- 27

Differentials by Female Educational Status in Delays of Marriage ----- 28

Differentials by Females Educational Status in Celibacy ---------------- 28

Proportion of Ever Married Women (15-49) Who Are
Married to Their First Cousin --- 30

Percent of Ever Married Women Who Married Their First Cousin
(Father and Mother Side) by Periods Before Survey ---------------------- 31

Percent of Ever Married Women who Lived in Someone else House at
Initiation of Marriage by Periods Before Survey --------------------------- 31

Percent Distribution of Ever Married Women
By Age Gap between Husbands and Wives ---------------------------------- 32

Percent Distribution of Ever Married Women
by Inter Spousal Educational Difference ------------------------------------ 33

Percent Distribution of Ever Married Women by Inter Spousal
Education Difference and Marriage Duration ---------------------------- 34

Among Those whose Wife Education is Higher than Husband The
Percent of Women Whose Educational Gap Is at Least Two Stages ---- 35

Percent of Females Never Joining Schools & Percent of
Females with Secondary+ Education for Different Cohorts --------------- 36

Percent of Wives Whose Husbands are Less Educated by Working Condition of Wives Before Marriage	36
Profile of Never Married Women in the Age Group 15-49	40
Percent Distribution of Female Heads by Residence, Age, Marital Status and Educational Attainment	41
Percent Ever Married	53
Number and Percentage of Marriage Contracts by Age Group, 1986 and 1996	54
Age Characteristics of Couples Marrying 1986 vs. 1996	55
Wife's Maiden Age at Time of Marriage Contract by Husband's Age	56
Bride's Side Real Marriage Costs, 1965-1995 (1979 LE)	94
Contributions to Marriage Costs by Region	98
Component Parts of Total Costs of Marriage, Urban/Rural, '99 Marriage Module	101
Total Marriage Costs Relative to Annual Household Expenditure Per Capita	107
Divorce Rate in Various Countries	127
Reasons for Divorce in Tunisia about 1970	128
Increase of Equipment in Tunisian Households (percent)	130
The Culture of Shame	134
Definitions Used in the Classification of Households	147
Distribution of Households and of Population by Type of Households (EDHS 1995)	148
Characteristics of Households and Their Population by Type of Household (EDHS 1995)	150
Characteristics of Households and Their Population by Household Headship (EDHS 1995)	152

Characteristics of Implicit Female Heads
and Their Households (EDHS 1995) -- 155

Characteristics of Single-Person Households by
Gender (EDHS 1995) --- 156

Characteristics of Older Persons and Their Households by
Gender (EDHS 1995) --- 158

Conceptual Framework of the Determinants and Dynamics of
Intra and Inter-Generation Gap --- 222

Percent Distribution of Adolescents in the Sample by Distant
Explanatory Variables Hypothesized to Impact
Both Intra- and Inter-Generation Dynamics -------------------------------- 226

Adolescents Responses Concerning What They Like Most
About the Person Identified as Role Model -------------------------------- 228

Attitudes of Never Married 16-19 Year-old Adolescents Living with
Both Parents and the Attitudes or Actual Corresponding
Experience among the Parents' Generation --------------------------------- 230

Attitudes of Selected Sub-Groups of Adolescents Regarding
Parameters of Family Formation and Marriage Relations ------------------ 233

Odds-Ratios of Reporting Either Parent as a Role Model and
Failure to Identify a Role Model at All by
Distant Background Variables --- 243

Multiple Classification Analysis: Index of Divergence from
the Average Experience of the Parent-Generation by
Distant Explanatory Variables-- 244

Socialization Style at Home; Odds-Ratios of Family Integration and
High-Level Inter-Generation Communication by Distant
Background Variables --- 245

Socialization Style at Home; Odds-Ratios of High Exposure
to the Mass Media and Less Restricted Mobility by
Distant Background Variables --- 246

Reduction of Divorce and Polygyny Rates in Egypt and Algeria ------- 271

Regional Patterns of Nuptiality in Egypt in 1935 and 1991 ------------- 272

INTRODUCTION: THE NEW ARAB FAMILY

NICHOLAS S. HOPKINS

The Arab family is a perennial topic. The Arab family is always itself, a comfortable framework within which people live, and always adjusting to new circumstances. The broad processes of social and cultural change in the Arab world guarantee that there is always something new to say on the subject.

On May 6 and 7, 2000, *Cairo Papers in Social Science*, in collaboration with the Social Research Center of AUC and the Population Council's Cairo office, held a conference on "The New Arab Family". This volume represents the revised versions of the papers given at that conference. The conference reflected considerable preliminary work by the organizing committee including Dr. Suad Joseph, Dr. Hoda Rashad, Dr. Barbara Ibrahim, and Dr. Nicholas Hopkins, thus covering anthropology, demography, and sociology.

The idea behind the conference was to focus attention on the family in the Arab world, thinking that this topic has been somewhat neglected in recent years. There has been a shift of interest away from family and towards gender. Of course there is a high degree of overlap between these two topics, but they are not identical, nor is one contained within the other. Hence we thought it would be useful to call attention once again to the family as an institution and a social setting.

The further idea was to combine two very different approaches to the study of the family--on the one hand demographic, on the other broadly sociological or anthropological, or as some would say, psychodynamic, that is to say focusing on dyadic or multi-member networks of relationships within the family. Some of these papers in turn focused on 'agency', the ways in which individual action fit into cultural and social frames.

Since each individual paper tends to take one or the other of these distinctive approaches, it is up to the reader to judge how successful the combination was. For those who were there, the approach certainly stimulated some fruitful discussions. We organized the panels so that papers with different approaches were paired with one another in order to foster cross-fertilization of that kind, and it worked, and we hope the organization of this volume will also work. We also solicited papers that covered a good deal of the Arab world, though in the end with a focus on Egypt. In addition to general papers relying on demographic data from different parts of the Arab world, we have case studies from Tunisia, Lebanon, and Saudi Arabia. It could be argued that we have understated the rural Arab world.

During the conference, and in these papers, we discuss a variety of topics dealing with the Arab family. Marriage, divorce, and related topics of course were center stage, particularly in the demographic papers. Demographically we can see that people are marrying later, and that celibacy is growing among women. We can also trace the shifts in educational level, and the linked occupational patterns. The slow transition from an extended family to a nuclear one was treated in a number of papers, together with the related shift from marriage as domination to marriage as companionship between equals. Inheritance, allowing for the transfer of wealth across the generations, came up in several papers, though none was devoted to it alone. Nonetheless, the role of the extended and nuclear family in the reproduction of social and cultural forms was stressed. One manifestation of this is the extent to which marriage is a family project.

The family is a collection of individuals whose understanding of their roles derives from cultural definitions. But the way in which the roles are acted out, in combination with parents, children, siblings, and others also reflects the individual personalities involved. Our papers include several that examine dyadic relations, between brother and brother, brother and sister, father and child, husband and wife. A particularly interesting contrast is between the brother-sister pair and the husband-wife pair. These dyadic relationships show how the cultural definition of the role is affected by the accident of the personalities involved. When we examine how the family as a kinship unit is organized as an economic unit for production or consumption, we think of the household, and consequently of the leadership of that small group. The kinship values and norms strengthen a pattern of interaction, and provide the ideological basis for the teamwork that is required to make this small group successful in social terms.

At the broadest level, the collective argument of these papers runs as follows. Changes in the economy and in access to education have affected people's behavior in the family, household, and married couple. There are now therefore new forms of household and family, or at least a change in the statistical prevalence of the major forms. Within these new or relatively new households and families there are changing psychodynamics or patterns of dyadic relationships. People who see themselves as family members still care for each other, quarrel with each other, sometimes even betray each other, as they always did, but now within a slightly different framework and with different stakes as the wider society changes. This combination of values, understandings, and behavior makes a new society that in turn promises to lead to changes in choices in the family, household, and marriage relationship.

We are grateful to all those who presented papers in May 2000, and also to those who chaired sessions or simply brought their interesting comments. We are particularly grateful to Dr. Afaf Mahfouz who gave one of the concluding talks summing up the conference. We are grateful to the staff of the *Cairo Papers in Social Science,* and to the staff of the AUC and Population Council more generally for their material and logistic support. Without the willingness of the authors to revise their papers and answer queries we would not have gotten this far. We hope the readers will share our enthusiasm for the issues raised by these papers, and will help us advance the intellectual discourse.

The funding for our conference came from the Vice-Provost's office of the American University in Cairo, from the regular budget of the *Cairo Papers in Social Science*, from the Population Council, and from the New Arab Demography Program co-ordinated by the Social Research Center of the American University in Cairo. We are grateful to all those who made the participation by such a wide range of individuals possible and fruitful.

FRAMEWORKS FOR STUDYING FAMILIES IN THE 21st CENTURY

CAROL B. STACK

Over the past thirty years I have studied family migrations and everyday lives within extended kin networks and across rural and urban spaces (Stack 1970). Constructs within the sociology of the family that isolate nuclear families fail to illuminate the inner workings of kin networks whose rights and responsibilities stretch across several households, regions, and nations. From anthropology, I could draw upon comparative studies of kinship and residence patterns, child-keeping and child-fosterage, and the distribution of rights and responsibilities among households (Stack 1974). But my hardest challenge has been to discover how to move between those two conversations.

Much is lost in translation between these social science disciplines, and much is gained. The study of kinship within anthropology has provided supple tools for understanding the complexities of patriarchal, patrilocal, and neolocal family patterns in the Middle East. But as these patterns shift, and family members participate in long and short term labor migrations, scholars are finding that they need to develop other, equally robust guides for understanding social processes or social change within and across the domestic sphere--what we might call kin and gender work in action, and across time.

Over the years I have tried to build theoretical bridges to talk about households and kinship patterns that did not take nuclear families as a starting point. Today, studies of changing families in the Middle East are confronting the same task, in the reverse. The challenge in Middle Eastern societies is to follow families and individuals as they travel from one place to another, and/or from traditional extended family, patriarchal arrangements, into "new couple," "conjugal," or "neolocal" households (Altorki and Cole 1989). In the effort to foreground such dramatic changes in the nature of formal and informal social ties, several scholars in this volume are turning their attention to the salience of dyads, the timing of life events, the reconfiguration of households, and the emergence of new marriage patterns. On these sites of personal and political struggle, in the cross-fire between interpretation and agency, changing ideologies provide sources of identity and conflict and dramatically influence individual lives.

What we have come to learn in the process is that people do not necessarily do what they are supposed to do for kin, but they know what they are supposed to do, when they should do it, and that kin will summon them to do kin work. What makes kin ties and fictive kinship intriguing is that they are both the product of what goes on in people's heads and the site of personal and political struggle. Ideologies within kin settings provide a constant source of identity and conflict, and play upon individual lives in the cross-fire between interpretation and agency.

The purpose of this paper is to present a framework for understanding gender, kinship and the property of social ties within the context of time, symbols, and lived lives. In 1993 my colleague, Linda Burton, and I introduced the notion of *kinscripts* as the play of ideology and performance which emerges from highly contested, yet deeply cultural, domains of *kin-work*, *kin-time*, and *kin-scription* (Stack and Burton 1993). In the first section of this paper I draw upon *kinscripts* as a framework that presses meaning and process into the idiom of kinship. In the second section, I introduce David Plath's discussion of the dilemmas of adulthood, so brilliantly developed in his 1980 book, *Long Engagements* (Plath 1980). Both perspectives examine the dilemmas of adulthood as time moves through lives and lives through history (Elder 1978; Hagestad 1986).

Part 1

We need fluid but vigorous frameworks within which to examine how kin as multi-generational collectives, and individuals embedded within them, negotiate the life course. As a conceptual scheme, *kinscripts* poses questions for family scholars to ask of their own data; provides a context for a critique of cohort analysis that tracks individuals and makes claims for families; and challenges some of the limitations of aggregate data. We have proposed a *kinscripts* framework for organizing our ethnographic observations of families and individuals who are negotiating and contesting everyday codes of behavior.

Life course research has traditionally focused on individual lives shaped within the context of significant others. These lives have been viewed as finely placed, but, in effect, cut off in the rich tapestry of families in transition. Much of the discussion in the literature focuses on individuals and dyads, rather than on the impact of families on individuals, and of individuals on families. From life course research, we have learned a great deal about the development of individual lives, but little about how individuals in kin settings re-write their scripts, or how kin collectively negotiate multiple scripts.

Along with other scholars, Linda Burton and I suggest that families have their own agendas, their own interpretation of cultural norms, and their own histories (Hagestad 1986; Reiss 1981; Tilly 1987). As they help individual members to construct their personal life courses, families, as collectives, create life courses of their own. Our notion of kinscripts is grounded in a theoretical approach that weaves together sociological studies of the life course and anthropological studies of kinship and the developmental cycle of families. Earlier studies of the life course looked at how individuals create their own biographies and identified patterns in the timing, duration, spacing, and order of life events (Elder 1978; Rossi 1980). We propose the study of interlocking pathways of family members within families as they sway and ultimately shape each others' life choices (Elder 1987; Plath 1980). Suad Joseph's elegant account of intimate selving in the Arab world provides the foundation for such exploration of Middle Eastern families. She shows how "intimate relationality" frames "notions of the self that do not conform to the individualist, separatist, bounded, autonomous constructs" of Western psychodynamic theory (Joseph 2000). Her study of the psychological formation of the self enormously enriches the conversation about families in which notions of maturity "valorize rather than pathologize the embeddedness of the self and other," and in which, nevertheless, "embeddedness still encompasses agency."

The fluidity of boundaries between self and other that Joseph describes is written in Western as well as in Middle Eastern family stories as personal and historical struggle unfolds within kin networks and as individuals work through and around the continuum of often competing ideological scripts. Family members do not simply follow cultural mandates or expectations across generations; as agents, they elect to situate themselves into kin obligations or they elect not to do so. Kin negotiate plans of action and respond to personal as well as social, economic, and political forces. They also revise their own family histories and memories.

Kinscripts, our designation for these complex dynamics, emerges out of three closely interwoven cultural domains: kin-work, kin-time, and kin-scription. Kin-work is the work that kin need to accomplish to survive over time. Kin-time directs the timing of individual transitions, charting movement and continuity through time. Kin-scription is the active recruitment or conscription of family members to take on kin-work. I will now describe these dimensions one at a time.

Kin-work

Kin-work is family labor. It is the collective labor expected of family-centered networks across households or family compounds and within them (di Leonardo 1987). It defines the work that needs to be done in families, which have long been conceived as the locus of women's active agency. Even recently, women have been treated by family scholars as if they were confined to families, and in some cultures and social classes, kin-work and power within family networks are synonymous with women (Finely 1989). Kin-work, however, is not limited to the labor of women. In culturally diverse racial, ethnic, and class-based settings in the United States, kin tasks are also distributed among men, children, and fictive kin—and this is increasingly the case in Middle Eastern families as well.

In Western as well as in Arab families, tradition held that the head of the household was responsible for feeding, nourishing, and sustaining all those who lived with or depended upon (almost inevitably) him (Fay 2000). But kin-work spreads (and democratizes) the burden of nurturance—emotional, educational, and financial—across the family. Kin-work is the consequence of gender-, class-, and culturally-constructed family obligations defined, in part, in the context of changing social, material, and political conditions. Kin-work regenerates families, maintains lifetime continuities, sustains intergenerational responsibilities, and reinforces shared values. It encompasses, for example, all of the following: family labor or reproduction; intergenerational care for children or dependents; economic survival including wage and non-wage labor; family migrations, and strategic support for kin across regions, state lines, and nations. Kin-work is very hard work, and it is always work-in-progress.

As patrilocal households give way to neolocal households, Middle Eastern families revise, improvise, and invent new family scripts for the organization of kin-work. In Saudi Arabia, for example, Soraya Altorki and Donald Cole argue, the revolution wrought by oil (*al-tufrah*, the boom or "mutation") led to the monetization of the economy and salaried employment for both men and women and brought radical change to the structure of family life and kin-work across three generations of families in Jiddah (Altorki 2000, Cole 2000). In the first generation, households had one kitchen, meals were shared, mothers, sons' wives, and daughters all worked under the mothers' directions. Mothers-in-law, not husbands, gave permission for outings, and mother-in-law/daughter-in-law relations were marked by tension and occasional conflict that sometimes involved the son/husband. In the third generation, young men and women, educated and salaried, make decisions about their own lives and those of their children that are more (or less) independent of parental influence. Women and men whose employment-time now unfolds outside the compound and/or the context of the extended family must make new arrangements for the kin-work on which family survival depends.

Among working-class families in Cairo, migration of male workers to the oil-rich countries of the Gulf served to generate more income and to improve the family's standard of living—and indeed, migration was seen both by husbands and by the wives they left behind as an act of sacrifice for the good of the family. That sacrifice transformed male-headed households into de facto female-headed households, Homa Hoodfar argues (1993), and wives, out of necessity, took on many of the tasks of their husbands. This marks dramatic reversal of the norm: Islamic code and Egyptian custom assigns responsibility for the household's day-to-day expenses to the husband. Wage-earning wives who proved that they could support their families on their own staked out new (and for many, hostile) territory within the domain of kin-work. Before migration, women were unwilling to spend their income on regular household expenses except under very exceptional circumstances. Now, they discovered, the disruption of the old order was to be permanent. While husbands had to endure loneliness, hard work, and bad treatment in their host countries, their wives now had new budgetary and household obligations: to protect their household they had to develop new skills and cement old networks. Migrants' wives identified the loss of their husbands' moral support as a great sacrifice. It bears repetition. Kin-work is very hard work, and it is always work-in-progress.

Kin-time

Kin-time represents the temporal scripts of families, providing determinations of when, and in what sequence, role transitions such as marriage and childbearing, and kin-work such as child-rearing, should occur (Hagestad 1986). Kin-time includes temporal guides for the assumption of leadership roles and caregiving obligations, and demarcates rites of passage or milestones within kin groups; for example, the handing down of property and power and tasks following the death of family elders. Chronological age, social time, family time, and historical time are played out when we appropriate and situate the temporal nature of the life course; and what appear to be outcomes can also be viewed, critically, as process.

Hareven (1977) defines family time as the "timing of events such as marriage, birth of a child, leaving home, and the transition of individuals into different roles as the family moves through its life course." Individual progression through these family stages is influenced by historical and social context and by the tensions between individual preferences and familial expectations. Hagestad describes how families, as cultural units, devise timetables for the movement of the group through predictable phases of development and changing generational structures (Hagestad 1986). Those timetables represent the shared understandings and interdependencies within kinship structures. Among Egyptian families whose father/husband intends to migrate to another country to work, kin-time usually postpones departure until the mother/wife has two or three children, and can live on her own respectably, as an established matron. If the young wife is still childless, kin-time usually demands that she move in with her parents (thus, she loses the autonomy that is one of the attractions of the married state.) But events outside the kin group can skew family timetables and disrupt interdependencies, as Erika Friedl (2000) documented in her research on three generations of families in rural Iran.

Friedl reasons back from the dramatic increase in the number of adult unmarried women after the Islamic Revolution in Iran to the circumstances their great-grandmothers and grandmothers confronted. Amongst her oldest respondents, she could find no one who remembered a man or a woman who lived by himself or herself. Marriage was seen as an institution willed by God to make ordered life possible in the world, and without it, survival was uncertain. When Friedl asked the women who are now grandmothers what they expected of the men who would be chosen as their mates, her respondents refused to answer the question, which they thought absurd. "No woman would tell me what she was looking for in a husband." Friedl writes. "She wasn't looking at all." Then, all an unmarried woman could hope for was to be reasonably well treated in her husband's house.

Three generations ago, parents set all the terms of marriage arrangements, and early marriage was seen as a good that careful fathers and mothers provided for their daughters. Structural and social change, in middle and upper class families before the Revolution and everywhere after 1979, has altered that belief, and now, even in poor villages in Iran, parents who allow their daughters to be spoken for early appear to be careless of their welfare. Kin-time is always under pressure from extra-familial events. With the proliferation of modernist institutions such as schools, wage-labor, and salaried positions for women, different choices appear possible for girls as well as boys. And, paradoxically, social programs and economic developments under the Islamic Republic have had the effect of weakening parents' authority and with it their will and power to select marriage partners for their daughters. The opening of university admission to women from rural areas was meant to integrate villages into the economic and administrative structures of the state, and, with the goal of strict gender segregation, to make it possible for women's needs to be served by other women. Although there aren't many rural women enrolled in universities, the idea that daughters might gain access to salaries and to some degree of freedom has changed kin-time in rural Iran.

From the 1970s onward, Friedl argues, many young Iranian men have been caught in social and economic limbo as unemployed high school graduates or unemployed college graduates. As they abandon their villages for study or joblessness in cities, young local women are left behind, still completely dependent on their fathers and brothers, confined to their courtyards by propriety and village etiquette, and with little to occupy them. Some go to school, and imagine different, less constrained lives, calibrated to new timetables and free from family interests and management. If or when they marry, they want husbands who are attractive, reasonable, well-paid, and willing to help with housework — unlike their grandmothers, they're forthright about their expectations. Kin-time is always under pressure from extra-familial events.

Kin-scription

It is important to understand how power is brought into play within the framework of kin-time and kin-work through the process we call kin-scription. Instead of accepting the attempts of individuals to set their own personal agendas, families are continually rounding up, summoning, or recruiting members for specific kin tasks. Some kin, namely women and children, are easily recruited. The importance women place on maintaining kin ties and connections to others has been well documented (Stack 1974; Gilligan 1982), and in Western and Middle Eastern cultures alike, women find it difficult to refuse kin demands. We are aware of the power dynamics that unevenly conscript women and children to carry out kin-work; the power women sequester for themselves within families in the face of external structures that ostracize them; and the power appropriated by kin who refuse conscription. And lest we forget, the men working in foreign lands, isolated from kin but religiously sending remittances back home, are deeply embedded in kin-work that summons them to keep active their responsibilities and allegiances, and their honor.

People who agree to, or who elect kin-scription are not, as some scholars would have it, simply determined and dominated by the needs of their families. It is especially useful, as Suad Joseph suggests (2000:15), "to view persons in Arab societies as embedded in relational matrices that shape their sense of self but do not deny them their distinctive initiative or agency." Members of Middle Eastern families, Joseph says (2000:11), "have often resisted, constructed alternatives, or created networks that crossed the boundaries of family, neighborhood, class, religion, ethnicity, and nation, emerging with notions of self that, while privileging relationality, are quite hybrid."

Annelies Moors (2000) examines the dynamics of kin-scription in her discussion of the competing claims of autonomy and family loyalty among women in the Arab World. Moors sets out to investigate when men and women identify with the family and when they see or act as if their interests are divergent. From her parents and sometimes her brothers, a daughter receives gifts of gold that prove how much she is valued in her natal family. These gifts endow the daughter with resources of her own, and often, Moors argues, have the effect of ensuring that daughter/sisters will refrain from claiming their shares in the agricultural land and urban commercial property in their fathers' estates, if the contending heirs are their brothers.

The legal right of women to inheritance is codified in Islamic law, so refraining from claiming that right, the daughter/sister strengthens her kin relations with her brother or brothers and, Moors says, provides herself with negotiating space among her kin. Thus, a woman's agency may be circumscribed by kin-scription, but it is also visible in her commitment to her natal family. In the context of growing emphasis on conjugality, a woman's attempt to reinforce her relationship with her brothers by giving up property rights not only reproduces the patrilineal family but also limits her dependence on her husband. The sister makes a gift to her brother, and the brother returns care, present and future, for her welfare. Kin-scription moves in both directions.

Some relatives may inadvertently play havoc with family expectations while simultaneously attempting to attach themselves to the family legacy. A sister/daughter who, perhaps under the urging of her husband, chooses to claim a share of the productive property of her father's estate, puts at risk her access to emotional and other kinds of support from her natal family. When kin act out or resist pressures to stay in line, families have been known to use heavy-handed pressures to make them conform, and failing that, to recruit other individuals to do kin-work. At the same time, kin may be well aware that family demands criss-cross and that it is impossible for individuals who are summoned to kin-work to satisfy everyone at once. Kin-scription is always contested. The life course of kin is produced on the deeply conflicted ground where kin-work, kin-time, and kin-scription converge. Our interest must be in the process by which kinscripts emerge from these three domains as negotiated discourses, exemplified by the generations maneuvering as agents through families over time.

Part 2

Centuries ago, people born into particular systems of kinship and descent faced every day the dilemmas posed by death, disability, war, and famine, events that shattered expectations and redistributed rights and responsibilities within families, sometimes catastrophically. But difficulties and disasters played themselves out in established contexts. During the past 50 years or so, however, modern economies and modern thought have transformed gender, kinship, and the property of social ties. As lives take on new meanings, as we entertain new options and make different choices about where and how to situate ourselves among kin and fictive kin, our practices are carried out within eyesight and earshot of the very people and institutions who organize to protect the meaning of cultural symbols

The everyday dilemmas of adulthood are among the most traumatic dilemmas of modern times. And they are far more complex than the ordering of family events by stages, transitions, or roles, or by age-linked or dyadic relationships, might suggest. Culturally defined roles and timetables--one focus of scholarship in anthropology, sociology, and psychology--camouflage biography, identity, and subjectivity.

To strip away that camouflage, I want to invoke the work of David Plath, whose book, *Long Engagements* (1980), stands as a classic. Plath's study of the rhetoric of maturity in Japan taps into the dilemmas of adulthood situated within the pressure points of lives stretched across time and place. The fabric of biography takes on new meaning when modern couples, for example, in New Arab families, hatch their own conjugal households. These couples, in collaboration with significant others in their dominion of trust, are authoring their own biographies. But they are not acting alone in the family legacies they are creating. On one hand, they may provoke and test their intimates. On the other hand, their actions must be affirmed, in some measure, by the kin to whom they are linked and the civic society to which they belong. This breaking of new ground takes place over generations, relies on coalitions, and, at last, calls for the consent of those who experience its consequences. Persons who act together, in a dominion of trust, acquire cultural strategies for construing and organizing experience, and for solving problems.

A little while ago, I cited research on Saudi Arabian families by Soraya Altorki and Donald Cole that traces changes across generations in the web of kin support, in the organization of the political economy, and in the expectations of women and men about how they will write their own lives (Altorki 2000; Cole 2000). Altorki and Cole explore residence patterns; the economic independence of men; the impact of women's work; and transformations in role relationships, marriage preferences, and the mutual obligations of spouses. Let me use their fine research as a springboard for what I am trying to say. I am interested in how these transformations across generations work themselves out in the everyday lives of young men and women--against, or in collaboration with intimate others. Who resists and who participates in authorizing new codes that guide young couples' lives? What changes does the presence of women in the work force trigger for them? What are the costs of those changes, and what constitutes the nature of worrisome dilemmas that arise when obstacles appear between individuals and cultural mandates? How does human character evolve as we face those who stand in the way or support our desire for change? These are crucial questions that family studies must address in this century.

All too often, anthropological and sociological studies of families imprison what David Plath calls (1980:12) the "drama of sociability and how it shapes character." All too often we lose sight of the dilemmas people face, and the ways they engage cultural symbols that identify experience. Ethnography counteracts that willful nearsightedness as it recognizes that family transitions and constraints are bundled into hundreds of stories of individual lives fettered together. Research on families in transition has the capacity to ponder the dilemmas of adulthood by specifying the options from which people choose, the questions they ask (of themselves and of others) about those choices, the choices they make, and the fruits of those choices. We know that people in the cultures we study write their own life stories. Those stories must also finally be sanctioned by those who live among us.

In the low-income African-American families I have studied for many years, different events—the birth of a baby to a young mother, for instance—trigger shifts in domestic arrangements. The baby must be cared for, so families assign responsibility for that care, often to someone other than the parent. In my first book, *All Our Kin* (Stack 1974), I wanted to take a snapshot of urban families as they assigned such responsibilities. My interest then was in portraying kinship and family organization, and in putting patterns such as child-keeping on the map. I was not asking how those patterns were enacted, whether they were processed or contested. In my more recent book, *Call to Home* (1996), I try to look at family relationships as they unfold over time, as people change and grow older, as new members are born or recruited into the kin group and as the elders die and leave their property and their work to others. I think of *Call to Home* as an album of family photographs. Through their descriptions of the return migration from the Northeast to the rural South, people narrate their own stories carefully and deliberately, as though they were turning over pages filled with pictures of themselves at different stages of their lives. They tell how kin-work spread out over time and space, creating an image of family trees branching across the landscape of the United States against a moving background of years. They tell how time passes through families, and they pay attention to events that trigger change. Their kinscripts are thick with details of how they make and remake their surroundings, the allies they find in faraway places or at home, and the help given or refused by family and friends as they confront the dilemmas of adulthood.

I mention this shift in my own work only to suggest further questions that family studies may want to follow. What do I owe myself? What do I owe others? How does loyalty to family figure in my life? Will I submit to kin-scription? For how long? At what cost to my own individual ambitions? These questions probe the processes by which women and men grow together in communities of kin or fictive kin and track the changes in those communities over the life course. In the working out of those processes, personal biography takes shape against an endless stream of family events and family needs. To see how that happens, how the dilemmas of adulthood establish the contexts in which women and men write and rewrite their lives, is, I argue, the business of family studies in our time, and across cultures. As the forces of radical change press Middle Eastern families into new configurations, it is a wonderful moment to be studying families.

References Cited

Altorki, Soraya. 2000. "Family in Changing Saudi Arabia (II): The Boom and Afterwards, ca. 1975-2000." Paper presented at the Conference on Family History in Middle Eastern Studies, University of California, Berkeley, April 7-9.

Altorki, Soraya, and Donald Cole. 1989. *Arabian Oasis City: The Transformation of 'Unayzah.* Austin, Texas: University of Texas Press.

Cole, Donald. 2000. "Family in Changing Saudi Arabia (1): Substantive Development, ca. 1955-1975." Paper presented at the Conference on Family History in Middle Eastern Studies, University of California, Berkeley, April 7-9.

Di Leonardo, Micaela. 1987. "The Female World of Cards and Holidays: Women, Families, and the Work of Kinship," *Signs* 12(3):440-453.

Elder, Glen H. 1978. "Family History and the Life Course" in T. Hareven, ed., *Transitions: The Family and the Life Course in Historical Perspective.* New York: Academic Press, pp. 17-64.

Fay, Mary Ann. 2000. "From Warrior Grandees to Domesticated Bourgeoisie: The Transformation of the Elite Egyptian Household into a Western-style Nuclear Family." Paper presented at the Conference on Family History in Middle Eastern Studies. University of California, Berkeley, April 7-9.

Finely, Nancy. 1989. "Theories of Family Labor as Applied to Gender Differences in Caregiving for Elderly Parents," *Journal of Marriage and the Family* 51:79-86.

Friedl, Erika. 2000. "Tribal Family Enterprises and Marriage Issues in Twentieth-Century Iran." Paper presented at the Conference on Family History and Middle Eastern Studies, University of California at Berkeley, April 7-9.

Gilligan, Carol. 1982. *In a Different Voice: Psychological Theory and Women's Development*. Cambridge MA: Harvard University Press.

Hagestad, Gunhild O. 1986. "Dimension of Time and the Family," *American Behavioral Scientist* 29(6):679-694.

Hareven, Tamara K. 1977. "Family Time and Historical Time," *Daedalus* 107:57-70.

Hoodfar, Homa. 1993. "The Veil in Their Minds and On Our Heads: The Persistence of Colonial Images of Muslim Women," *Resources for Feminist Research* 22, nos. 3-4:5-18.

Joseph, Suad. 2000. *Intimate Selving in Arab Families: Gender, Self, and Identity*. Syracuse: Syracuse University Press.

Moors, Annelies. 2000. "Women's Gold: Shifting Styles of Embodying Family Relations." Paper presented at the Conference on Family History in Middle Eastern Studies. University of California, Berkeley, April 7-9.

Plath, David. 1980. *Long Engagements*. Stanford CA: Stanford University Press.

Reiss, David. 1981. *The Family's Construction of Reality*. Cambridge, MA: Harvard University Press.

Rossi, Alice. 1980. "Aging and Parenthood in the Middle Years" in P. Baltes and O.G. Brin, eds, *Life Span Development and Behavior*, vol. 3. New York: Academic Press, pp. 137-205.

Stack, Carol. 1970. "The Kindred of Viola Jackson: Residence and Family Organization of an Urban Black American Family" in N. Whitten, Jr., and J. Szwed, eds., *Afro-American Anthropology: Contemporary Perspectives*. New York: The Free Press, pp. 303-312.

----------. 1974. *All Our Kin: Strategies for Survival in a Black Community*. New York: Harper and Row.

----------. 1996. *Call to Home: African Americans Reclaim the Rural South*. New York: Basic Books.

Stack, Carol and Linda Burton. 1993. "Kinscripts," *Journal of Comparative Family Studies* Vol. 24(2):157-170.

Tilly, Charles. 1987. "Family History, Social History, and Social Change," *Journal of Family History* 12:320-329.

NUPTIALITY IN ARAB COUNTRIES: CHANGES AND IMPLICATIONS[1]

HODA RASHAD AND MAGUED OSMAN

The purpose of this study is to provide a regional comparative overview of changes occurring in the prevalence, timing, and characteristics of marriages in Arab countries. The implications of these changes are many, including the shaping of a number of social groups with special needs and new concerns. The sheer size of these groups, the different nature of their needs. and the clear absence of targeted strategies and policies all point to an important direction of social research. There is a clear need for research efforts that go beyond describing the boundaries of nuptiality change to investigating the content of such change, and its consequences on the well being of individuals and the functioning of the society. Such a research effort needs to guide the choice of appropriate new social policies.

The study is divided into four sections. The first provides a general background on marriage patterns and their evolution across time. The second documents the changes occurring in Arab countries. The third section describes characteristics of marriage and the final section discusses the implications of changes in nuptiality on Arab societies and points to needed research and guided policy interventions related to these implications.

Marriage Patterns and their Evolution in Time

The existence of three distinctive female marriage patterns during the early decades of the twentieth century has been documented. These patterns are: "One of late marriage and high permanent celibacy, the 'Western European'

---

[1]This paper is an integral component of the many research pieces presented by the New Arab Demography Program (NAD) to the Cairo Papers symposium. The New Arab Demography Program is a collaborative effort between Arab scholars, national and international institutions. It is co-ordinated by the Social Research Center (SRC) of the American University in Cairo (AUC) and supported by Mellon, Hewlett and the Ford Foundations. The authors would like to thank Dr. Sahar El-Tawila, Dr. Laila El-Zeini and Dr. Zeinab Khedr for their comments. The assistance of Ms. Eman Mostafa in preparing tables for this paper is appreciated.

pattern, which characterized the Western European countries of the time; one of early and universal marriage, the 'non-European' pattern, which pertains to the less developed regions; and a third with a later marriage timing patterns than the developing countries and high marriage prevalence, the 'Eastern European' pattern, found in a number of areas of that sub-region" (United Nations 1990:5, based on Hajnal 1953, 1965).

Two interesting observations discussed in the UN study (1990) deserve a special mention. The first is the fact that the three marriage patterns prevailed in typically agrarian societies. The late marriage patterns prevailing in Western Europe (which were brought over to North America and Oceania) were reported as far back as the eighteenth century when these countries were neither industrialized nor urbanized (Hajnal 1965). A multitude of factors were proposed to explain this late pattern. Among them: the relatively higher prevalence of independent nuclear family[2] (demanding a more secure economic base before initiating a family), pressure on land, as was evidenced in Finland and Norway (Drake, 1972; Lutz, 1987), dowry customs, the institution of servants (domestic and agricultural laborers postponed marriages until they acquired necessary savings), as well as various other factors such as taxes on bachelors to finance wars and migration of males.

The second interesting observation is the fact that the movement across time is not unidirectional from early marriages to later ages at marriages. Western Europe actually experienced a trend towards younger marriages (United Nations 1990). This occurred during the final phase of the shift from an agricultural rural society to an industrialized urbanized society. Explanations of this downward shift included declining family authority, increasing income through greater job independence and opportunities, decline of large land holdings, population movements towards industrial areas (Hofstee, 1968, cited in Heeren, 1973), and gainful urban employment for women.[3] This trend towards younger age of marriage is the opposite of

---

[2] The UN study explains that: "It was during the eighteenth century that values giving increasing importance to companionship in marriage, to the role of the mother and the raising of children became more prominent (Aries, 1948; Stone, 1979). This development strengthened the formation of an independent nuclear family (Badinter, 1980)" (1990:33).

[3] Habakkuk (1971:43) cited in United Nations (1990) noted that "men were more ready to marry girls or young women who were themselves earning money."

what occurred in the societies of the third world when they underwent industrialization.

The current position of Arab countries in terms of the three specified marriage patterns and their evolution across time will be investigated in the next section. The purpose is to know whether Arab societies have moved away from the non-European marriage type.

Changes in Marriage Patterns in Arab Countries

Despite the paucity of existing data, there is a consensus that the position of the Arab marriage pattern during the first half of the twentieth century was similar to the non-European marriage type characterized by early marriages and a relatively low proportion of single men and women.

This pattern is clearly influenced by a number of economic, cultural, and social factors that operated in many developing countries. In particular "The agrarian production system and the family organization appear as major bases of the early-marriage pattern. The extended (joint) family system, characterized by strong common economic and family ties, is able to provide readily the economic support for newly married couples. In this family system, children do not leave the family at marriage; they are integrated into the family production system and acquire immediately an economic basis for establishing their marriage" (UN 1990:35, quoting Wolf 1988). Furthermore, marriage in Arab society is a legally and socially well-defined turning point in the life of both males and females that reflects status attainment.

The image of the life cycle of a typical female in an Arab country not very far in the past is: she marries at an early age, probably moves in with her husband's family, her marriage partner is very likely a relative, he is older than her and indeed, in a good proportion of marriages, the age gap is quite large. Given the low educational level in general, they are both uneducated or the educational gap is in favor of males. Whether married or not, house chores and/or agrarian activities are a major occupation.

The contemporary marriage picture is expected to have undergone important changes. The following analyzes the nuptiality transition that took place in the Arab region recently. To describe the transition, two dimensions are considered: timing of marriage and celibacy.

Table 1 provides the proportion ever married for women aged 15-49, 20-49 and 40-49 from a time period as far back in time as data allow.

Table 1

Proportion Ever Married in a Specified Base Year for Women Aged 15-49, 20-49 and 40-49 in Different Arab Countries

Country	Year	% Ever married 15-49	% Ever married 20-49	% Ever married 40-49
Egypt	1960	84.6	93.1	98.5
Libya	1973	84.3	96.4	99.5
Sudan	1973	84.9	94.6	98.2
Jordan	1961	73.6	88.7	97.2
Kuwait	1970	76.4	90.8	98.1
Syria	1970	74.2	88.7	97.2

Source: U.N. Demographic Yearbook for different years.

Taking account of the fact that the available statistics cover the relatively recent period of the 1960s and the early 1970s, we note that during the 1960s and up till the early 1970s at least three quarters of females aged between 15-49 were ever married. If we exclude age group 15-19, which is likely to have experienced recent shifts, the proportion of females ever married in age group 20-49 increases considerably. For the cohort of females aged 40-49, during the 1960s and early 1970s, marriage is almost universal. This indicates that the prospects of marriage for the young cohorts of the mid-1930s were almost certain.

Moving to a contemporary period, Table 2 shows that during the 1990s (only thirty years after the previous table) important changes in the proportion ever married have occurred in many Arab countries. The proportion of ever married women in most (12 out of 17) of the countries considered does not reach 60 percent of those aged 15-49. For the remaining few, this proportion ranges from 60 percent to 72 percent.

Table 2

Proportion Ever Married in a Specified Recent Year, for Women Aged 15-49 and 40-49 in Different Countries

Country	Year/ Source	% Ever Married 15-49	% Ever Married 40-49
Libya	1995/1	38.8	97.7
Lebanon	1996/1	52.2	85.1
Algeria	1992/1	53.6	97.4
UAE	1995/2	54.2	99.2
Jordan	1997/3	54.6	95.1
Bahrain	1995/2	54.7	95.6
Tunisia	1994/95/1	55.2	96.2
Syria	1993/1	55.8	94.2
Saudi Arabia	1996/2	55.8	98.5
Kuwait	1996/2	56.4	93.6
Morocco	1995/3	57.5	96.5
Qatar	1987/4	58.0	93.6
Sudan	1992/93/1	60.7	97.6
Oman	1995/2	64.4	99.3
Iraq	1987/5	65.5	95.8
Egypt	1995/3	70.1	98.5
Yemen	1997/3	71.7	98.8

Source: (1) Maternal and Child Health Surveys
(2) Family Health Surveys
(3) Demographic and Health Surveys
(4) Child Health Survey in Gulf Countries
(5) U.N. Demographic Yearbooks

In viewing the proportion of women aged 40-49 who are ever married, it is obvious that the universality of marriage that characterized the marriage cohort of the mid-1930s continues to be a feature of the marriage cohort of the mid-1960s to mid-1970s. Clearly whatever changes are affecting the proportion ever married, they have occurred after the mid-1970s.

The components (delay and/or celibacy) of the decline in proportion of females ever married are illustrated in Table 3. The delay in marriage is evidenced by the decrease in proportion married by age 20, while the increase in celibacy is indicated by the change in the percentage of females not married by age 30-39.[2]

Table 3 confirms that all Arab countries have experienced delays in marriage (though with a varying degrees) and that many Arab countries are also signaling a departure from universal marriage. For these countries (10 out of 15) a proportion between 10 percent and 27 percent remain never married by age 30-39.

Table 3

Indicators of Delays in Marriage and Increase in Celibacy for Different Countries and Years

Country	% of women 20-24 married by age 20		% Female 30-39 never married		
	25 years ago	Recently between 1992-97	Base year	At base year	Recently between (1992-97)
Algeria	85.6	23.6			10.0
Bahrain	77.3	20.6			14.5
Egypt	64.8	41.4	1960	2.5	3.9
Jordan	55.0	26.5	1961	4.4	15.4
Kuwait	65.2	29.3	1970	2.6	14.1
Lebanon	44.3	20.6			27.0
Libya	82.9	8.7	1973	0.8	20.6
Morocco	72.7	29.2			16.5
Oman	95.8	55.5			1.6
Saudi Arabia	82.7	38.6			4.7
Sudan	83.6	35.7	1973	2.3	11.7
Syria	64.5	37.0	1970	4.7	13.3
Tunisia	67.2	19.6			12.6
UAE	88.3	33.3			6.0
Yemen	87.5	63.6			3.0

Source: Same as tables 1 and 2

The distribution of Arab countries according to their current stage in the nuptiality transition is illustrated in Figure 1. Countries falling in the lower right corner (stage 1) of the graph experience the non-European pattern of

---

[2] The age group 30-39 may of course include residual effect of marriage delays but the recency of change in nuptiality patterns supports its use. Graph (1) provides this measure for the older ages 35-39.

early and universal marriage while countries falling in the upper left corner (stage 3) follow the Western European pattern. Stage 2 represents an intermediate stage where marriage is late but universal. Countries like Lebanon, Kuwait, Jordan and Libya are very far off in their nuptiality transitions and there are only a few Arab countries remaining in stage 1. Most Arab countries are in the intermediate stage. The classification by stage indicates little similarity across the region. Furthermore, the clustering of countries within each stage is surprising. Egypt, with a long history of women's education and productive employment, remains in stage 1 next to Yemen and Oman while a conservative society such as Saudi Arabia is in stage 2. Countries similar with respect to culture and social structure such as the Gulf States are spread over the three stages.

The clustering of countries is related to some extent to female literacy. Countries in stage 3 have a higher female literacy level (90 percent in Lebanon, 79 percent in Jordan, 75 percent in Kuwait and 63 percent in Libya) while countries in stage 1 experience a much lower level of 46 percent in Oman, 39 percent in Egypt and 39 percent in Yemen (UNDP 1998). However, female literacy does not explain a large amount of variability in nuptiality, which suggest that other forces are contributing to changes in marriage patterns. The nature of these forces and their effect are not necessarily similar across all Arab societies.

It is interesting to investigate the differentials in the experience of delays in marriage and celibacy by educational status, which is summarized in Tables 4 and 5 respectively. The role of education in delaying marriage is very evidenced in Table 4. The chances of an uneducated woman being married at ages 20-24 are around twice the chances of the educated. Actually, in some countries (e.g., Algeria and Yemen) her chances are more than three times as much.

Figure (1)

Distribution of Arab Countries by their Current Stage in the Nuptiality Transition

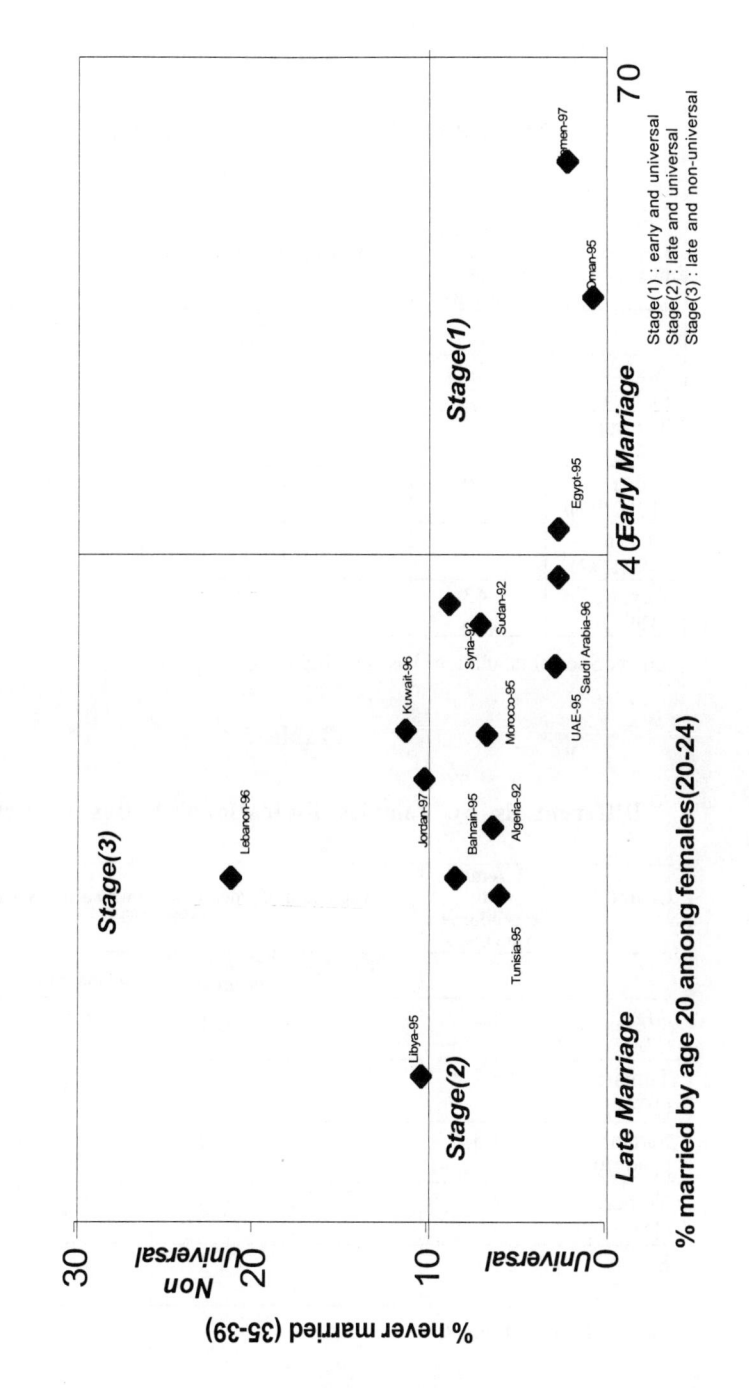

Stage(1) : early and universal
Stage(2) : late and universal
Stage(3) : late and non-universal

Table 4

Differentials by Female Educational Status in Delays of Marriage

Country (Year)	% female with secondary+ education	Proportion of women 20-24 who are ever married (1988-1995)			
		<Primary	Primary & Preparatory	Secondary+	Total
Algeria (1992)	24	39.3	28.3	11.3	29.6
Tunisia (1988)	27	43.6	37.8	21.0	35.4
Sudan (1992/93)	20	57.6	29.1	21.9	39.9
Yemen (1991/92)	7	77.9	59.0	23.5	71.8
Egypt (1995)	43	77.5	68.3	37.5	58.6

Source: Special tabulations based on MCHS and DHS data

Table 5

Differentials by Females Educational Status in Celibacy

Country	% female with secondary+ education	Proportion of women 30-39 who are never married (1988-1995)			
		<Primary	Primary & Preparatory	Secondary+	Total
Algeria (1992)	6.2	7.8	16.1	26.2	10.1
Tunisia (1988)	13.7	7.0	10.6	9.4	8.5
Sudan (1992/93)	12.3	9.1	11.8	26.8	11.7
Yemen (1991/92)	2	1.7	7.2	17.4	2.2
Egypt (1995)	26.2	3.4	3.5	5.4	3.9

Source: Same as Table 4.

Differentials in celibacy by educational status are not uniform across the Arab countries. They are marked for Algeria, Sudan and Yemen but negligible for Tunisia and Egypt. In Algeria and Sudan, about one quarter of educated women are not married. In these countries, celibacy is clearly prevalent for this group of women. Actually, even if we confine the analysis to age group 35-39, the level of celibacy remains as high as 25 percent and 17 percent (Algeria and Sudan respectively).

Two interesting observations are inferred from Table 5. First the small changes in the pattern of marriage in Egypt, which remains in the first stage of the nuptiality transition, are not confined to the uneducated. Those with higher education in Egypt experience the same low levels of celibacy as the less educated. Also, the delays in marriage in Egypt are notable only after secondary education is achieved (those with primary and preparatory are not different from those with less than primary). The second observation is that in countries with overall moderate levels of celibacy (Algeria, Tunisia, Sudan), the uneducated as well as those with little education do experience their fair share of celibacy.

Characteristics of Marriage

Five aspects of marriage are likely to play a key role in the dynamics of the relationship. They are: blood relationship between couples, establishment of independent households, gap in age, gap in education, as well as the wife's command over resources (whether education or income). The characteristics of recent marriages along those five dimensions as well as changes occurring in them are summarized below.

1) Consanguinity. The percentage of ever married women (15-49) having a blood relation with their husbands is generally high. Table 6 shows that it ranges from 18 percent (Lebanon) up to 56 percent (Sudan) and that in 7 countries (out of 13) at least 30 percent of ever married women (15-49) are married to their first cousin.

Table 6

Proportion of Ever Married Women (15-49) Who Are Married to Their First Cousin

Country	Year /Source	%
Algeria	1992 [1]	26
Bahrain	1989 [2]	23
	1995 [3]	24
Lebanon	1996 [1]	18
Libya	1995 [1]	43
Egypt	1991 [1]	31
	1992 [4]	25
	1995 [4]	24
Kuwait	1987 [2]	30
	1996 [3]	26
Oman	1988/89 [2]	33
	1995 [3]	34
Qatar	1987 [2]	35
Saudi Arabia	1987 [2]	36
	1996 [3]	31
Sudan	1992/93 [1]	56
Syria	1993 [1]	35
U.A Emirates	1987 [2]	26
	1995 [3]	24
Yemen	1991/92 [4]	31
	1997 [4]	34

Sources: [1] Maternal and Child Health Surveys.
[2] Child Health Surveys in Gulf Countries.
[3] Family Health Surveys.
[4] Demographic and Health Surveys.

Table 7 confirms that the changes across time in consanguinity are not very significant.

Table 7

Percent of Ever Married Women*
Who Married Their First Cousin (Father and Mother Side)
by Periods Before Survey

Country	Year	Periods before survey		
		> 5	10-14	15-19
Egypt	1995	21.0	24.8	24.8
Algeria	1992	24.2	25.3	27.4
Yemen	1991/92	34.8	32.5	31.3
Sudan	1992/93	54.3	57.3	62.2

Source: Same as Table 4.
* Confined to women married once and their age at marriage ≤ 35.

The qualification of age and marriage is imposed to achieve comparability as it avoids the censoring bias caused by upper ceiling of age 50.

2) Establishing Independent Homes. Table 8 shows a very large proportion of ever married women initiating their marriage in someone else's house. Surprisingly, there is a decrease across time in the proportion setting up their own homes. The economic and housing situation are probably very much linked to this trend.

Table 8
Percent of Ever Married Women* who Lived in Someone Else's House at Initiation of Marriage by Periods Before Survey

Country	Year	Periods before survey		
		>5	10-14	15-19
Egypt	1991	57.8	51.2	53.1
Sudan	1992/93	63.4	49.5	45.0
Yemen	1991/92	72.6	66.0	64.1
Algeria	1992	85.9	82.0	86.0

Source: Same as Table 4.
* Confined to women married once and their age at marriage ≤ 35.

3) Gap in Age. Table 9 shows that the age gap remains in favor of husbands. This is very much evidenced in Sudan, where in about 18 percent of marriages, the husband-wife age gap exceeds fifteen years. In the remaining three countries husbands in six percent of marriages are older than their wives by at least 15 years. On the other hand, except for Sudan, a non-negligible percentage of women (between 6 percent and 9 percent) are also older than their husbands.

Table 9

Percent Distribution of Ever Married Women*
By Age Gap between Husbands and Wives

Country	Year	Age gap between husband and wife			
		H ≤ W	0-9	10-14	15+
Algeria	1992	9.2	71.0	13.9	5.9
Egypt	1995	5.9	68.0	20.2	5.9
Sudan	92/93	2.8	52.7	26.7	17.8
Yemen	91/92	8.7	73.5	11.9	5.9

Source: Same as Table 4.
* Confined to women married once and their age at marriage ≤ 35 and married during five years preceding survey.

4) Gap in Education. Table 10 shows a higher than expected proportion of recent marriages with an educational gap in favor of females. In Algeria and Sudan in about two out of every ten recent marriages the wife's education was higher than her husband's. The percentage of recent marriages that fit the typical picture of a husband more educated than his wife is less than 50 percent in many countries.

Table 10

Percent Distribution of Ever Married* Women by Inter Spousal Educational Difference

Country	Year	Education of husband compared to wife			
		H> W	H=W; no education	H=W; same education	H<W
Algeria	1992	23.6	12.2	26.7	37.5
Egypt	1995	15.8	9.7	36.4	38.1
Sudan	1992/93	22.0	16.8	21.0	40.2
Tunisia	1988	9.2	10.7	34.1	46.0
Yemen	1991/92	8.7	23.1	6.5	61.7

Source: Same as Table 4.
*Confined to those married once and whose age at marriage ≤ 35 and married during five years preceding the survey.

Table 11 allows us to study the trend in the educational gap across time. Clearly the percentage with both couples uneducated has decreased significantly across time and is being replaced mainly by couples with similar education or where the wife has the higher education.

In cases when wives are more educated than their husbands, the gap in education status is not negligible. For example Table 12 shows a good proportion with very large differences.

Table 11

Percent Distribution of Ever Married Women* by Inter Spousal Education Difference and Marriage Duration

Period before survey	H<W	H=W; no education	H=W; same education	H>W
Algeria (1992)				
<5	23.6	12.2	26.7	37.5
10-14	15.1	29.2	19.6	36.1
15-19	11.1	39.1	15.5	34.3
Egypt (1995)				
<5	15.8	9.7	36.4	38.1
10-14	12.6	19.3	26.7	41.4
15-19	11.3	23.4	23.6	41.7
Sudan (92/93)				
<5	22.0	16.8	21.0	40.2
10-14	15.4	33.6	16.7	34.3
15-19	10.3	45.5	14.7	29.5
Tunisia (1988)				
<5	9.2	10.7	34.1	46.0
10-14	10.1	26.3	24.2	39.4
15-19	9.1	44.2	17.2	29.5
Yemen (91/92)				
<5	8.7	23.1	6.5	61.7
10-14	2.9	45.0	2.9	49.2
15-19	1.1	50.8	1.0	47.1

Source: Same as Table 4.
*Confined to women married once and their age at marriage ≤ 35.

Table 12

**Among those whose Wife Education is Higher than Husband*
The Percent of Women whose Educational Gap is
at Least Two Stages****

Country	Year	%
Algeria	1992	46.2
Egypt	1995	52.3
Sudan	92/93	35.3
Yemen	91/92	43.5

Source: Same as Table 4.
* Confined to women married once and their age at marriage ≤ 35 and married during five years preceding the survey.
** For example those complete secondary are married to someone less than preparatory

5) Command over Resources. The two assets of education and economic independence are critical in the dynamics of the marriage relation. A wife's autonomy, decision-making power, and responsibilities are clearly affected by her command over these two basic resources. The investigation of improvement of resources over time is conducted by comparing the educational assets of younger (aged 15-19) and older cohorts. Table 13 shows a significant change across time in joining schools and continuing to secondary levels.

A comparison between the percent of females never joining schools in the two cohorts indicates a dramatic change especially in Algeria (from 86 percent to 19 percent). Younger females are more likely to finish secondary education. The percentage of females in the age group 45 to 49 with secondary education was only 11 percent in Egypt and less than 5 percent in Tunisia, Algeria, and Sudan, and increased substantially among the younger cohort (20 to 24 years old) to reach 43 percent in Egypt and 20 to 27 percent in the other three countries.

Table 13

Percent of Females Never Joining Schools & Percent of Females with Secondary+ Education for Different Cohorts

Country	% of females never joining schools in age group		% of females with secondary + education	
	15-19	45-49	20-24	45-49
Algeria, 1992	19.0	86.0	24.2	1.0
Egypt, 1995	19.4	54.7	43.2	10.8
Sudan, 1992/93	22.2	79.0	19.7	1.5
Tunisia, 1988	27.7	88.3	26.8	4.2

Source: Same as table 4.

The economic participation of women not only influences the dynamics of the marriage relation but also the characteristics of the husband. Table 14 shows that women are more likely to marry a husband who is less educated than them if they ever worked before marriage.

Table 14

Percent of Wives* whose Husbands are Less Educated by Working Condition of Wives Before Marriage

Country	Ever worked	Never worked
Algeria, 1992	30.2	12.7
Egypt, 1995	14.3	12.9
Sudan, 1992/93	14.2	12.9
Tunisia, 1988	12.9	6.8
Yemen, 1991/92	16.4	3.2

Source: Same as Table 4.
* Confined to women married once and their age at marriage ≤ 35.

Implications of Nuptiality Changes

The study indicates that most Arab countries are undergoing a nuptiality transition resulting in a delay in marriage and an increasing proportion of females who will eventually remain in a state of celibacy.

In addition, the changes taking place with respect to the prevalence of celibacy and the timing of marriage are associated with changes in the characteristics of marriages. As a result of development, both education and age gaps are getting narrower with wives having more command over resources.

A surprising change, and one that seems to contradict with development, is the decrease across time in the proportion who are setting up their own homes. The high population growth rate and the trend towards increasing urbanization in the 1960s and the 1970s created a huge demand on housing units. Such demand was not satisfied and has been reflected in the cost of housing which might explain the decreasing proportion of newly married couples setting up their own homes. Another dimension that appears not to have been altered is the percentage of couple consanguinity.

The changes in marriage patterns and in the characteristics of couples within marriage have a number of important implications. Among them are the introduction of new social groups with special concerns, and functional changes in terms of role and contribution of women to the household. Also, the nuptiality transition has a number of demographic and age compositional consequences with far-reaching effects. These changes exert pressure for more sensitive public policies and more balanced gender relations.

(1) Youth. The recent significant demographic movements on the fertility and mortality front are changing the age structure of the population. The Arab population is moving now from a very young age structure to a situation where the two groups of Adolescents and Youth (10-24) constitute one-third of the total population in the region, a significant figure that approaches 85 million people (Population Reference Bureau 1998).

The increase in size accompanied by delays in marriage and different intergenerational perspectives highlight the need to understand the new situation of youth, their characteristics, problems, and demands.

Youth have currently been placed on the international research and programmatic agenda. In the Arab region, the recent past has witnessed major research efforts[3] and the establishment of youth ministries. Both developments are a step in the right direction.

El-Tawila (2000) notes two types of underlying thinking framing the interest in youth: a prevalent "deviant" paradigm reflecting apprehension and negative expectations about this group, and a new developmental approach with a broader vision of growth and development reflecting recognition of young people's potential.

Young people in the Arab region are characterized by higher levels of education attainment among both sexes, markets that are incapable of absorbing the influx of these young cohorts, poor access to programs concerned with life skills and family life education, and postponed marriages. The profile of young people, their contemporary needs, and the cultural context governing their identity, inclusion, and behavior call for a broad research agenda.

El-Tawila discusses in detail possible research directions encompassing the need to incorporate social marginalization or power in the international operational definition that is solely based on age, to develop a comprehensive understanding of the social and health needs of young people, to study the effectiveness of counseling services and NGO interventions, to better appreciate the attitudes/values and aspirations of the young generation, as well as possibly the need to develop an age-sensitive approach to the study of the realities and consequences of current economic policies in the region.

The better understanding of young people's sexuality is another area of concern. The restrictive norms in Arab countries taboo sexual relations and prohibit any discussions of sexual needs. Young people rarely discuss sexual matters explicitly with their parents or with adults older than themselves. A recent study (El-Tawila et al, 1999) showed that adolescents need sexual

---

[3] The concern with this group of the population is guiding a number of research efforts currently adopted by the Social Research Center of AUC in collaboration with the Population Council and a number of local partners. The national study of adolescence in Egypt conducted during 1997, the establishment of a regional working group on youth as well as the launching of a new study on "Patterns of Marriage and Family Formation among Youth in Egypt" are all illustrations of this justified new direction.

information and prefer it to be provided by their parents. Parents, on the other hand, are very reluctant to provide such information and in turn need assistance as far as what information should be conveyed, at what time, and how.

Furthermore, the region exhibits all the warning signs for anticipating rising rates of sexual activity: rising age of marriage, growing autonomy of teenagers, gender equality, and exposure to Western media (quoted from Furstenberg 1998). Findings from recent empirical research provide evidence that premarital sex may be on the rise (El-Zanaty and Abdalla, 1996), and that the practice may not be as rare as believed. Indeed, the emerging common-law (*'urfi'*) marriage among young couples in Egypt, as well as other non-conventional forms of marriage, may represent a coping strategy among youth as a compromise to the economic constraints to marriage and the cultural denial of extra-marital sexual relations.

(2) Celibate Women. The nature of nuptiality changes occurring in Arab countries suggest that a larger proportion of women may live in permanent celibacy. The implications of these changes on the well-being of women are very much linked to their individual traits and resources, familial and societal support systems, as well as opportunities for self-fulfillment beyond the role of mother and wife.

The existing data on the profile of single women, their engagement in new forms of marriage, their sexual health, their level of dependency, and their support network are very slim. A more focused research effort is required. The very limited data provided in Table 15 suggest a high level of dependency in terms of personal traits and ability to earn a living.

Table 15

Profile of Never Married Women in the Age Group 15-49

Country	Year	Proportion with primary education or less (no schooling)	% Working	% Working for cash
Algeria	1992	62.4 (19.9)	7.5	6.6
Egypt	1995	29.4 (16.4)	13.3	12.25
Sudan	1992/93	62.3 (40.7)	13.0	9.97
Yemen	1991/92	84.6 (71.2)	4.6	2.99

Source: Rashad and Khadr (forthcoming)

The importance of education and productive careers for the fulfillment of women's lives should be central in any social policy agenda. Unfortunately, societal recognition and support systems appear to revolve around the roles of women as wives and mothers and the family remains very much the basic focus. The continued re-discussion of the value of women's work, in view of the high unemployment rates, not only ignores the psychosocial dimension of females' well-being but also the situation and needs of the unmarried.

(3) Female Headed Households. Another area of policy research that requires increased attention is the situation of female-headed households and their share of societal support.

The recent past has seen increased recognition of the existence of a high proportion of households with female heads. Recent data reveal that at least one out of every ten households in Arab countries is headed by a woman. Table 16 shows different characteristics of female headships in selected Arab countries. For example, while in Algeria and Egypt more than half of female heads reside in urban areas, the majority of those female heads reside in rural areas in Sudan and Yemen. Sudan and Yemen also show a higher proportion of female heads who are younger (than those in Algeria, Egypt and Tunisia) and are currently married. Clearly there are different underlying contexts surrounding this phenomenon in these countries.

Table 16

Percent Distribution of Female Heads by Residence, Age, Marital Status and Educational Attainment.

	Algeria	Egypt	Sudan	Tunisia	Yemen
% of female headed households	10.6	12.6	12.4	11	12.2
Percentage distribution by different characteristics:					
Place of residence					
Rural	41.0	48.9	64.6		86.3
Urban	59.0	51.1	35.4		13.7
Age					
<30	1.9	3.2	14.9	7.9	18.8
30-49	27.8	36.2	38.9	28.5	47.2
50+	70.3	60.6	46.2	63.6	34.0
Marital status					
Never married	1.1	2.4	1.2	2.7	1.3
Married	11.7	10.4	42.3	22.6	60.9
Widow	71.7	80.9	44.3	68.9	32.4
Divorced	15.5	6.3	12.2	5.8	5.4
Education attainment					
<primary	94.4	83.1	89.4	84.5	98.2
Primary or Preparatory	3.4	8.7	6.8	11.8	1.4
Secondary +	2.2	8.2	3.8	3.7	0.4

Source: Same as Table 4.

The available data on female headships do not provide a detailed and complete picture on the profile and needs of this group. Furthermore, the sparse available research and data on female headships are built on the use of the heavily criticized criterion of self-definition or acknowledgement of the female head by household members. Such a definition underestimates the prevalence of these households and does not capture the real situation of female headships. Khadr and Farid (1999) discuss the different criteria for headships and shows that only a few small-scale studies (for example see Fergany 1998) have used the criteria of possessing the power of decision making or being the major economic supporter in the household.

The widely used definition conceals important categories of female heads. Among them three call for special attention:

1) Widows/divorced women living in their paternal households or absorbed by other kin households. Khadr and El-Zeini (2000) show that more than 90,000 households in Egypt host a widow or a divorced woman with her children and pose the question: who is the real head of this subfamily?

2) Females who fulfill all the duties of headship in conjugal marriage, while the patriarchal cultural tradition accords her husband the headship.

3) Older females living in single person households which constituted more than 25 percent of all female headed households in Egypt.

The difference in the nature of female headship and the characteristics of the different types reveal the need for further thorough examination of the context, causes, and determinants of this phenomenon in order to identify policies to address their needs.

(4) Gender Relations. The changing characteristics of married couples and the different societal contextual[4] forces not only influence the roles of husband as the main breadwinner and the household head but they are also affecting the dynamics of the relation and the functioning of the family.

The adaptation of the family to different forces of change and its functioning are areas requiring further investigation. Efforts since the late 1970s to change personal status and the unexpected resistance to such a change illustrate the need for research and advocacy efforts to guide policy formulation (Zulficar 1995).[5]

---

[4] The increased education, urbanization and changing economic conditions are all redefining the role of women in the public and domestic spheres.

[5] A law was passed in 2000 that was more responsive to the needs of women and children when a divorce occurs. The law significantly simplified the procedure for

(5) Demographic Consequences. Fertility, age composition, and family demography consequences are clearly associated with nuptiality changes outlined earlier. Rashad (1997) discussed the significant recent fertility transition in Arab countries and demonstrated the role played by marriages in precipitating such a change.

The future directions of fertility change are very much related to the ongoing changes in nuptiality as well as possible changes in marital fertility patterns to offset the fertility inhibiting effects of later marriages. Understanding determinants of nuptiality change, the response of married females to shorter fecund periods of life and the health consequences of different reproductive patterns are all areas of research that are needed to guide future planning.

The already well advanced demographic transition is now producing important fundamental transformations. At the aggregate level, the age structures are shifting towards a greater concentration at middle and older ages. At the household and individual level, the demography of the family is changing dramatically as individuals live longer, marry later, and have fewer children.

A number of recent studies have started to investigate some aspects of the consequences of demographic change in the Arab region. The recent conference on "Population Challenges in the Middle East: Towards the 21st Century" organized by the Economic Research Forum discussed the implications of the Arab demographic dynamics for labor markets and concluded: "Yes, there is a demographic window of opportunity due to a notable decline in fertility, but the success in benefiting from this demographic gift would very much depend on the policies that will be adopted by the different countries of the region" (Forum Newsletter 1999, p. 1). In the same conference Rashad and Khadr (forthcoming) noted that although populations in the region are currently far from aging, the on-going demographic changes are building up the needed momentum for rapid aging of these populations.

These studies are a step in the right direction, but much more focused effort is needed to identify the nature of macro level demographic changes and their demand on the economy and the provision of social services. Also,

---

a wife to obtain divorce and allowed her in effect to obtain divorce without her husband's consent.

much more attention should be given to exploring the implications of the transition on the well-being of the various segments of the population.

References

Abdel-Azeem, F., S. Farid and A. Khalifa (eds).1993. *Egypt Maternal and Child Health Survey 1991*. Cairo: Central Agency for Public Mobilization and Statistics and PAPCHILD/League of Arab States.

Algeria Maternal and Child Health Survey: 1992. 1994. Algiers: National Office of Statistics (Algiers) and Cairo: PAPCHILD/League of Arab States.

Al-Mazrou Y., and S. Farid, (eds.). 1991. *Saudi Arabia Child Health Survey 1987*. Riyadh: Ministry of Health.

Al-Muhaideb, A., A. Abdul-Ghafour, and S. Farid, (eds.). 1991. *United Arab Emirates Child Health Survey 1987*. Abu Dhabi: Ministry of Health.

Al-Qassimi, S., M. Fikri, and S. Farid (eds.). 1996. *United Arab Emirates Family Health Survey 1995: Preliminary Report*. Abu Dhabi: Ministry of Health.

Al-Rashoud, R., and S. Farid. 1991. *Kuwait Child Health Survey 1987*. Kuwait: Ministry of Health.

Al-Rashoud, R., and S. Farid (eds.) 1997. *Kuwait Family Health Survey 1996: Preliminary Report*. Kuwait: Ministry of Health.

Ariès, P. 1948. *Historie des populations françaises et de leurs attitudes devant la vie depuis le XVIIe siècle*. Paris: Editions du Seuil.

Azelmat, M., M. Ayad and E. Housni. 1996. *Enquête de panel sur la population et la santé 1995*. Rabat: Ministère de la Santé Publique and Calverton, Maryland, USA: Macro International Inc.

Badinter, E. 1980. *L'amour en plus*. Paris: Flammarion.

Drake, M. 1972. "Fertility controls in pre-industrial Norway" in D.V. Glass and Roger Revelle, eds. *Population and Social Change*. London: Edward Arnold, pp. 185-198.

Economic Research Forum. 1999. *Newsletter of the Economic Research Forum for the Arab Countries, Iran and Turkey*, 5(4).

Al-Tawila,S., B.Ibrahim, S. Sallam, F. El Sahn and O. El Gibaly. 1999. *Transitions to Adulthood: A National Survey on Adolescents in Egypt*. Cairo, Egypt. The Population Council Regional Office for West Asia and North Africa.

Al-Tawila, S. 2000. *Youth in the Population Agenda: Concepts and Methodologies*. West Asia and North Africa Cairo: MEAwards Regional Papers No.44, Population Council.

El-Zanaty, F., H. Sayed, H. Zaky, and A.A. Way. 1993. *Egypt Demographic and Health Survey, 1992*. Cairo: National Population Council and Calverton, Maryland, USA: Macro International Inc.

El-Zanaty, F. and E. Abdalla. 1996. "Behavioral Research among Egyptian University Students." Unpublished report. Cairo: International Medical Technology Egypt (Medtric), Family Health International, Behavioral Research Unit, December.

El-Zanaty, F., E.M.Hussein, G.A.Shawky, A.A. Way and S. Kishor. 1996. *Egypt Demographic and Health Survey, 1995*. Cairo: National Population Council and Calverton, Maryland, USA: Macro International Inc.

Farid, S. 1992. *Bahrain Child Health Survey 1989*. Manama: Ministry of Health.

Fergany, N. 1998. "Human Capital Accumulation and Development: Arab Countries at the Close of the 20th Century." Economic Research Forum, Arab Fund for Economic and Social Development, Conference on Population Challenges in the Middle East and North Africa, Cairo, Egypt, 2-4 November 1998.

Furstenberg, F. 1998. "The implications of Western Experience with Teenage Childbearing for Developing Countries," *Studies in Family Planning* 29(2):246-253.

Habakkuk, H. J. 1971. *Population Growth and Economic Development Since 1750*. New York: Humanities Press.

Hajnal, J. 1953. "Age at Marriage and Proportion Marrying," *Population Studies* 7(2):111-136.

Hajnal, J. 1965. "The Marriage Boom" in Joseph J. Spengler and Otis Dudley Duncan, eds., *Demographic Analysis: Selected Readings*. Glencoe. Illinois: The Free Press. Pp. 80-101.

Heeren, H.J. 1973. "Marriage as a Demographic Variable." International Population Conference, vol. 2, pp. 9-17. Liege: International Union for Scientific Study of Population.

Hofstee, E. W. 1968. "Population Increase in the Netherlands," *Acta Historicae Neerlandica* 3:43-125.

Jordan Population and Family Health Survey 1997. 1998. Amman: Department of Statistics, Amman and Macro International Inc., Calverton, Maryland USA.

Khadr, Z. and I. Farid. 1999. "Who is the Head: An Anthropo-demographic Perspective on Female Headed Households in Egypt." Paper Presented to IUSSP Committee on Anthropological Demography Seminar on Social Categories in Population Research, Cairo, Egypt, September 15-18, 1999.

Khadr, Z and L. El-Zeini. 2000. "Families and Households: Headship and Co-Residence." Paper prepared for the Symposium on the New Arab

Family, Cairo Papers in Social Science and Social Research Center, The American University in Cairo.

Khoja, T. A., and S. Farid (eds.). 1997. *Saudi Arabia Family Health Survey 1996: Preliminary Report*. Riyadh: Ministry of Health.

Lebanon Maternal and Child Health Survey 1995, 1996. Beirut: Ministry of Health (Beirut) and Cairo: PAPCHILD/League of Arab States.

Libya Maternal and Child Health Survey 1995, 1997. Tripoli: General Committee for Health and Social Security and Cairo: PAPCHILD/League of Arab States.

Lutz, W. 1987. "Finnish Fertility since 1722: Lessons from an Extended Decline." Publication Series D. No. 18. Helsinki: Population Research Institute in collaboration with the International Institute for Applied System Analysis.

Population Reference Bureau. 1998. *World Population Data Sheet*.

Rashad, H. 1997. "A Comparative Analysis of Fertility in Arab Countries: Explaining the Anomalies" in Basia Zaba and John Blacker, eds., *Brass Tacks: Essays in Medical Demography*. London: Athlone Press.

Rashad, H. and Z. Khadr. Forthcoming. "The demography of the Arab region: new challenges and opportunities." Paper presented to Economic Research Forum Conference, Cairo, 2-4 November 1998, to appear in Sirageldin, I. (ed.), Population Challenges in the Middle East and North Africa: Towards the Twenty First Century.

Salman, A., K. Al-Jabar, and S. Farid (eds.) 1991. *Qatar Child Health Survey 1987*. Doha: Ministry of Health.

Stone, L. 1979. *The Family, Sex and Marriage in England 1500-1800*. New York, Harper Colophon Books.

Sudan Maternal and Child Health Survey 1992/93. 1995. Khartoum: Federal Ministry of Health and Cairo: PAPCHILD/League of Arab States.

Sulaiman, A. M., A. Al-Ghassany, and S. Farid (eds.) 1992. *Oman Child Health Survey 1988-89.* Muscat: Ministry of Health.

Sulaiman, A. M., A. Al-Riyami, and S. Farid, 1996 (eds.). *Oman Family Health Survey 1995: Preliminary Report.* Muscat: Ministry of Health.

Syria Maternal and Child Health Survey 1993. 1995. Damascus: Central Bureau of Statistics and Cairo: PAPCHILD/League of Arab States.

Tunisia Maternal and Child Health Survey 1994/95. 1996. Tunis: Ministry of Health and Cairo: PAPCHILD/League of Arab States.

UNDP. 1998. *Human Development Report, 1998.* New York: Oxford University Press.

United Nations. 1979. *Demographic Yearbook Historical Supplement.* New York.

United Nations. 1982. *Demographic Yearbook.* New York.

United Nations. 1990. *Pattern of First Marriage: Timing and Prevalence.* New York: United Nations.

Wolf, A.P. 1988. "Family Systems in Agrarian Societies." Paper prepared for the Rockefeller Foundation workshop on women's status in relation to fertility and mortality. Bellagio, Italy, June 6-10, 1988.

Yacoub, I., T. Nasseb, and S. Farid (eds.). 1996. *Bahrain Family Health Survey 1995: Preliminary Report.* Manama: Ministry of Health.

Yemen Demographic and Maternal and Child Health Survey 1991/92. 1994. San'aa: Central Statistical Organization, Cairo: PAPCHILD/

League of Arab States (Cairo), and Calverton, Maryland USA: Macro International Inc.

Yemen Demographic and Maternal and Child Health Survey 1997. 1998. Sana`a: Central Statistical Organization, and Calverton, Maryland USA: Macro International Inc.

Zulficar, Mona. 1995. *Women in Development: A Legal Study*. Cairo: UNICEF.

AGE-DISCREPANT MARRIAGE IN EGYPT

MAGUED OSMAN AND LAILA S. SHAHD

Introduction

Nuptiality trends in the last two decades indicate an increase in age at marriage among Egyptian females. This shift in age at marriage is probably due to an increase in female education and/or economic hardship and has been observed in nearly all Arab societies. An upward shift in age at marriage is expected to result in a larger proportion of females who never marry. Despite the increase in age at marriage among Egyptian females and contrary to what has happened in other Arab societies, the prevalence of celibacy among older women has not increased which suggests that the dynamics of family formation might have been subject to change.[1]

Furthermore, statistics on the singulate mean age at marriage by sex show that the age difference between spouses has only changed slightly during the last 30 years and that the universal pattern of men preferring to marry younger women still persists. In 1960, the gap between spouses reached an average of 6.1 years, while in 1991, it reached 5.2 years (CAPMAS, 1960; Abdel-Azeem et al, 1993).

Three dimensions, namely prevalence, timing, and characteristics of spouses are usually used to describe changes in nuptiality. Few changes occurred in Egypt with respect to prevalence and timing in the last two decades. A new trend that has not been documented elsewhere is the significant increase in the number of older wife/younger husband marriages

---

[1] This paper is an integral component of the many research pieces presented by the New Arab Demography Program (NAD) in the Cairo Papers Symposium. The New Arab Demography Program is a collaborative effort between Arab scholars, national and international institutions. It is co-ordinated by the Social Research Center (SRC) of the American University in Cairo (AUC) and supported by Mellon, Hewlett and the Ford Foundations. The authors would like to thank Prof. Nicholas Hopkins and Dr. Somaia al-Sadani for their comments.

(or age-discrepant marriages) since the 1990s. Changes in the characteristics of spouses is the main focus of this paper.

Age-discrepant marriage is defined as a marriage in which the individual is by societal standards considered to have transgressed the boundaries governing the selection of a mate (Berardo et al 1983). The society attributes the violation of prescriptions on what are "ideal" and "acceptable" age differences between mates to unusual traits of the participants in such unions. It is even expected that their marriage will have undesirable results (Vera et al 1985). Furthermore, the age-discrepant marriage is a marriage that involves people who are at different phases of life; e.g. one of the partners may be approaching retirement, while the other may be in the middle-years (Berardo et al 1983).

Certain changes in the society may result in alterations in the age-mating gradient norms of individuals seeking marriage. These include, first, the imbalance in the sex-ratio, second, the postponement of first marriage by large numbers of women in favor of education and/or career accompanied with the increase of women's economic independence (Wheeler and Gunter 1987).

In Egypt, educational attainment is considered as one of the main factors leading to the increase in age at marriage for females. The percentage of ever married is 78 percent among females with no education and 38 percent among females who completed secondary. On the other hand, the percentage of never married among females 30 to 39 years old is not associated with educational attainment. The percentage of celibacy is 3.4 percent among females with no education and 5.4 percent among females who completed secondary (El-Zanaty et al 1996; EFS 1983).

Source of data

Indicators reflecting timing and prevalence of marriage can be calculated from censuses or demographic surveys. However, demographic survey data do not include all necessary variables related to the nuptiality experience of males. Another source of data that might provide a wealth of data is marriage statistics. In the current study, census data and annual marriage statistics are used in describing the trend and dynamics of marriage.

A more qualitative approach has been adopted to supplement these data by conducting in-depth interviews with *ma'zoun*-s (religious registrars) as key informants. Further data on characteristics of spouses have been collected by examining *ma'zoun* records. Data can be considered as a convenient sample and is by no mean representative. However, an attempt has been made to include geographical areas (the *ma'zoun*'s catchment area) with different socio-economic characteristics.

Recent Changes in Characteristics of Spouses

Census data on marital status support the universality of marriage among females over 30 and males over 35. Between 1986 and 1996, the prevalence of celibacy increased slightly for females below 30 and for males below 35; however marriage is nearly universal for both females above 30 and males above 35 (Table 1).

Table 1

Percent Ever Married, 1986 and 1996

	Females		Males	
	1986	1996	1986	1996
20-24	63	56	19	12
25-29	86	87	56	49
30-34	93	95	85	82
35-39	95	97	94	94
40-44	95	98	96	98

Source: Calculated from Population Census (CAPMAS)

Marriage statistics suggest that family formation has not been subject to decline. On the contrary, the annual number of marriage contracts increased from 400 thousand in 1992 to nearly 500 thousand in 1997. This increase of 25 percent is higher than the growth in the number of adults. However, the characteristics of couples marrying changed in the 1990s. The traditional pattern of marriage of spouses belonging to the same generation with husbands a few year older is not the only prevalent pattern any more.

Results from marriage statistics indicate that a sharp increase in the number of marriages took place within the following three categories:

"husband 20-24 and wife 25-29," "husband 20-24 and wife 30-34," and "husband 25-29 and wife 30-34." The percentage of marriage contracts within these three categories was less than 10,000 cases in the beginning of the 1990s. Then it increased to more than 50 thousand cases in 1994 and to 133 thousand cases in 1996. As illustrated in Table 2, these three segments represented one fourth of all marriage contracts in 1996. This is a large increase over the figure of 2 percent in 1986.

Table 2

Number and Percentage of Marriage Contracts by Age Group, 1986 and 1996

Wife's age	Husband's age	1986	1996
25-29	20-24	4569 (1.1)	37297 (7.6)
30-34	20-24	708 (0.2)	54792 (11.2)
30-34	25-29	2650 (0.7)	41395 (8.5)
Total		6891 (2.0)	133484 (27.3)

Source: Calculated from Marriage Statistics (CAPMAS)

In the mid-1980s, the largest three types of marriages were between wives below 25 marrying husbands 5 to 10 years older (45 percent of all marriage contracts). In the mid-1990s, age-discrepant marriages with wives between 30 and 34 years and husbands older by 5 to 10 years represented 20 percent of all marriage contracts (Table 3). The appearance of such a larger number of marriages in this segment of the population might be explained by the increase in age at marriage during the 1980s, which has left a larger number from the female cohort born in the 1960s unmarried. When this cohort reached the age group 30 to 34 in 1990s, they did not find the socially accepted match and a large portion of this cohort got married to males who were on the average 5 to 10 years younger.

Table 3

Age Characteristics of Couples Marrying 1986 vs. 1996

1986			1996		
Wife	Husband	%	Wife	Husband	%
<20	20-24	16	20-24	25-29	14
20-24	25-29	15	30-34	20-24	11
<20	25-29	14	25-29	30-34	9
20-24	20-24	9	30-34	25-29	9

Source: Calculated from Marriage Statistics (CAPMAS)

The median age of wives at the time of the marriage contract did not change significantly between the 1960s and the 1980s. The median was slightly below 20 and increased to 25 in the mid-1990s. The change in the median age of the wife correlates with the age of the husband. As presented in Table 4, the change is inversely related to the husband's age. The younger the husband the larger the increase in the wife's age. Between 1962 and 1994, the median age of wives married to males below 30 at the time of the marriage contract gained around 5 years. On the other hand, the gain was around 2.5 years for older males.

It is interesting to notice that among husbands below 20, the wife was at least seven years older than her husband in at least 50 percent of the cases. The number of marriage contracts where the husband is below 20 years was 10 thousand cases in 1962 and 15 thousand cases in 1994. The distribution of marriages by wife's age shows that in 83 percent of the cases in 1962 the wife was in same age group. In 1994, the percentage decreased to 13 percent. Meanwhile a large number of males in this age group were involved in age-discrepant marriages (about 10 thousand out of the 15 thousand marriage contracts) where the wife is between 25 and 29.

Similarly, the distribution of marriage contracts where the husband is 20 to 24 years old by his wife's age changed significantly between 1962 and 1994. In 1962, in 72 percent of the cases the wife was below 20 and in 23 percent of the cases the wife was in the same age group. The percentage of older wife-younger husband was only 5 percent. Three decades later, the distribution changed significantly. In only 15 percent of the cases, the wife was younger (<20), in 34 percent the wife was from the same age group and in 51 percent of the cases the wife was older (25+).

Table 4

Wife's Median Age at Time of Marriage Contract by Husband's Age

Husband age	1962	1972	1982	1994
18-19	<20	<20	<20	26.3
20-24	<20	<20	<20	25.1
25-29	<20	20.4	20.9	24.5
30-34	21.2	22.1	23.0	23.6
35-39	24.3	23.2	25.1	26.5
40-44	27.7	24.7	26.9	30.3
45-49	30.1	27.2	28.5	32.8

Source: Calculated from Marriage Statistics (CAPMAS)

Social Change or Statistical Artifact

It is important to find out whether the sharp increase in older wife-younger husband marriages reflects a social change in Egyptian society or is only a statistical artifact. An attempt has been made to check whether other sources of data support these results. A comparison of the sex composition of the never married in the last two censuses (1986 and 1996) indicates a decrease in the sex ratio (number of males per 100 females) among the never marrieds in the age group 20 to 24 from 241 to 218, which indicates that a larger proportion of males in this age group is leaving the state of celibacy.

If the sex ratio were constant between 1986 to 1996, the number of never married males in the age group 20-24 would have increased from 2,319,000 to 2,565,000, a difference of 246,000 males. This difference is close to the number of marriage contracts taking place in the period 1994-1996 among males in the same age group (229 thousand marriage contacts) and older females.

It should be noted that the decrease in sex ratio between 1986 and 1996 occurred in both urban and rural areas, which might suggest that this new pattern of marriage is occurring in both urban and rural areas (from 192 to

174 in urban areas and from 329 to 279 in rural areas). Furthermore, the sex ratio among the population (ever married and never married) in the age group 20 to 24 did not change from 1986 to 1996, which indicates that the change occurring in the sex ratio among the never married is not a result of migration (from 99 in 1986 to 100 in 1996). The fact that analysis of census data agrees with marriage statistics suggests that the older wife-younger husband is not a statistical artifact.

The *Ma'zoun* Study

In an attempt to determine recent marriage changes in Egypt, age-discrepant marriages, specifically marriages where the wife is older then the husband, were investigated. *Ma'zoun*-s (official marriage registrars) were interviewed to determine their views on the characteristics and on the motives of marriages of older wives and younger husbands. In addition to in-depth interviews with *ma'zoun*-s, data on particular aspects including age-gap between spouses, dowry as mentioned in the marriage contract, previous marital status of husband and wife, educational level and occupation of husband and wife were analyzed. The data collected through interviews with the *ma'zoun*-s are preliminary but can be helpful in directing the research into much more precise and concrete research areas.

The interviews with *ma'zoun*-s focused on several areas including the prevalence of marriage between older women and younger men in different socioeconomic areas in Cairo; the age gap between younger husbands and older wives; the age category of men/women more likely to marry older wives/husbands; men's and women's motives for marrying older wives/younger husbands; the educational gap between older wives and younger husbands; and the instability of marriage between younger husbands and older wives.

The phenomenon of older women marrying younger men was studied in different socio-economic areas in Cairo governorate; lower, middle, and upper socioeconomic areas represented by Zeinhom, El-Sayeda Zeinab, and Garden City/Manshiet al-Bakry respectively. It is more likely to be prevalent among males from the lower socioeconomic categories of the middle class and it is relatively limited among males from the lower and the upper classes.

The age gap between the younger husband and the older wife ranges between 10–20 years in the different socioeconomic groups. According to *ma'zoun*-s, there is a positive relationship between age gap and marital status of the wife. The age gap in older wife-younger husband marriages increases among women who were previously married. According to *ma'zoun*-s, it might be difficult for a divorcee or a widow to find a husband of her own age or a bit older since she is not by social standards a privileged woman. Such woman can be considered as an advantage to younger men coming from lower economic standard. For the younger husband, marrying an older wife is an advantage since he can marry without having to take on the financial burdens of marriage, such as providing an apartment. For the older wife, her younger husband is a privilege since she can have a "husband" when it is difficult for her to find one.

The *ma'zoun*-s observe that the age of women who marry younger men ranges between 30 years old and 55 years old, while the age of men who marry older women than themselves ranges between 22 years old and 28 years old.

Concerning the reasons why men marry older women, *ma'zoun*-s argued that they are purely economic. The man may not have enough financial capacity to buy an apartment, and pay the *mahr* (paid by the groom's side), and the engagement gift (*shabka*) for a girl who is from his age or younger than him. As a result, he may think to marry an older woman as long as she will not burden him financially. This woman might be single, having passed the socially expected age of marriage, or might be a widow or a divorcee. In most of the cases, males willing to marry older females come from a lower socioeconomic class than that of females. Even though their families perceive such a marriage as socially unacceptable, they are not against it since their sons are relieved from the financial costs of marriage. Furthermore, the parents' satisfaction with their sons' marriage increases as there is a great probability that they will move to a higher socioeconomic level.

As for the motives of women who marry younger men, *ma'zoun*-s explained that they differ according to the previous marital status of women. For the single woman who did not marry during the socially appropriate time/age for marriage, finding a husband is an advantage. When she gets married, she overcomes the great social pressure against single women, and fulfils her own psychological needs of having a partner.

For the divorced/widow woman, finding a husband (even if he is younger) is an advantage for providing her with security and protection from people's gossip about her behavior and from the attempts of brothers or fathers to dominate her mobility.

The age gap is often associated with an educational and occupational gap. *Ma`zoun*-s argued that a large educational gap between the older wife and the younger husband may exist. According to data obtained from the *ma`zoun*-s, among the women married to younger men, 16.9 percent are professionals who are married to workers. One *ma`zoun* registered an older wife-younger husband marriage contract where the wife is a journalist and the husband is a merchant of vegetables. Another *ma`zoun* said that he handled a marriage contract where the wife is a university professor while the husband graduated from an intermediate industrial school.

Ma`zoun*-s emphasized that the woman who marries a younger man usually feels insecure in her marriage. She is keen to keep him as her husband, and, to achieve this, she imposes obstacles for divorce by requesting a large amount of deferred payment *"mu`akhar sadaq" in the marriage. This amount may reach LE10,000-15,000. Furthermore, a woman marrying a younger husband may insist on documenting in an appendix to the marriage contract a list of household items she owns (e.g. furniture or electrical appliances) at the time of marriage in order to keep these items for herself in the event of divorce.

The stability of marriages in which the husband is younger than his wife is limited. According to most of the *ma`zoun*-s, the divorce rate among these marriages is high. Only 15 to 20 percent of these marriages continue. If a woman has children from a previous marriage and gets married to a younger husband, tension in relations between her children and her new husband will affect her marriage stability.

Conclusion

Marriage statistics revealed a sharp increase in the number of younger males marrying older females, a new trend that has not been documented before. Three age categories (wife 25 to 29 and husband 20 to 24, wife 30 to 34 and husband 20 to 24, and wife 30 to 34 and husband 25 to 29) represent more than one fourth of marriage contracts in 1996. Marriage contracts in these three segments were only 2 percent of all marriage contracts one decade earlier.

Analysis of census data on marital status agrees with findings of marriage statistics and rules out that these findings resulted from errors in age reporting and therefore suggests that a change in pattern of family formation is taking place.

The emerging of such a larger number of marriages in this segment of the population might be explained by the increase in age at marriage during the 1980s, which has produced a larger number of females unmarried and then willing to marry even if the direction of the age difference is socially devalued. Economic factors play a role in correcting the balance in sex ratio within the marriage market. Young males will marry older wives who are more likely to be in a better economic status to free themselves from the financial burdens associated with marriage.

The recent increase in age-discrepant marriages suggests further studies. Research areas that need to be considered by social scientists include dissolution of older wife-younger husband marriages, decision-making and power within the family, and level and pattern of fertility.

References

Abdel-Azeem, F., S. Farid, and A. Khalifa, eds. 1993. *Egypt Maternal and Child Health Survey 1991.* Cairo: Central Agency for Public Mobilization and Statistics (CAPMAS) and PAPCHILD/League of Arab States.

Berardo, Felix M., Hernan Vera, and Donna H. Berardo. 1983. "Age-discrepant Marriages," *Medical Aspects of Human Sexuality* 17(1):57-76.

Central Agency for Public Mobilization and Statistics (CAPMAS). 1960. *National Population Census.* Cairo.

Central Agency for Public Mobilization and Statistics. 1983. *Egyptian Fertility Survey (EFS), 1980.* Volume 1.

El-Zanaty, F., E.M. Hussein, G.A. Shawky, A.A. Way, and S. Kishor. 1996. *Egypt Demographic and Health Survey, 1995.* Cairo: National Population Council and Calverton, Maryland: Macro International Inc.

Vera, Hernan, Donna H. Berardo, and Felix M. Berardo. 1985. "Age Heterogamy in Marriage," *Journal of Marriage and the Family* 3 (August):553-566.

Wheeler, Raymond H. and B.G. Gunter. 1987. "Change in Spouse Age Difference at Marriage: A Challenge to Traditional Family and Sex Roles," *The Sociological Quarterly* 28(3):411-421.

RATIONALES FOR KIN MARRIAGES IN RURAL UPPER EGYPT

HANIA SHOLKAMY

Introduction

This paper is about the ubiquity of kin marriages in Egypt. Unfortunately, the study of family, marriage, and kinship is by and large 'old country' as far as anthropology is concerned. Gender and the individual are our new frontiers! Thirty odd years having passed since kinship and kin marriages were topics worthy of theorizing and analysis (Antoun 1972, Bourdieu 1977, Holy 1989). But a look at Egyptian demographic data from the late 1990s shows that almost half of all marriages are between men and women who are related. So while this paper may not offer a new theory or revelation, it will describe the rationales that make youth in the 1990s seemingly continue to make choices similar to those of their ancestors.

The paper relies on ethnographic data from a small village in the governorate of Asyut, Upper Egypt. The inhabitants of this village are of Arab Bedouin origin.[1] They differentiate themselves from neighboring Upper Egyptian peasants by referencing this heritage and following in its traditions. Young people in this village identify with this heritage but have to contend also with the expediencies of a changing society, economy, and environment.

To meet three main objectives, the paper will closely look at the practices of a young couple and their friends and relatives. The first objective is to illustrate how new 'old' forms of marriage unions take place. The second is to consider the implications of these choices on how the young view their past, present, and future. And the third is to postulate on the meaning and significance that women in this village give to kin marriages.

The argument that follows does not generalize from these specific data.[2] It also does not claim that the practices of these men and women are

---

[1] The inhabitants of the village were nomadic until they settled about eighty years ago.
[2] These data are derived from fieldwork undertaken in 1992-95.

symbolic of anything. The paper hopes to enrich our understanding of how the so-called New Arab Family is forged in a particular village and to comment on the social principles that guide marriage unions. It attempts to go beyond the abstraction of these marriage choices and rules of prescription and to understand the conditions that make them favorable options for those who engage in them. I do not assume that kin marriages are antithetical to modernity or development. Indeed this paper illustrates that these matches are what people make them and that love, longing, and the effervescence of youth have a place even within the most classical of unions.

After this introduction there follows a brief review of anthropological writings on consanguinity and the theoretical considerations of marrying kin. The paper then presents a description of one patrilateral parallel cousin marriage from the village of Rihan.[3] The last section offers the exegesis of villagers for the choice of kin marriages and so places these choices in familial, social, and historical context as constructed by the villagers, particularly women themselves.

Kinship and Anthropology

Kinship studies, once the bread and butter of anthropology, have highlighted the significance of marriage prescriptions of the Mediterranean and the Arab world. On the whole, the ethnography of Middle Eastern societies has posited kinship and marriage rules as the organizing principles of people's lives (Eickelman 1989:124-34), with *bint al-'amm* (FBD/S) marriage[4] at the heart of these principles. The analysis of this practice cites consolidation of property and of family honor (protection of women) as the reasons why men choose *bint al-'amm*. Tillion offers a feminist explication of these unions that centers on the oppression of women by patriarchy and designates societies where patrilateral parallel marriage prevails as "The Republic of Cousins" (Tillion 1983). From the feminist point of view, this marriage form is a principle of political and not just social organization.

---

[3] Rihan is a pseudonym for the village, so chosen to guard the privacy of its inhabitants.

[4] Or marriage between patrilateral parallel cousins, the offspring of a pair of brothers.

I would like to differentiate between the principle of marriage to *bint al-'amm* and its practice. The principle makes it a unique type of endogamous marriage that seems to defeat the purpose of marriage itself. As viewed in a global context and as explained by structuralist analysis marriage is about exchange rather than conservation (Lévi-Strauss 1969). In this paper I shall argue that practice removes it from this perceived uniqueness and places this along with other kin marriages in a social and historical context. Whether one chooses his uncle's daughter or that of his second cousin twice removed, the logic and justification may be similar. It is this logic as illuminated by the individual practices, perceptions, and expectations of young men and women that this paper will address.

Using the logic of practice, Bourdieu has suggested dismantling the rigid principle of father's brother's daughter marriage since ".. [A]ny two marriages between parallel cousins may have nothing in common" (Bourdieu 1977:48). The alliance is not between a man and his father's brother's daughter. It is between two individuals whose actions reference not only their lineage but their emotions, land, position in society, and social relationships. Bourdieu criticizes the very language of prescription, wondering if

> ... [W]e can make the genealogical definition of groups the only means of differentiating between social units and of assigning agents to these groups without implicitly postulating that the agents are defined in every respect and for all time by their belonging to the group, and that, in short, the group defines the agents and their interests more than the agents define groups in terms of their interests? (Bourdieu 1977:32).

He thus re-focuses the issue on the practice of individuals of this form of marriage. One can extend this argument to other forms of kin unions. By so doing the issue relates to concepts and perceptions of kin and family rather than considerations of structures of kinship.

Others working in the Arab region have similarly argued for an understanding of each event of cousin marriage (Antoun 1972:114-141). While this point has been aptly made, less attention has been given to the role of women in structuring and defining these unions and the kinship ties that ensue (Boddy 1992). But kinship maps that only chart patrilineal descent ignore the essential and critical affinal and matrilateral relationships which are as pertinent to kinship as are agnatic ties (Boddy 1992, Bourdieu

1977). Individuals may be equally related from both mother's and father's side, yet in studies of societies where FBD/S marriage exists as an ideal, only the father's side is considered (Bourdieu 1977:36, 43. Also see Barth 1970; Khuri 1970:610-18; Davis 1987; Eickelman 1989:129).

Students of Egyptian and other Arab (as well as Middle Eastern and Mediterranean societies) have long argued that the theory of parallel cousin marriage is not borne out by the frequency of its practice. At best it is a preference that is subject to circumstances, the most obvious of which is the availability of a suitable cousin. Perhaps the assumption of such marriages as an interesting social phenomenon lies in the extent to which they linger in our idealized social imaginations. Another reason for the assumed ubiquity of this and other kin marriage preferences can be placed at the ethnographer's feet. By abstracting a principle from a practice and highlighting patrilineal relations over other markers of identity, thus isolating this practice from its historical and social contexts, ethnographers have ignored the diversity of reasons that make some cousins marry one another. The purpose of this section is to stress the importance of the practice of patrilateral parallel cousin marriages, and thus place them in the same domain as other kin marriages. For that is what this lens of practice suggests. It shows that patrilateral parallel cousins may also be related through their mothers and that these other ties are as influential in questions of choice of partner. It also tells us that the logic for marrying close can inform the choices of youth even if the partner is not their direct cousin. So what is the practice in Egypt?

Despite falling fertility rates, which have limited the number of cousins from which one can choose a spouse and until 1991, more than 30 percent of all marriages in Egypt were between first cousins (both parallel and cross from both the father's and mother's side). By 1995 the rate had fallen to approximately 24 percent of all marriages but with a ten percent increase of marriages between other relatives which stand at 15.2 percent of all marriages. Of the total marriages between relatives, which in 1995 are almost 40 percent of all marriages, the most common blood tie is that of the first cousin on the father's side (Egypt DHS 1995).[5] In other words cousin marriage is still a statistically significant phenomenon. Moreover the recent

---

[5] This is a reading of cross tabulations between type of relationship and current marital status.

decline in frequency has been coupled with a surge in marriages between relatives in general.

Not only is this the practice but it is also the stated preference of women in particular (Hoodfar 1997, Rugh 1984). Hoodfar attempts to explain these marriage choices in terms of the security of kin marriages but points out that for urban dwellers neighbors often replace kin, since people find the kind of assurances that marrying a relative offers present in life-long relationships based on proximity.

Some analysts have indicated an antithetical relationship between kin marriages and the forces of modernization. Mobile individuals migrating in search of work and a new life may not be inclined to marry their kin (Haj 1988). But others have challenged this assumption and showed that endogamy and kin marriages are thriving (Holy 1989, Rugh 1984). The figures just cited from the Egypt Demographic and Health survey of 1995 support that conclusion.

The question then is how do people juggle the demands of modern life and modern economies and the particular type of often individualistic rationality that clash with the necessities of cultural and social structures and the values that they promote? Hirsch (1999) has considered marriages amongst Mexicans living at home and others who have migrated and has shown how the meaning and significance of marriage has changed over time. Love, sexuality, and procreation may remain as basic elements of marriage but their construction and implications/functions have differed greatly. A similar argument can be made for the 'old' practice of marrying kin. This marriage preference is not an old choice; but rather it is a new one. Each time a young couple embark on such a union they are creating a new family and structuring a new relationship.

The Modern Practice of Marrying a Cousin

In Rihan there are a surprising number of people who are married to their patrilateral parallel cousins. Marriage also cuts across generations with people marrying their classificatory aunts and uncles. In the old days the inhabitants of this village were too poor and too unruly to be concerned about marriage prescriptions. They kept their women to themselves and added to them with marriage to others. Even in those old and wild days marriage for females was endogamous. But the men married any woman who would agree to have them. As old Ghelmy remembered:

> *At the time life was easy. What was marriage? A word with the male responsible for the woman, a silver anklet or two, some food, and the women would bring their own 'barazi' (the woolen tent set up for the married couple outside the nucleated settlement area) to marry in. When he left her, she and her children would live as everyone else did. They would remarry other men. So men married and divorced and the result is this village.*

It becomes clear from tracing the descent lines of different households in the village that concerns about marrying from within the patriline came as a consequence of the sedentary life style which villagers had adopted when they settled in Rihan. The income they got from guarding land and crops and their subsequent acquisition of land and property enabled them to create a pool of cousins from which sons and daughters could marry. In other words, the adherence to the rule of marriage preference for parallel cousins, although a highly esteemed Arab ideal and practice, became more important with the relative upward mobility of some of the inhabitants. Perhaps an illustration would help explain the point.

Ni'mat's grandfather married 7 women and had 10 boys and a number of girls--she is not sure of the exact number. She can remember 8 of her aunts. The boys include her own father, her husband's father, her sister's husband's father, her other sister's husband's father who is also the brother-in-law of her two younger brothers and the ex-father in law of her third brother who has divorced her cousin for a Cairene. Her third sister is married to the son of her father's cousin (from his father's side). She and two of her sisters and her three married brothers[6] are married to their patrilateral parallel cousins. The ten sons of Ni'mat's grandfather fathered 48 sons and 35 daughters, including those who did not survive till adulthood.

---

[6] Her fourth brother is still a young boy of 12 and is in school, and her step mother has three children all of whom are under the age of seven years.

Her mother and father are not related although her mother is an Arab and her grandparents from her father's side were unrelated, moreover her paternal grandmother was a peasant.

Her daughter is engaged to her own father's brother's son and her eldest son is supposed to take his father's brother's daughter but does not want to for personal reasons.

The family prides itself on its ability to inter-marry. Constant comparison is made with the other families in the village who are less numerous and so have not managed to achieve an equal number of cousins or other family marriages. As one prominent member of the Sewify family explains comparing his own family with that of the Moroukh who live in the southern part of the village:

> *We have many men and fewer women but they, aha, the wonders of God, have many daughters. So we take from them but we do not give to them. It is very rare that we give them Sewify women. But it has happened. But this was before we fell out. And so, they have a lot of unmarried women amongst them. It is not only that they have few men, but also because their men take from the outside because by their own admission, their women are bad. They wish that they had enough sons to take their daughters like we do.*

Indeed, the Sewifys derive a part of their social prestige from the fact that they have enough men for their own women. They can adopt the famed Upper Egyptian and old Arab Bedouin ways of arranging marriages from childhood and so avoiding the anxiety that partner-less girls precipitate.

The second generation of one branch of the Sewify family illustrates this marriage preference clearly. This generation ranges between the age of 56 years and 3 years. Of the 34 men who are married, 17 (50 percent) are married to their patrilateral parallel cousins. Of the remainder, 5 are married to other cousins, 10 to more distant relatives or to women from other families in the village, and only two have taken complete strangers.[7]

---

[7] One of them is a radical Muslim whose bride was chosen by his cell, not by himself or his family. In fact, his family only learned of his marriage by coincidence when he was caught and imprisoned.

For some of the Sewifys the boundaries of the family are almost the boundaries of the village. A male elder proudly boasted: "There was no village, but we brought children and filled the world, and now there is a village."

However, even among this same group issues of personal choice and preference are not absent from the consciousness of individuals. A closer look at the experiences of marriage and at the deliberations and considerations involved will illustrate this well.

Al-Nina and Mansour

Al-Nina has a reputation for being one of the most eligible girls in the village. She used to do most of the work on behalf of her mother who admits to making her work like a slave and describes how. "She used to get up before dawn and start mixing the dough for bread, and then clean under the animals and make dung cakes, then collect fuel for the oven, all before I even woke up."

Al-Nina's two brothers are married to their patrilateral parallel cousins (FBD). The two girls have different mothers, one from Cairo and one from the village. The elder girl is the Cairene who fell in love with her cousin who is a very attractive young man. The younger girl, 15 years old, married his brother because the fathers arranged it. Due to her jealousy of her Cairene sister, and despite or because of her youth, she likes to say that she too had eyes for her cousin.

When al-Nina's brothers "took" their wives, their uncle and future father-in-law made it a condition of his approval that their family consent to "giving" al-Nina to his 19-year-old son, Mansour. al-Nina and Mansour had been clutching hands on the landing and sharing mementos and subtle hints for some years. She had no objections to the idea whatsoever. Neither did her father and brothers. Indeed, once her uncle had asked for her, there was not much anyone could do. She is Mansour's rightful bride to take or leave. In claiming her he had only done the right thing.

However, her family bestow al-Nina with many virtues and talents. They see her as being a perfect bride. She has 'family', beauty, the correct demeanor and disposition, and a reputation for being a very hard working girl. So while no one could deny her to Mansour, they did balk when it came to the details. They organized the official signing of the marriage contract (*katb al-kitab*) on the same day as her brothers' wedding, but wanted to postpone the celebration and consummation of the contract for a year. The groom refused and insisted on getting married in June. This was seen as small-mindedness and inconsiderateness. June is a parched month. People have spent their money and have not yet harvested cotton, the main cash crop in the area. No one has money in June, no one can invite, celebrate, and make the appropriate gift offerings to the newly weds. But he insisted and who can deny a man his legal wife ?

The family was completely split on the issue. Many cousins swore that they would not attend. Some said that this was the work of women. The groom's mother and sisters were blamed for this awful timing, but neither he nor his father would back down. Needless to say, when the day came, the celebrations were extensive and much food was consumed. All did attend, and Mansour and his father made their point clear. As al-Nina's sister put it: "when you are giving the woman, you are the weaker party." Fathers for this reason do not attend their daughters' weddings. It is unbearable for their dignity and for their sense of modesty to attend this event. Indeed, a woman cannot lift her eyes to her father's until a reasonable period of time has passed.

Al-Nina entered into the perfect match. Mansour is an "*areeb*" (relative) not a "*ghareeb*" (stranger). He cannot discard her. Her sister explained that if he did not keep her because she is his wife he would have to because she is his cousin. It is also a happy coincidence that they have been "in love" for some time.

Yet this very obvious alliance was never taken for granted and was not free of distress. When I was discussing the issue with al-Nina's sister several months after the wedding and saying that all is well that ends well, she agreed with reservations. They would never forget what a hard time Mansour's family gave them. But what does it matter, I asked? Her retort was:

> Well, haven't you noticed that she has not been to visit her father's home yet. Mansour is playing hard with her. But she has become as bad as they are. She has not left the house once since they married. She did not come to visit me after I gave birth. She herself says that it is because her own brothers did not let their

wives visit their father's house till many months after the wedding. Do you not remember that they did not attend the wedding?! Well even if my brothers did that, she should try to go and see her mother!

Understanding the framework of blood ties against which people make individual choices is requisite for the understanding of the significance of events and of decisions. The linkages are a background against which people live their daily lives. These ties are more pronounced at times than at others. However, when called into play in day-to-day life they do not act in isolation. In the realm of the mundane, personal likes and dislikes, as well as affections, emotions, bad habits, and economic hardships, have room to design and structure the interaction of individuals and families.

In the case of al-Nina and Mansour, their match was at once condoned and anticipated by their blood ties, but it was made by them and colored with tension and obstinacy by their mothers, sisters and brothers. One can argue that all of the details don't really matter since the commonly held general principles and preferences seem to prevail in any case. But to understand parenting, child rearing, and the situation of women as mothers, boys as sons, and girls as daughters demands an understanding of the details and a sensitivity to the relationship between structuring axioms and daily life. Perhaps one can even locate the potential for change in these details.

Explanations and Conclusions

Men and women choose, or wish, to marry patrilateral parallel cousins because marriage is not just a way to consolidate wealth, control women, or to compete for power (Barth 1970, Bourdieu 1977). Marriage is a route to personal security (Hoodfar 1997) and to the creation of a secure environment for procreation (Sholkamy 1997). This becomes evident when analysis transcends marriage and looks at married life, especially from a woman's point of view.

Children make or break marriages. Procreation is the essence of marriage and should not be absented from the discussion. Islam defines descent through the father, hence the predominance of agnatic links. But the mother and her family have an important cultural role to play in the lives of children. The romance of the mother and father rearing their own children in their own way has yet to delude villagers. Children are born into households and into families. Marrying close means knowing whom the extended and very influential kin of sons and daughters will be.

It makes sense for both men and women to be safe in the knowledge that their children will be born into a known and secure network. Choosing the mother of the child-to-be is an implicit choice of a future head of a household. For many new brides of today are the matriarchs of tomorrow. Most men would choose to marry a patrilateral parallel cousin, if an eligible one existed, so as to consolidate the heritage, if not the inheritance of their children.

Marriage is also a source of security for women. Aziza explains:

You get educated and when you finish you have the guarantee of your job that gives you a monthly salary. Here our guarantee is our children. If a woman has no man her brothers won't let her starve but they have wives and families too. With no children a man can throw her out but not if she is his blood and has nowhere to go. Even if he is made of stone he could not throw out his own blood. Of course you never know and we hear of all sorts of things happening these days. As Arabs we have many divorces and marriages but now people have hardly enough to feed their families and no one can afford a divorcee or single woman. No, marriage is the way for women.

Aziza talks of marriage, marriage to kin, and the children that result as well as the economic and social security they extend to the mother as one thing. By and large these things are interconnected. They are the perfect benefits, which a mother aspires to see her daughter enjoy. However, this clear design and the security that it extends do not negate the individual concerns of girls and of families when venturing on a marriage agreement and celebration.

The historical meaning of security has influenced choices of marriage partners. Labor migration to the Gulf resulted in fathers preferring a rich "*ghareeb*" to a poor "*areeb*". But in Rihan, security still meant blood ties that created respect and a welcoming home.

Often cousins are like brother and sister before they marry, but as the saying goes "*illy yetkissef min demoh ma-yekhlefsh*" (He who is shy of his blood will never have children). Indeed, some divorces are explained by the man's inability to approach the woman because he feels that she is like a sister to him. This is an extreme case, which has been known to happen, but families try to protect their children from such mishaps by separating cousins who are eligible from quite an early age.

It is well acknowledged that close marriages do not always work and there are even some notions floating around concerning the development of genetic defects when successive generations of cousins intermarry. But there are other considerations for women in particular. For a woman, marrying a stranger can be a dangerous bet. Women in Rihan know that they can consolidate but cannot forge alliances. A woman who marries a stranger cannot create an alliance with his family. At best, she can offer only herself. In case of divorce, she is not entitled even to her own children.

Batta, for example, lives with her mother and daughter since her divorce. She had married a stranger from Arab Matteer. He is a drug addict and has abused her to the extent that she asked for a divorce. She had a daughter and son by him. His family took the boy and refused to take the girl.

He is a stranger. I have no leverage over him except by the courts but I cannot go to court, his family would scandalize me and my mother. Now he pays me nothing. I wanted him to take the girl too as I can't feed her but he won't. His mother said, the boy belongs to them and that I can take the girl since they do not want her.

If a tie already exists between the two families, a daughter's marriage can consolidate this tie. But a woman cannot be a link between families who are unrelated. Consequently there is very little security for a peasant woman who marries a stranger.

In Rihan matrilateral ties are recognized but only if they exist against a background of agnatic ties, even if distant ones (for Sudan see Boddy 1992). Such ties are highly regarded and are seen to create affections and intimacy between people who are thus related. They also create an alternative marriage pool for men and women.

Women play an important role in structuring the pool of marriageable partners not just through marriage, but also through breast-feeding. Fostering of children through milk ties, which makes marriage impossible, is a means for women to regulate marriages (Khatib-Chahidi 1992:109; Altorki 1980). Marriage in general has been portrayed as a male concern, but the role of women in structuring incest and thereby defining legitimate partners is of great importance.[8] While this point does not relate to FBD marriages per se, it is an important silent ingredient in the construction of marriage and marriage preferences.

The marriage of a daughter is both a blessing and a loss. Once they are married off, they really do not belong to the father's family any more. This is no less serious for those marrying a cousin. A woman's labor belongs to her new home. She must keep their secrets, be prudent when it comes to their belongings, food, and animals, she must be very clear as to whose household she now belongs. But keeping women within the family is judged to be better then letting them disperse.

Young girls know that they are headed for marriage, and some of them do not relish the idea. For them it means going to live with another family, having children, working very hard, baking, and breeding animals. Marriage for a woman signifies departure--a departure from home and the life they have always known. She is leaving her family, hopefully for good. She must therefore be assured of a dignified reception and place in another family, and who would take better care of her than her own kin?

A woman who marries within the family is assured a minimum in terms of dignity and fair treatment. More importantly, she is assured a place in her own patriline. Because girls are viewed as belonging to their husband's family, and not their own, they are often treated as strangers within their own homes. The saying has it that "*al-banat marbat-hin khaly*" (The stable of women/girls is empty). In other words, you cannot rely on a girl giving returns on her parents' investment in her future. One cannot, when poor, afford to invest in girls as they leave home and join their husbands. His and his family, their problems, joys, sorrows, responsibilities, and projects become hers. And "...when they come to tell her that her father has died she goes to scream at the grave and then returns to her husband's home, fills her belly with food, and forgets all about the dog who died," said one man who has five daughters.

A girl who marries into her own patriline reconfirms her own ties to the family. She also remains amongst her family and friends, and she keeps her children close to their maternal kin but, more importantly, they become part of her own patriline.

---

[8] Islam prohibits children who have been breast-fed by the same woman to marry.

If a woman marries out she has fewer guarantees. She may be lucky in terms of her husband loving her or even by just being a good man who will take care of her. She may be unlucky and in that case she can only rely on her kin to argue her case if the need arises. Alternatively, her security may lie with her children and in the role of 'mother', not that of 'bride'. Over time, and as she grows older, she may become completely estranged from her paternal kin.

Perhaps people do idealize FBD marriages because married life, divorce, polygyny, and above all procreation are present in the mind and the imagination when marriage looms on the horizon. The contemplation of these potentials is not confined to men. Women have a role in choosing to be chosen as partners.

The dry and abstract concept of FBD mistakenly relays an image of a dry and abstract act of consolidation and alliance (Bourdieu 1977:43). In Rihan the most passionate of couples were direct cousins. At least they had a chance to know each other before marriage. Sexual encounters between engaged cousins are not unknown. Couples had time and space to nurture love and compassion. Unrelated couples in rural areas cannot afford this luxury.

Kinship as an abstraction of an official representation that is only valid in particular situations is not really helpful in understanding marriage preferences, how they structure society, and the functions that they perform in maintaining and reproducing it. Perhaps at one level FBD/S alliances exist as a 'white lie', as Bourdieu calls it, which serves to reaffirm gender and the sexual division of labor by completely denying the role of other relationships and markers of identity (Bourdieu 1977:43-4). But this view ignores the fact of women as marriage partners and sees them only as representatives of a group of kin. In accepting to marry their patrilateral parallel cousins, women in Rihan are not just acquiring affines; they are securing agnates.

Marriage is also a life-step, what could be called in the context of modern discourse, a career move. It has profound implications for the personhood of the woman and all its individual manifestations. Marriage is important and marrying close is a calculated tactic even at the personal level. Marriage is getting a husband and access to children, status, a different position in another house, and in many cases it means re-admission into a network of mothers and of grandmothers, but as a married woman.

The importance of endogamous marriage is a testimony to the importance of kinship to social life. Security, identity, and the future still lie within the folds of kinship. Men and women do not only marry cousins, they also vote for, work with, migrate to, and invest in kin. The continued advocacy of the FBD marriage, and endogamous marriage in general, also indicates a lack of trust in modern social indicators of status and of security. Despite the ascendance of money, moral righteousness, and education as markers of status and as desirable assets the importance of networks of kin remains the mainstay of social relations.

The individual is an unreliable partner; the group is a safer bet. Marrying close consolidates the group but it also assures both parties in the marriage that their alliance is guaranteed by their co-membership and their equality within that group. This provides the couple and their children with protection from the outside and with the language and rules with which to communicate within their group.

This does not mean that social ties are stagnant or conflict-free. On the contrary, brothers fight and cousins can become worst enemies. People are not denied the frustrations and tensions, which clutter social relationships. But maintaining consolidated patrilines in which women play an important role remains a way by which many people want to define, negotiate, and live in society.

Thus goes the reasoning presented by those who have married their close kin and those who intend to do so. One fourteen-year-old girl in the village was promised to a cousin who had migrated to Jordan in search of a job. Along came a wealthier but more distant cousin who had a very good position in Saudi Arabia. Her greedy father opted for the wealthier man and so she was betrothed to him. She hardly knew either of them and while impartial to the two men, she was attracted by the wealth of the new suitor. Some villagers called it a sign of the times that this was happening. Others said that material things had always mattered even if you harkened back to ancient times. Her mother found solace in the fact that they were related to both men.

The family is just like the village. You fall out with some and are very close to others. This is always happening in all families and they are kin. What would it be like with strangers?!

Are these testimonies and experiences of significance when we revisit kin marriages in Egypt? I hope they are. They tell the reader of how youth in one part of Egypt rationalize their world and their future, and how they relate to heritage and responsibilities. They also show that the story is never one of individuals making life choices by referring only to their free will. Nor are they just objects controlled by inherited ideals and strictures.

They also show how women in this village view their future and their security. They highlight the precarious nature of womanhood as it is socially constructed in modern Egypt and the extent to which women's personal choices strive to fortify this position and overcome its burdens.

The paper cannot claim to have shown whether marrying kin is a good or bad thing. It has perhaps shown that it is a viable option for youth in Egypt and one which can extend the benefits that women in particular seem to be seeking.

Bibliography

Altorki, S. 1980. "Milk Kinship in Arab Society: An Unexplained Problem in the Ethnography of Marriage," *Ethnology* vol. XIX, 2:233-44.

Antoun, Richard. 1972. *Arab Village: A Social Structural Study of a Transjordanian Peasant Community*. Bloomington: Indiana University Press.

Barth, F. 1970. "Father's Brother's Daughter Marriage in Kurdistan" in L.E. Sweet, ed., *Peoples and Cultures of the Middle East*. Vol. 1. Garden City, New York: The Natural History Press.

Beck, L. and N. Keddie, eds. 1978. *Women in the Muslim World*. Cambridge, Mass.: Harvard University Press.

Boddy, J. 1992. "Bucking the Agnatic System: Status and Strategies in Rural Northern Sudan" in J. Brown & S. Vatuk, eds., *In Her Prime: New Views of Middle Aged Women*. Urbana & Chicago: University of Illinois Press.

Bourdieu, P. 1977. *Outline of a Theory of Practice*. Trans. R. Nice. Cambridge: Cambridge University Press.

---------------. .1990. *The Logic of Practice*. Trans. R. Nice. Stanford: Stanford University Press.

Davis, J. 1987. "Family and State in the Mediterranean." in D. Gilmore, ed., *Honor and Shame and the Unity of the Mediterranean*. Washington DC: American Anthropological Association.

Demographic and Health Survey 1995. Cairo, Egypt.

Eickelman, D. 1989. *The Middle East: An Anthropological Approach*. 2nd ed. Englewood Cliffs, NJ: Prentice Hall.

Haj, M. 1988. "Kinship and Modernization in Developing Societies: The Emergency of Instrumentalized Kinship," *The Journal of Comparative Family Studies* 36(3):311-328.

Hirsch, J. 1999. "Companionate marriage, Sexual Intimacy, and the Modern Mexican Family." Paper presented to IUSSP workshop on Social Categories in Population Research. Cairo, Egypt.

Holy, L. 1989. *Kinship, Honour and Solidity. Cousin Marriage in the Middle East.* Manchester: Manchester University Press.

Hoodfar, H. 1997. *Between Marriage and the Market: Intimate Politics and Survival in Cairo.* Berkeley: University of California Press.

Khatib-Chahidi, J. 1992. "Milk Kinship in Shi'ite Islamic Iran" in V. Maher, ed., *The Anthropology of Breastfeeding.* Cross Cultural Perspectives on Women. Oxford/Providence: Berg.

Khuri, F. 1970. "Parallel Cousin Marriage Reconsidered; A Middle Eastern Practice that Nullifies the Effects of Marriage on the Intensity of Family Relationships," *Man* (N.S.) 5(4):597-618.

Levi-Strauss, C. 1969. *The Elementary Structures of Kinship.* Boston: Beacon.

Rugh, A. 1984. *Family in Contemporary Egypt.* Syracuse: Syracuse University Press.

Sholkamy, H. 1997. Children's Health and Well Being: An Ethnography of an Upper Egyptian Village. Unpublished PhD Thesis, Anthropology, London School of Economics.

Tillion, G. 1983. *The Republic of Cousins: Women's Oppression in Mediterranean Society.* London: Al Saqi Books.

THE COST OF MARRIAGE IN EGYPT: A HIDDEN VARIABLE IN THE NEW ARAB DEMOGRAPHY

DIANE SINGERMAN AND BARBARA IBRAHIM

Introduction

Marriage is an event infused with multiple meanings in the lives of Egyptians. It is a civil contract between two families with legally binding conditions on both parties. Marriage is a means for consolidation of social status, and, in a conservative society, it also provides the only approved access for young men and women to sexual and reproductive partners. In the Arab world in general, and in Egypt in particular, marriage is considered a "social pinnacle and major turning point in the lives of both men and women," heralding the transition to full-fledged adulthood (Shafey 1998:39). Finally, though this aspect is often overlooked, marriage is the occasion for a major intergenerational transfer of wealth, larger in many cases than the inheritance following a parental death. In this paper we contend that contemporary marriage arrangements absorb the highest investment of financial resources that most Egyptians will accumulate throughout their lives. Marriage is thus a major economic project, demanding significant family energy and assets, often over a considerable period of time.[1]

---

[1]The authors gratefully acknowledge support for the development of this research provided by the Population Council, the American University Senate Research Award (Washington, D.C.), the New Arab Demography Project of the Social Research Center at the American University in Cairo, and the Mellon Foundation. Invaluable research assistance was provided by Amina Hegazy, David Spielman, Fatma El-Hamidi, Rania Salem, Maria Buzdugan, and David Richards. Helpful advice at various stages of the analysis was offered by Ragui Assaad, Omaima el-Gibaly, Fredric Shorter, Rachel Kranton, Magued Osman, and Saher El-Tawila. Special thanks are due to Akhter A. Ahmed and Lawrence Haddad at the International Food Policy Research Institute (IFPRI) for sharing their data and

Despite the centrality of marriage to Egyptian life, the material exchange itself and the total cost of getting married remains under-researched and under-theorized. Yet our preliminary analysis suggests that in total Egyptians spend more than 13 billion Egyptian pounds annually on the costs of getting married. On average, families spend four and a half times GNP per capita ($1,290 in 1998 [IBRD/World Bank 2000:12]) on the costs of marriage or LE20,194 (approximately $5,957 in 1997). The marriage burden is particularly harsh for those households living below the poverty line in rural areas, as this paper will demonstrate.[2]

For too long, culture-blind economic analysis has not recognized the place of marriage in national economies like Egypt or in the economic priorities of young people and their families.[3] Considered an "incidental expenditure" in household expenditure surveys, marriage costs can, in fact, absorb years of collective savings, and these family accumulation strategies must be repeated an average of 3.3 times (total fertility rate) for Egyptian households (EDHS 1995). Yet there has been almost no creative statistical analysis of existing data to understand the cost of marriage in the national economy and its place in economic decision-making.

Approaches to the Study of Marriage Formation

Marriage formation has received most attention from anthropologists interested in kinship patterns, or more recently from demographers seeking to make sense of shifting ages at marriage. Throughout the Arab region, longstanding marriage patterns are undergoing change in a process widespread enough to qualify as a "nuptiality transition." While mid-20th century patterns varied somewhat from country to country, marriage prior to

---

agreeing to add a battery of questions on the cost of marriage in Egypt to one of their surveys.

[2] A poverty line represents the income or expenditure level below which a minimum, nutritionally adequate diet plus essential non-food requirements are not affordable (UNDP Human Development Report 1997, 238).

[3] For comparative work on marriage and personal status law in the Middle East and North Africa see Tapper 1991; Hoodfar 1997; Singerman 1995; Rugh 1984; Mir-Hosseini 1993, 1999; Joseph 1996; Sonbol 1996; Women Living Under Muslim Laws 1996; Lloyd and Naguib 1994, and Tove 1997.

that time was generally both early and universal. Before the advent of girls' education, most females in the Arab world could expect to marry soon after reaching physical maturity, while men married somewhat later but typically before age 30 (EDHS 1997). Newly formed couples most commonly resided in the husband's household, especially in rural areas.

The trend in most Arab countries since that time has been toward later ages at marriage, larger percentages of nuclear households, and increasing numbers of men and women who remain celibate (unmarried) into middle age or later (Rashad and Khadr 1998; Rashad and Osman 2000).[4] The trend toward later marriage ages is associated with reduced fertility and thus it has been welcomed by demographers and policymakers concerned with high rates of population growth. More recently, however, public discourse in Egypt and elsewhere in the region has raised new concerns over the social "cost" of delayed marriage. Delay may bring with it unintended consequences, when young people are able neither to marry at the time they want nor to find socially acceptable paths to adult partners and independent living arrangements. This paper makes problematic the way marriage timing has previously been addressed by scholars who see later marriage ages as an unambiguous good (Singh and Samara 1996). It draws attention to the neglected economic dimension of marriage in Egypt and asks how material costs may impact both marriage timing, economic decision-making, and patterns of cultural and gender norms.

We hypothesize that the cost of marriage in Egypt plays a greater role in delaying marriages than has previously been supposed. Other factors have more often been cited by demographers, such as increased female education and labor force participation, or male needs for increased skill training before taking up employment (McClamroch 1996). In an economic environment that has produced both higher growth and higher poverty rates in the 1990s, it becomes essential to understand the economic behavior surrounding marriage. This will improve the robustness of economic indicators such as household expenditure levels and assessments of households living below a given level of poverty. It could also assist policy

---

[4]For comparative research on marriage age and informal marriages see Greene and Rao (1995).

makers in devising appropriate and informed policies to respond to the current financial burden marriage places on individuals and families.

Casual observation of daily topics of conversation, reinforced by perusal of popular news media, reveals a widespread perception that marriage costs are both high and rising relative to income (Shahine 1998; Hoodfar 1997:68). Popular discourse on the subject places the total costs for jewelry, housing, furniture, and ceremonies so high that entire families must save and sacrifice over many years for their child's marriage. This high cost of marriage is thought to have a number of secondary consequences, such as labor migration, second jobs for men (Abu Hashish and Peterson 1999), or deployment of women to the labor force.

In response to the perceived high costs of marriage, NGO groups in Egypt have experimented with alternatives to traditional marriage such as mass ceremonies where costs are subsidized (El-Magd 1998).[5] Religious groups have promoted the idea of marriages based on only token exchanges of material goods and low bride price (with seemingly few takers). News accounts in the media suggest that *'urfi* or customary, common-law marriages that are either secretive or unregistered (and thus carry a social stigma) are increasingly popular among young people because these types of marriage reduce expenses while meeting the minimum requirements for marriage under Islamic law (Allam 2000; Shahine 1998; Ezzat 2000).

For the vast majority of Egyptians, however, publicly acknowledged marriage remains the norm, and large sums of money must be accumulated to meet the expectations of each party to the union. The typical strategy pursued by young people and their families in order to marry can dominate financial, social, occupational, and educational decisions, possibly for years. Ethnographic studies suggest that schooling, migration, and employment decisions and consumption, investment, and savings patterns may all be implicated in the project to marry (Hoodfar 1997; Ibrahim and Wassef 1999).

---

[5]Marriage societies, subsidized by governments, private and religious organizations are not exclusive to Egypt. In Jordan, mass marriages have been organized by Islamic non-governmental organizations in response to the high cost of marriage and consequent social anxieties (Wiktorowicz and Farouqi 2000).

Given this salience of marriage requirements, it is striking that so little is known about the cost of marriage and its consequences in Egypt. Our attempt to marshal existing evidence for this paper revealed that policy makers, economists, and other social scientists pay little attention to this issue.[6] We do not know if the real cost of marriage has indeed risen over time or at what rate, whether it is relatively higher among certain groups or exactly how it impacts nuptiality patterns. We know little about how macroeconomic phenomena impact the cost of marriage or vice versa. Have privatization and globalization of the Egyptian economy increased consumptive norms, thus increasing the cost of marriage? How do inflationary trends affect the 'purchasing power' of a marriage? Has the rising education and employment of women allowed them to demand more material assets from grooms and their families? Does the higher cost of marriage discourage marriage or change the age patterns of newlyweds? Is the cost of marriage more burdensome to urban or rural households, the lower or middle classes, grooms, brides, or their families? How have economic pressures altered the sharing of marriage costs between individuals and households?

These research questions imply a major program of study and cannot all be addressed in this paper. Many of them would require detailed data on marriage costs that are not currently available. Our more modest objectives are first to establish the importance of this neglected economic transaction, by attempting to verify the magnitude and trend in costs over the last few decades relative to household expenditures. Next we will sketch out a map of the contributions to marriage and examine its rural-urban, class, and gender variations. We hypothesize that one effect of the rising cost of marriage is to encourage more sharing of expenses between grooms' families--who traditionally bore most of the costs--and brides' families. We will also suggest ways in which the cost of marriage may be implicated in the delay of marriage in Egypt. Factoring in the cost of marriage suggests some new lines of inquiry for poverty studies, and underscores the need for improved data collection.

---

[6]The exception to this statement is ethnographic accounts of local community practices, which are numerous and richly detailed. See Hoodfar 1997, Singerman 1995, and Rugh 1984.

Conceptual Framework

Marriage costs are clearly a calculus of both cultural and economic factors. We opt for a model that sees both of these forces in play at any given time. "Tradition" in a given community is invoked to justify particular patterns of spending on marriage. Those patterns may even function as boundary markers, distinguishing one village from its nearby neighbor (Ibrahim and Wassef 1999). But within those traditions, accommodation is made for new material realities such as technological change, economic recession, or new consumption norms (see Singerman and Hoodfar 1997). Thus the advent of electricity in a community creates in its wake more demand for electrical appliances, as part of the package of goods deemed necessary to begin marital life. Some groups are exposed more forcefully to the effects of socio-economic change, like migrants or women entering the workforce for the first time, and those groups may be among the innovators. Innovations in behavior at one point in time become the tradition or 'norm' in succeeding marital negotiations. This dynamic model of change allows us to understand long-standing geographic diversity of marriage patterns in Egypt, as well as some of the similarities that are emerging as economic restructuring and globalization affect the entire society.

The cost of marriage in any society will mirror local, national, and international economic forces. Complex markets affect prices in Egypt. Thus the unit cost for major items such as housing is largely influenced by costs of land and construction. The cost of domestically produced or imported furniture and appliances for the newlywed domicile has increased since the introduction of the Economic Open Door Policy in 1974, so that this item is now a major factor in the overall cost. Our data confirm that the total cost of marriage increased significantly after the introduction of this policy, particularly through the 1980s. Other items are more likely to be shaped by local custom or family expectations, such as the cash amount to be paid for the bride price, or how lavishly to entertain at marriage celebrations. Our conceptual framework predicts that macroeconomic factors indirectly affect these social norms by changing perceptions of what is an acceptable standard of living for a newly married couple.

Previous approaches to the study of marriage costs were unsatisfactory in providing a full explanation for our data. Central to the neo-classical economic paradigm is the notion that marriage is a market, much like a market for any other good or service with supply and demand determining prices (Lundberg and Pollak 1997; Bhat and Halli 1999). The simplest economic analysis states that if the price of a good or service rises, the demand for it will fall. If the price of any of the material components of marriage rises, demand for marriage would fall and the incidence of marriage would decrease. Much of this research has focused on the ways in which the numerical availability of men or women affects the price of dowry, or other prices associated with marriage (Goldman, Westoff, and Hammerslough 1984; Lampard 1993; Behrman, Birdsall, and Deolalokar 1995; and Rao and Bloch 2000). Yet, this paradigm seems less useful when trying to model marriage as negotiation involving financial sharing among parties to the marriage and invoking as it does in Egypt religion, law, custom, and gendered norms.

At the same time, it is clear that we need to better understand the relationship between factor endowments (for example, geography, wealth, education, and gender norms) and the specific and aggregate cost of marriage. From anthropological literature we can borrow from a lively debate over whether dowry (payment from the bride's family to the groom's family) comes to replace bride price (payment by the groom's family to the bride's family) in communities where women's economic value in their new marital household declines (Tapper 1991, Van der Veen 1972; Schlegel 1993; Schegel and Eloul 1988; Gaulin and Boster 1990; and Goody and Tambiah 1973). According to this hypothesis, Egyptian women should be able to command greater prices from grooms' families as their economic utility in the marketplace increases. Yet, as will be described below, as Egyptian women become wage earners they seem to share more of the marriage expenses rather than be in a position to demand a larger bride price.

We posit that given the high value Egyptians place on marriage and the many social and economic functions it facilitates for them, families are responding to the high price of marriage with more than one strategy. First, some couples are accepting "substitutes" for marriage in the form of informal or secret unions that avoid costly exchanges of goods (Allam

2000). Others are breaking with long-standing tradition by accepting unions between younger men and older women. Magued Osman and Laila Shahd recently found that twenty-seven percent of husbands who married in 1996 married older women (15 percent married women five years older; 11 percent married women ten years older). As recently as 1986, only 2 percent of grooms married older brides. When marriage registrars were asked about the cause of this new age pattern, they suggested that the grooms did not have the requisite financial means to marry women their own age and that these older women, whose age decreased their value in the marriage market, bore most of the costs of marriage (Osman and Shahd 2000). We present further evidence below for increased sharing of what were once exclusively grooms' financial responsibilities.

Why would such significant shifts in marriage formation and a major financial transaction not figure more prominently in social analyses of Egypt and similar countries? We see a parallel in the way that measurements of work and income once ignored women's economic contributions. It took a long overdue application of a gendered analysis of labor force participation to uncover the significant role of women's domestic, informal and non-salaried sources of income (see Shukri 1999, 18; Moghadem 1993). Similarly, measurements of consumption and expenditure also need revision in order to capture the important cost of marriage. Like women's work in previous times, marriage costs may not have been perceived as serious enough for economists' or policymakers' attention, a "soft" social issue that occurred at irregular intervals and in relative obscurity. We hope that this initial exploration of the cost of marriage will provoke more extensive analysis on the intersection of nuptiality patterns, gender, and economic investments.

Finally, while cultural norms obviously shape economic decision-making, they also reflect and are reflected by political structures and policy. It is important to remember that attempts to change the laws that regulate marriage and divorce have been, and continue to be, at the center of some of the most contentious political debates in Egypt since the early 20th century (Ahmed 1992; Badran 1991). In January 2000 the Egyptian Parliament passed a controversial reform in Personal Status Laws by a narrow margin. The reformed law allows a woman to divorce her husband (*khulla*) if she relinquishes all her financial claims upon him, including the *mu'akhar sadaq*.[7] This same reform bill also simplified the procedure for divorce in a common-law (*'urfi*) marriage and for proving paternity. Below the rhetorically charged debate on gender norms and Islamic law that this bill generated, one finds equally controversial economic issues about the resources that men, women, and their families contribute to marriage and can thus claim control over in the future. The issue of marriage remains a deeply political and sensitive issue in Egypt that must be put in its political as well as economic context.

Similarly, a new standard form of the marriage contract that obligates newlyweds to place their fingerprints on the contract and attach photographs to it (to counteract proxy and underage marriages) was issued in June 2000 by the Ministry of Justice. The couple must declare that they have no "serious diseases," the divorce history of the couple must be declared and any previous wife's address and name provided. A woman may check off an option in the contract that allows her to maintain the right to divorce. Previously Muslim women did not have access to divorce without proving through a court that her husband had wronged her. With this new check-off option on the marriage contract, a woman may stipulate at the time of the marriage that she maintains the right to divorce without showing cause (known as keeping the right to divorce 'in the bride's hand') (Leila 2000). At the same time however, in conformity with the newly revised Personal Status Law of 2000, if a woman forgoes that option and later asks for a "no-fault" divorce, she must give up all financial claims.

Marriage Practices in Egypt

In anthropological terms, marriage in Egypt more closely resembles a closed than open system, meaning that certain ascribed characteristics are sought by families in the process of selecting a spouse for their son or daughter, and these considerations take precedence over personality and individual choice. Once a potential match is found, the two families enter into financial

---

[7]Typically, a divorced woman is entitled to whatever property she brought into the marriage as well as the *mu`akhar sadaq*, or the deferred part of the bride price that is stipulated as a payment to the wife in the advent of divorce or death of the husband.

negotiations over the amounts and timing of marriage payments. As in many societies with patriarchal traditions, negotiation over marriage terms may take place solely between the couple's fathers, but more typically today, negotiations include the couple and a number of family members (particularly mothers) and involve protracted discussions (Singerman 1995; Hoodfar 1997).[8]

The cost of marriage is an aggregate figure that includes items that custom and/or religious law dictate that the parties purchase or acquire before a marriage can occur.[9] Typical marriage costs in Egypt include housing, furniture and appliances, gifts of gold to the bride (*shabka*), bride price (*mahr*), celebrations, the bride's trousseau (*kiswa*), kitchenware, less expensive furnishings including lamps, carpets, sheets, etc., (*gihaz*), and other gifts exchanged during the courtship period. The quality and quantity of each of these requisites varies across groups considerably, as will be demonstrated below.

Marriage in Egypt typically takes place in publicly observed stages. Not all of the stages are observed in all areas or among all social groups, but at least two or more of the following stages should normally occur: *fatiha* (sealing the agreement between two families by reading the opening verse or *sura* of the Quran), *shabka* ('tying' the couple with a gift of rings or gold), *katb al-kitab* (formal signing of the marriage contract), and *dukhla* or *zifaf* (celebration of the first night of joint residence). When standard surveys in Egypt ask whether an individual is married using the term *gawaz*, it is commonly understood that this reference is to the final stage of establishing joint residence. Each stage with the possible exception of *fatiha* is normally accompanied by economic obligations on one or both parties to the marriage.

---

[8]Eighty percent of women in one recent survey said their marriages had been arranged (CAPMAS 1992 as cited in Abu Hashish and Peterson 1999).
[9]While marriage is a civil contract, its form is dictated by religious norms for Muslims and Christians respectively. Unless otherwise noted, the analysis in this paper refers to the marriage practices of the Muslim majority. Christian marriages differ only slightly from these patterns, largely due to the prohibitions on divorce and different registration procedures for the contract.

Sources and Quality of Data

Despite the strong inference that marriage forms a substantial financial outlay for Egyptian households, marriage cost data are rarely collected in household expenditure surveys (see for example CAPMAS Income and Expenditure Surveys). This may be because marriage is thought of as a one-time event rather than a recurring expense. In reality, funds for marriage expenses are accumulated over a number of years, usually by two households, and thus may escape the scrutiny of expenditure surveys that ask questions about a particular reference period. Finally, the cost of marriage may not be captured in Egypt and elsewhere because survey designs are often adapted from Western models, where marriage may not be seen as a significant financial event in the life of the household. Fortunately, recent surveys in Egypt have begun to remedy that situation.

In 1999, for the first time in Egypt, a household expenditure survey collected detailed information on the total costs of marriage. Prior to that, in 1997, the International Food Policy and Research Institute (IFPRI) in conjunction with the Egyptian Ministry of Agriculture and the Ministry of Trade and Supply, launched a 2400-household, nation-wide expenditure survey (Egypt Integrated Household Survey, EIHS). This study was designed to assist in policy formulation and improved targeting of commodity subsidies for low-income households (see Datt, Jolliffe, and Sharma 1998, and Bouis and Ahmed 1998). A sub-sample of the 1997 households was re-interviewed in 1999 in order to create longitudinal data on poverty and subsidy policies. IFPRI generously invited the authors to add a module of questions addressing marriage costs and strategies (Haddad and Akhter 2000).[10]

For the purposes of this study, we designed a detailed set of questions on marriage costs and negotiations. Based on previous ethnographic

---

[10]Some of the same questions from the 1999 survey were included in the 1997 survey, but the 1997 questionnaire was richer in data on various aspects of household characteristics. It consisted of 18 sections on a series of topics, which integrated monetary and non-monetary measures of household welfare and a variety of household behavioral characteristics. The questionnaire was administered to 2,400 households from 20 Governorates using a two-stage stratified selection process (see Datt, Jolliffe, and Sharma 1998, 6-7).

research and field experience, the module collected data about major component costs of marriage, methods of accumulation, and which party to the marriage paid for them (bride, groom, bride's family, or groom's family). This questionnaire module was administered to every household in the EIHS survey reporting a marriage event in the preceding five years (1992-1997). It resulted in 105 complete cases drawn from seven governorates in Upper and Lower Egypt, out of the larger sample of 380 households.

More than a quarter of the 380 households in the 1999 EIHS reported a marriage in the past five years. If the figure reflects national rates, then approximately one household in twenty experiences a marriage each year in Egypt. That figure in itself suggests that marriage is a process that affects a great many Egyptians at different stages in their life. We believe this is the first time detailed quantitative data on marriage expenses have been collected for Egypt.

The 105 survey cases are not fully representative of national households.[11] The sampling method favored somewhat lower income communities, however those households reporting marriages displayed a similar income profile to all households in the 1997 parent survey (see Haddad and Akhter, 2000). Future data collection efforts will hopefully provide larger representative samples with which to test the findings presented here. We are able to supplement the EIHS findings with data from the 1995 Egypt Demographic and Health Survey (EDHS 1996). That national survey of 12,000 ever-married women aged 15 to 49 asked several questions about costs of the woman's first and most recent marriage. We constructed cohort data representing five-year marriage intervals from 1965 to the present and adjusted those figures for inflationary trends. Because the EDHS only asks about contributions from the bride's family, it has limited utility in estimating total marriage costs. However, questionnaire items about the relative share of costs borne by the bride and her family enable us to look at trends in cost and cost-sharing over time.

---

[11]The 1999 EIHS selected seven of the original 20 Governorates, and returned to 347 households out of 2,450 originally sampled in 1997. A careful statistical analysis of the two samples showed close correspondence in terms of income and expenditure patterns and other population parameters (see Haddad and Ahmed 1999).

Together these data sources allowed us to begin to estimate total amounts spent on marriage; draw a profile of expenditures for each component of marriage costs; allocate costs between bride, groom, and their respective families; consider differences in marriage expenses between urban and rural households; and examine how households and individuals accumulate the sums needed to complete their marriages.

How High are Marriage Costs in Egypt?

One way to measure the relative cost of marriage across population groups is by creating a ratio of average costs to per capita annual income, assets or expenditures. When this calculation has been made in societies like India, where dowry costs are a significant social, economic, and political issue, one study found that the net value of goods and services transferred equals two thirds of the total assets of a rural Indian household. In parts of northwestern India the dowry rate (only part of the total marriage costs) is equal to the annual income of the bride's father (Bhat and Halli 1999:130). Other countries where data is available include Taiwan, where the real mean value of average dowries constitute about six months' earnings for men or ten months' earnings for women. In Taiwan communities practicing exchange of bride-price, that amount constitutes approximately three months' earnings for men and six months' earnings for women (Zhang and Chang 1999:798).

From an international comparative framework, the total marriage costs we estimate for Egypt are substantially higher. In the 105 cases of completed marriage transactions in the previous five years, average costs of marriage were LE20,194 (US$5,957 in the mid 1990s). Total marriage costs were thus four and a half times higher than GNP per capita (gross national product) estimates of $1,290 in 1998 (IBRD/World Bank 2000:12). In rural areas the average cost was LE17,373 ($5,125) or four times GNP per capita and in urban areas, LE24,969 ($ 7,365) or almost six times GNP per capita.

Another way to think of the magnitude of these costs is to apply them to the estimated total number of marriages per year in Egypt. We estimated that 1/20 of all 13 million households in Egypt experience a marriage in a year. Our estimate of the national cost of a marriage in Egypt equaled

LE20,164. Thus, the national cost of all 650,000 marriages equals LE13.11 billion ($3.867 billion), a figure which dwarfs the figure for total economic aid to Egypt from the United States in 1999-$2.1 billion (U.S. State Department 2000:2). Clearly, marriage transactions are financially significant and deserve greater research and policy attention.

Is the Cost of Marriage Rising?

While we do not have panel data for Egypt that allow for estimation of total costs of marriage over time, the 1995 EDHS does provide some useful approximations. This national survey of ever-married women asked a series of questions about which of the two families had contributed to various marriage costs, and whether the bride's family's contribution had been less than, greater than or equal to that of the husband's family. The survey also asked the respondent to estimate the total cost contributed by herself and her family.

To construct trend data we first created a set of cohorts based on the year of a respondent's marriage, defined as establishing joint residence. Among the surveyed women, the earliest marriages took place in the 1960s. We grouped cohorts into five-year intervals and calculated average marriage costs (borne by brides' families only) for each cohort. We then indexed these costs to changes in the consumer price index (CPI) over the three decades (CAPMAS 1999:298-299).

Table 1

Bride's Side Real Marriage Costs, 1965-1995
(1979 LE)

Year	Urban Bride's Side Real Marriage Costs 1979 LE	% change	Rural Bride's Side Real Marriage Costs 1979 LE	% change	Average Bride's Side Real Marriage Costs 1979 LE	% change	Real Per Capita GDP Growth Over Previous Period (%)
1965-69	743	--	381	--	523	--	--
1970-74	1032	39 %	508	34 %	716	37 %	7 %
1975-79	1287	25 %	491	-3 %	781	9 %	38 %
1980-84	1314	2 %	468	-5 %	796	2 %	25 %
1985-89	859	-35 %	423	-10 %	592	-26 %	-4 %
1990-95	533	-38 %	255	-40 %	352	-40 %	2 %

Source: EDHS 1995

Results of this analysis are shown in Table 1. After adjusting for inflation, we see that marriage costs for a bride's family rose dramatically in the years following 1965. In absolute terms, the median costs roughly doubled in each five-year interval, leveling off somewhat in the 1990s. The largest cost increases were experienced between the later years of the 1970s and the early 1980s, a period marked by accelerated opening of the Egyptian economy to global influences, increased pace of urbanization and expansion of rural electrification. The bride's cost of marriage in real terms for those marrying in 1970-75 increased by 37 percent over the costs of those who married between 1965-69. For the cohort of brides that married between 1975-79, their costs were 49 percent higher than their counterparts in the late 1960s. The next cohort of brides (1980-84) spent 52 percent more on marriage than their earlier counterparts. In the later 1980s and 1990s, the increases rose more gradually and then declined (in adjusted not actual amounts) to the point that in 1990-1995, the bride's side appeared to have contributed 33 percent less than those who married between 1965-69.

The pace of cost increases appears most pronounced in the 1970s and slows down during the second half of the 1980s, probably reflecting economic recession and later, the consequences of the Gulf War. It is plausible that labor migration in the 1970s and early 1980s contributed to increases in the total cost of marriage as migration fueled higher incomes and wages both abroad and in Egypt. During this period Egypt also experienced high real GDP growth per capita. By that time, however, actual marriage costs for a bride's family had risen ten times over 1965 levels (unadjusted for inflation), i.e. from LE 300 in the mid-1960s to LE 3,542 by 1990-95. Because this 30-year time interval corresponds roughly to one generation, it also means that parents of young men and women currently experiencing the marriage market will make these ten-fold cost comparisons to their own earlier marriages.

There are limitations to using brides' total costs as a proxy indicator of the way overall marriage costs have changed, because the proportional contribution of brides could be shifting over time. We know from ethnographic studies, backed by case study data, that considerable regional and social class variation exists in the proportional contribution brides and their families make to marriage costs. Over time, the EDHS trend data reveal a significant increase in the proportion of costs women say their families contribute towards marriage.

The traditional Egyptian pattern, where the bulk of marriage costs were borne by the groom's side, is shifting to a significant degree. For example, the percentage of women reporting equal sharing of costs with their grooms increased from only four percent in the 1960's marriage cohort to 25 percent in the 1990-1995 cohort. Even more revealing, because of the role reversal it implies, 15 percent of marriages contracted in the 1990s involved a lower contribution from the groom's side (compared with only 6 percent reporting a lower groom's contribution in the 1960s, data not shown). The range of marriage items once exclusively contributed by grooms and now shared more by brides has also expanded recently, a phenomenon that will be discussed further below.

Does the High Cost of Marriage Contribute to Marriage Delays?

The issues of cost and timing are closely linked in the minds of Egyptians, who comment frequently on the frustrations experienced by youth who are unable for financial reasons to marry as early as they would like. When parents of adolescents, defined as children between the ages 10-19, were asked in 1997 about the main problems facing youth, 59 percent identified buying an apartment or house for marriage, followed by 21 percent replying that youth lacked money, while 10 percent identified problems in furnishing the marital home (Ibrahim et. al. 2000:3). Thus the three leading problems for young people, according to their parents, are directly related to the financial burdens of marriage.

Average ages of marriage have risen significantly over the past 30 years. The proportion of women aged 20-24 who were married by age 20 in 1970 was 64.8 percent, while this proportion dropped to 41.4 in 1995 (Rashad and Khadr 1998). Similarly, the median age of first marriage for the age cohort 25-29 in 1970 was 18, while in 1995 it increased to 19.2 (Rashad and Khadr 1998). Some caution is necessary in linking marriage financing to delays, however, since many other factors, including legal constraints, military service, and extended education can also account for increases in the age of marriage. Hardship in accumulating the necessary sums for marriage could also be linked to recession or war or other macro-level events.[12]

The inference would be strengthened if evidence is found for a pattern of lengthening time between the initial commitment of a couple and the final stage of establishing joint living arrangements. In fact, some particularly compelling evidence for this kind of delay can be drawn from 1986 and 1996 Egyptian census trends. In those two rounds (only) a question was asked which distinguishes between the stage of marriage registration, *katb al-kitab*, and the final stage of establishing marital

---

[12]Multivariate analyses of these relationships are forthcoming for Egypt and neighboring countries as part of the New Arab Demography Project. Here we sketch out the broad figures for Egypt. For example, societies such as Lebanon, Kuwait, and Jordan that have recently experienced war or civil strife have the highest rates of never-married women in the 30-39 age cohort (see Rashad and Osman 2000).

residence, *gawaz*. Couples in the first stage are in fact legally married in Egypt but are not yet living together, often because the preparation of a new apartment or home is not complete. We compared the number of individuals 'caught' in the *katb al-kitab* stage as a proportion of all eligible adults in the population in the two time points and found a four-fold increase from 1986 to 1996 (CAPMAS 1987; 1997).[13] By contrast, the annual rate of marriages registered officially (*katb al-kitab*) only increased slightly, from 8.5 to 8.7 percent. An increase of four times in the delaying couples in ten years seems highly significant, and verifies the lay person's perception that marriage preparations are becoming a protracted, arduous process for brides, grooms, and their families.

Who Pays for Marriage?

The EIHS marriage module collected data on the four main parties contributing to marriage costs: the groom, the groom's family, the bride's family, and the bride. In earlier times, the responsibility fell almost entirely on family elders, but now it is assumed that grooms will also contribute, and increasingly so will brides. What each individual and family contributes is related to the gendered conventions and local traditions that govern the sharing of marriage costs in a particular location. Additionally, each specific item of expense is traditionally contributed by one party to the marriage.

As Table 2 shows clearly, the bulk of the financial obligations of marriage are still borne in Egypt by the groom and his family. Traditionally for the large majority, these costs would not have been great, consisting of gifts of jewelry, new clothes, and a legally required *mahr* (Hoodfar 1997, 68). These items would be transferred from the groom's family to the bride's at the time of marriage and were considered sufficient in rural communities where the expectation was that in return, brides would leave their natal homes to join the extended household of their husband.

---

[13]Results were nearly the same using all married adults or all adults of marriageable age as the denominator. The absolute numbers of men and women in this stage rose from 275,500 in 1986 to 1,351,000 in 1996 (CAPMAS 1987; 1997).

Table 2

Contributions to Marriage Costs by Region

Region	Urban	Rural	Total
Groom's family	28	45	38
Groom's share alone	44	34	37
Total	**72**	**79**	**75**
Bride's family	24	19	22
Bride's share alone	5	5	2.3
Total	**29**	**21**	**24**

While grooms and their families still contribute the lion's share to marriage, we found a trend in most parts of Egypt toward increasing contributions from brides' families as well. This phenomenon could be seen as representing a decrease in the status of young women. We suspect however, that the primary reason is a change in the earning patterns within families, such that women, and in particular younger women, now contribute increasingly to household wages. The ability of young unmarried women to work, and therefore contribute to marriage costs, is relatively new in Egypt.

There is some evidence, though numbers are too small for strong inferences, that brides' contributions are increasing and are linked to the availability of new employment opportunities. In rural Upper Egypt, where wage work for women is still scarce, only .03 percent of brides in our 1999 sample contribute to marriage expenses, as opposed to almost seven percent of urban brides in metro and Lower Egypt (EIHS, data not shown). Confirmation of this pattern is found in a recent study by Nagah Hassan, who compiled case studies of young women working in industrial areas of Port Said, Mansura and Helwan (Amin and Hassan, forthcoming). Her informants almost all reported that the main reason for taking a factory job was to save for the expenses of a pending marriage. It is primarily urban women and those in peri-urban areas who have access to wage labor and therefore are in a position to begin sharing the costs of marriage with their families and fiancés. Since the mid-1960s, women who work contribute more to marriage costs than those who do not (EDHS 1996). Similarly, more educated brides seem to contribute more to the costs of marriage and/or are able to leverage higher contributions towards their marriage from their own families, according to the EDHS cohort data (data not shown).

In our 1999 sample, the bride's family provides anywhere from one tenth to a quarter of the marriage costs. Regional variation is significant; in rural Upper Egypt, for example, there is little contribution from the bride's family (only 13 percent), thus conforming most closely to the traditional pattern of full funding from the groom's side (data not shown). When the sample is divided into strata by per capita expenditures, the richest third of brides' families contribute most to marriage expenses. This would not be expected if purely economic considerations were operating. We posit that well-off families are perhaps less sensitive to maintaining traditional norms, while also having the means to assure that their daughters will begin married life in comfort and at a standard of living commensurate with their own. If this pattern spreads, as is suggested by the EDHS trend data, then greater sharing of marriage costs will continue in the future.

The Distribution of Cost Sharing for Marriage

The 1999 EIHS collected data on the major cost items of marriage, including the bride price (*mahr*), marriage jewelry (*shabka*), housing, furniture, celebrations, and the less expensive furnishings such as clothing and kitchenware, known as the *gihaz* or preparations for marriage. The bride price is a contractual obligation of Islamic marriage and therefore almost always is paid by the groom or his family. The bride and her family may use the portion of bride price they receive to purchase their contributions to marriage (the *gihaz*, small furnishings, minor appliances, carpeting, etc.). Another portion of the bride price, the *mu`akhar sadaq* is stipulated in the marriage contract to be given to the wife only in case of later divorce. Some couples, particularly in urban Egypt, stipulate a merely symbolic amount for the bride price as it is registered in the marriage contract. According to the EDHS cohort data, 37 percent of the cohort that married between 1990-95 did not exchange a bride price. There is great regional variation in this trend (65 percent non-expenditure in Cairo; low of 26 percent in Rural Upper

Egypt). In our 1999 EIHS sample, only 27 percent of the couples reported exchanging a bride price. If households do not demand a large bride price from the groom, they nevertheless expect the groom to purchase a greater share of costly furniture and appliances. In other words, there may be a trend toward shifting resources away from the bride price in favor of contributions to necessary items like furniture and furnishings.

The *shabka* is typically paid exclusively by the groom and his family, although some sharing is reported, and the exchange of *shabka* in general has become more widespread over the past few decades (EDHS cohort data). This trend is significant because the *shabka*, which is almost always a gift of gold or precious gems, is given directly to the bride. Thus it becomes her property throughout the marriage and even in the case of divorce. Unlike some of the costs born by the bride and/or her family to furnish and supply the marital household, jewelry largely keeps its value over time and is thought of as a kind of insurance against personal or household emergencies. It is common for women to sell their jewelry to finance major initiatives such as the costs of migration abroad for another family member or investments in a new business venture. Jewelry can always be sold quickly to finance a medical emergency for children or the woman's own financial crisis in the case of a husband's death or divorce.

The costs of housing are generally born by the groom and his family, although there have been minor increases in sharing the costs of housing as well. Most couples prefer not to marry until they arrange to rent, purchase, build, or renovate a separate dwelling, but financial constraints appear to have slowed down an earlier trend toward nuclear households. A sizable proportion of newlyweds remain in extended family household residences in both urban and rural areas. Newspapers are filled with stories concerning the hardship of finding apartments for newlyweds, particularly for the poor and middle class. Parents may begin saving for purchases of land for their children's apartments or adding additional floors or rooms to their present dwelling years before their children are ready to marry.

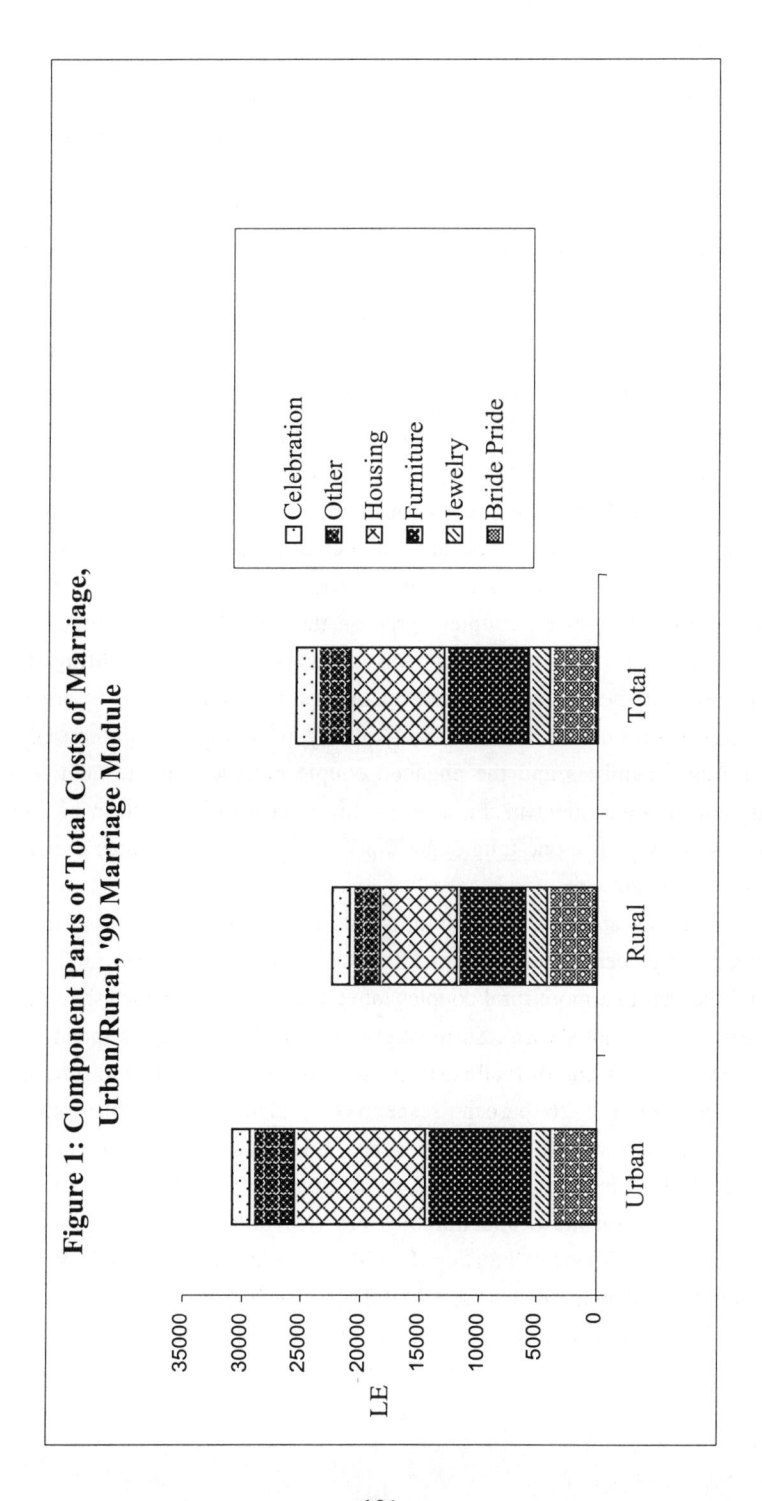

Figure 1: Component Parts of Total Costs of Marriage, Urban/Rural, '99 Marriage Module

The higher average cost of marriage in urban (LE24,969), as opposed to rural areas (LE17,373) is largely explained by the higher amounts spent on furniture and housing. In urban areas, families spend one and half times the amount that rural families spend on furniture and 1.7 times what rural families spend on housing, even though the percentage of the total costs spent on housing and furniture is relatively comparable.

A groom with an apartment he has inherited or whose family has purchased or built one for him is typically able to marry in a shorter time than others. Our data demonstrate that the cost of housing is approximately a third of the total costs of marriage, and furniture purchases follow closely behind (31 percent and 28 percent respectively). It is not only necessary to find a physical space before a couple can marry, but that space must be furnished, finished, decorated, and supplied in particular ways, according to the norms of particular classes, communities, and regions. During the long period of engagement, couples agree on the most basic of items such as housing as well as the most trivial (cookware, pictures, lighting, fans, glasses, bed sheets). It is also not uncommon for engagements to break up over disputes about the cost and quality of the goods purchased for marriage. Families and the engaged couple believe that the quality and amount of investment in the new dwelling place is a reflection of family status, as well as a one-time opportunity to raise the new couple's material living standard.

In urban areas the proportion spent on housing is more than in rural areas (36 percent as opposed to 28 percent), reflecting higher land values and the fact that more rural couples move into add-on or refurbished family quarters (data not shown). Surprisingly, we found that couples spend nearly the same proportion of total costs on furniture in both urban and rural areas (29 percent and 26 percent respectively). The considerable expenses incurred for furniture in 1999 is supported by analysis of the Consumer Price Index, in both urban and rural areas in the 1990s, where price increases in furniture and durables are two to three times higher than increases in the cost of housing. In addition, prices in rural areas are often rising faster than in urban areas (CAPMAS 1999:298-299).

Why should furniture increase as a proportion of total marriage costs in recent decades?

The domestic furniture and appliance industry expanded in the late 1970s and 1980s, and importing furniture and appliances became more possible under the Economic Open Door Policy. In addition, the standard of living has risen for some groups, and consumptive norms broadened the basket of goods now considered necessary for marriage. While having a television as part of one's *'afsh* may have been an innovation in the 1960s, in the 1970s and 1980s in urban areas at least, one needed as well a washing machine, fans, cassette recorder, stove, refrigerator, etc.

Not surprisingly, housing costs vary by residential pattern, whether nuclear or extended. Our 1999 sample and the EDHS cohort data for marriages in 1990-1995 found fairly high rates of extended family living in both urban and rural areas. In the 1999 EIHS, 39 percent of the households who had married in the past five years lived in an extended family. Thirty-one percent of all urban couples lived in extended family arrangements and 44 percent of all rural households lived with extended families. The housing costs of couples living with their families were significantly lower than for couples that set up housekeeping as nuclear families (for example, twelve grooms in the sample contributed nothing to housing costs). The average housing cost for the groom's side in a nuclear residential pattern was LE 8,566 (21 percent more than the total mean), compared to LE4,801 in an extended family situation (32 percent less than mean housing costs). Housing costs remain fairly significant, however, even for extended living arrangements. This is presumably because the new couple may renovate their space or add additional rooms to the family dwelling.[14]

What Are the Strategies for Accumulating Marriage Costs?

The 1999 EIHS asked respondents in the marriage module households what means had been employed to save the requisite amounts for their marriage.

---

[14] In the DHS survey, among the cohort of women who had married between 1990-1995, the pattern of extended family residence was even greater. Sixty-three percent (N=1617) reported that they began married life in an extended family (79 percent of rural and 33 percent of urban women). These figures are much higher than national household surveys of residential patterns from the same period, suggesting that this kind of newlywed residence may be temporary. Further research on this disparity is warranted.

Interviewers asked for information on the contributions of four categories: bride, groom, bride's family, and groom's family. The responses suggest that families are employing multiple strategies to meet their obligations. Twenty-six percent of grooms found second jobs to save for marriage, as did 6 percent of all brides, the bride's family members, and the groom's family members. The fact that few brides are involved in financial accumulation is not surprising, giving the previous discussion of work opportunities, but some of them take on a second job to finance their share of the marriage. However, the 40 percent of groom's families who report not participating in accumulating marriage costs does go against expected norms in Egypt. Another surprising finding is that labor migration as a strategy plays a relatively minor role (less that 5 percent of groom's family and less than 10 percent of grooms report migrating abroad to prepare for a marriage.) Once an important channel of employment, external migration has decreased significantly since the late 1980s.

On the other hand, participating in a savings group (*gama'iyya*) was reported as a strategy employed by at least one fifth of brides' family members, grooms, family members of grooms (6 percent of brides, 32 percent of grooms, 31 percent of bride's family, and 20 percent of groom's family). This relatively understudied informal financial mechanism operates among neighbors, kin, and work colleagues. It enables those participating to deposit savings with the group on a regular basis; the collected amounts are then distributed to the members on a rotating basis. The *gama'iyya* enforces savings over several months or years, usually for the purpose of buying something expensive. It avoids banks and other financing mechanisms, such as time purchases, which may impose charges, and are perceived as rigid and ultimately expensive. Widespread use of the *gama'iyya* for wedding preparations deserves more attention from those attempting to reform credit and savings policies and ameliorate financial burdens on families (Singerman 1995; Baydas, Bahloul, and Adams 1995).

Some additional evidence is available about family accumulation strategies from the 1997 ASCE adolescent survey (Ibrahim et al, 2000). Parents of adolescents were asked to suggest possible remedies for the high costs of marriage. Overall, parents expect the groom to work more or take on additional jobs as the primary accumulation strategy. Brides were more likely to be expected to contribute in urban areas and Lower Egypt, again confirming the link between work opportunities and changing marriage customs. In urban areas, housing was mentioned as the largest obstacle, and parents said that the government should be doing more to help. Differences by socio-economic strata and education were in a predicted direction. Those with less education and lower status are more likely to favor living with in-laws as a strategy to reduce costs, while high status and more educated parents, by a wide margin, believe the government should be doing more to help. The fact that those most in need of outside assistance are least likely to ask for it, raises interesting questions about public policy and its role in family economics.

Do the Poor Pay More for Marriage?

Poverty rates are debated in Egypt, but the 1997 EIHS concluded that 27 percent of the Egyptian population was living in poverty (29 percent of the rural population and 23 percent of the urban population) (Datt, Jolliffe, and Sharma 1998). In the smaller 1999 EIHS, 33 percent of the households fell below the poverty line, an increase of 6 percent (Haddad and Akhter 2000:11).[15] Adams also found a slight increase in both the depth and severity of poverty between 1981-82 and 1997 (2000:263). Assaad and Rushdy argue that "at least one quarter of Egypt's population is poor by any standards and another quarter lives on the margins of poverty (1999:11)." Nagy argues that 37.3 percent of the households he surveyed in 1995 were objectively poor (2001:42).

While the causes and measurement of poverty are extremely complicated we posit that ignoring the effects of the cost of marriage on expenditure data may unnecessarily distort poverty measures and, more importantly, distort the ability of policymakers to better target and formulate poverty alleviation strategies. If current measurements of poverty underestimate the welfare and poverty effects of inter-household transfers of assets by ignoring the largest single expenditures that families make, it is not surprising that policies designed to improve the economic and social conditions of Egyptians may falter.

---

[15]The poverty line is the break even level of expenditures by a household needed to meet a minimum of food and non-food requirements (Adams 2000:261). See note 2.

To be sure, marriage solves some of the immediate issues surrounding vulnerability of the poor: it houses a couple, allows for the reproduction of children who provide security and labor for later support; it directs assets of gold and furniture to the new couple that can be sold during a financial crisis, and it provides a healthier environment in a new or refurbished physical space for a newlywed couple and their ensuing children. On the other hand, marriage can indebt families for years, it can force women or men into arranged marriages that they do not want, and it can encourage conspicuous consumption rather than direct limited funds for savings, investment, education, and other skills-training.

The financial challenge that marriage poses for the bride, groom, and their families is demonstrated by Table 3 below. The cost of marriage we estimate nationally equals almost five times GNP per capita, which was $1,290 in 1998 (IBRD/World Bank 2000:12): LE20,194 (approximately $5,957). In rural areas the figure was LE17,373 (four times per capita income) and in urban areas, LE24,969 (almost six times per capita income). But the burden that marriage places on households becomes even more apparent when we examine data at the household level. As Table 3 suggests, the average cost of marriage nationally, is fully eleven times annual household expenditure per capita.

Given these high ratios of cost to family outlays, we must expect the expenditures a family makes on marriage to affect other kinds of consumption for food and health care, for example. This suppression of other types of expenditure is difficult to measure with available data. However, by separating families into those living either below or above the poverty line, we can demonstrate the relative weight of these expenditures.

One-third of the 1999 EIHS households were found to be living under the poverty line (Haddad and Akhter 2000:11). The national cost of marriage for these households is LE9,466, dwarfing their annual household expenditures per capita twelve times over. For households living above the poverty line, the costs of marriage (LE24,688) are only somewhat lower and equal eleven times per capita expenditures. However, rural-urban distinctions are more dramatic. In urban areas, Egyptians living below the poverty line spend nine times per capita expenditures on marriage. Yet, the greatest burden is carried by Egyptians who live below the poverty line in rural areas and spend *fifteen* times their annual household expenditures per capita on the cost of marriage. The financial challenge that marriage poses for the rural poor clearly deserves more detailed attention in order to understand both its causes and its consequences.

Table 3

Total Marriage Costs Relative to Annual Household Expenditure Per Capita

	Urban	Rural	Total
Total Cost of Marriage for Household			
Above poverty line	34,012	19,680	24,688
Below poverty line	8,822	11,219	9,466
All households	24,969	17,373	20,194
Total Cost of Marriage Relative to Households Expenditures Per Capita			
Above poverty line	11	10	11
Below poverty line	9	15	12
All households	10	12	11

While households may be forced to reduce short-term expenditures in order to meet the costs of marriage for their children, newlywed households naturally gain materially from those sacrifices. There is a strong economic rationale for investing large resources in marriage in order to launch the new generation into a higher economic position. Indeed, our analysis suggests the existence of a positive "newlywed bounce" in Egypt. Only 19 percent of newlywed households fell under the poverty line, compared to 27 percent of all households surveyed (data not shown).[16] Investing in marriage means that younger households enjoy relative prosperity, although it is very probable that this newlywed bounce evens out as couples have children,

---

[16]Nine percent of entire 1997 EIHS were defined as newlywed households (211). Newlywed households were defined as such if the family had four or fewer children below five years or if their durables were less than five years old and the head of the household was younger than forty.

increase their expenses, and eventually begin reducing their expenditures to save for the marriages of their own children.

Conclusion

As we have demonstrated throughout this paper, Egyptian families make significant financial sacrifices in order to invest in the next generation. The burdens are not evenly distributed among social groups, however, and in relative terms the poor pay more. How can we explain the strength of cultural norms that shape years of financial sacrifice in order to fulfill the goal of marrying off one's offspring? One explanation may lie in the apparent short-term benefit of increased well-being: resulting new couples are more likely to escape poverty, at least in the early years of marriage. This enhanced standard of living may also provide a healthier context for bearing and raising children which typically occurs in the early years of marriage.

The very public way that marriage is celebrated and goods are displayed in the newlywed home in Egypt suggests that marriage expenses are also a means of consolidating a family's social standing in the community, a "signaling" effect of social status, as Rao found in his study of rural South India (2001). It may be plausible that investments in marriage should be understood in terms of "purchasing" upward mobility, expressed through the shared perception of an improvement in the physical standard of living from the natal household to the newly established marital household. A caution is needed here however: the "newlywed bounce" that was discussed above is the consequence of impressive savings strategies, stretched out over a number of years. Yet this strategy may be the cause of financial insecurity for aging parents in the future who may not "recover" from these marriage expenses for years as their earning power diminishes.

While macro-economic trends of growth, poverty, employment, and globalization are difficult to predict, as are the resulting changes in the state's commitment to social welfare and public services, Egyptians will continue to launch accumulation strategies to invest in the next generation. This clearly influences the economic decision-making and life choices that young women and men and their families make. The cumulative effect of these household patterns needs to be better understood within the context of macro-economic trends in consumption, savings, and investment. There are many significant questions that remain unanswered around these choices and their consequences. Our hope is that the findings presented here will spark further attention from researchers and those charged with policy decisions affecting Egypt's youth.

Works Cited

Abu Hashish, Shireen Ali and Mark Allen Peterson. 1999. "Computer *Khatbas*: Databases and Marital Entrepreneurship in Modern Cairo," *Anthropology Today* 15:7-11.

Adams, Richard H. 2000. "Evaluating the Process of Development in Egypt, 1980-97," *International Journal of Middle East Studies* 32: 255-275.

Ahmed, Leila. 1992. *Women and Gender in Islam: Historical Roots of Modern Debate.* New Haven and London: Yale University Press.

Allam, Abeer. 2000. "'*Urfi* Delivers the Goods, at Half Price," *Middle East Times* (February 18).

Amin, Sajida and Negah Hassan. 2001. "Female Employment in the New Free Zones." Population Council, New York.

Assaad, Ragui and Malak Rouchdy. 1999. "Poverty and Poverty Alleviation Strategies in Egypt." *Cairo Papers in Social Science* 22: 1.

Badran, Margot. 1991. "Competing Agenda: Feminists, Islam and the State in Nineteenth and Twentieth-Century Egypt" in Deniz Kandiyoti, ed., *Women, Islam, and the State*, pp. 201-236. Philadelphia: Temple University Press.

Baydas, Mayada M., Zakaria Bahloul, and Dale W. Adams. 1995. "Informal Finance in Egypt: 'Banks' within Banks," *World Development* 23: 651-661.

Behrman J., N. Birdsall, and A. Deolalikar. 1995. "Marriage Markets, Labor Markets, and Unobserved Human Capital: An Empirical Exploration for South-Central India," *Economic Development and Cultural Change* (April) 43:585-601.

Bhat, P.N. Mari and Shiva S. Halli. 1999. "Demography of Brideprice and Dowry: Causes and Consequences of the Indian Marriage Squeeze," *Population Studies* 53:129-148.

Bouis, Howarth E. and Akhter U. Ahmed. 1998. "The Egyptian Food Subsidy System: Impacts on the Poor and an Evaluation of Alternatives for Policy Reforms." International Food Policy Research Institute. Food Security Research Unit of the Agricultural Policy Reform Program in Egypt in Collaboration with the Ministry of Agriculture and Land Reclamation and the Ministry of Trade and Supply. March 31, 1998. International Food Policy Research Institute. Washington, D.C.

Central Agency for Public Mobilization and Statistics (CAPMAS). 1999. *Statistical Yearbook 1992-1998*. Nasr City, Egypt.

_____. 1987. *Population, Housing, and Establishment Census 1986: Preliminary Results*. Nasr City, Egypt.

_____. 1997. *Population, Housing, and Establishment Census 1986: Preliminary Results*. Nasr City, Egypt.

Datt, Gairav, Dean Jolliffe, and Manohar Sharma. 1998. "A Profile of Poverty in Egypt." FCDN Discussion Paper No. 49. Food Consumption and Nutrition Division. International Food Policy Research Institute. Washington, D. C. (August).

"Egypt Demographic and Health Survey, 1995." 1996. National Population Council (Egypt) and Macro International Inc. Calverton, MD.

Ezzat, Dina. 2000. "Sacred Knots and Unholy Deals: The Road Towards Pro-Women Legal Reform in Egypt" in Judith Mirsky and Marty Radlett, eds., *No Paradise Yet*, pp. 39-60. London: Panos/Zed Press.

El-Magd, Nadia. 1998. "Anniversary Wedding," al-*Ahram Weekly* 398 (October 8-14).

Gaulin, Steven and James Boster. 1990. "Dowry as Female Competition," *American Anthropologist* 92: 994-1005.

Goldman, N., C. Westoff, and C. Hammerslough. 1984. "Demography of the Marriage Market in the United States," *Population Index* 50: 5-25.

Goody, Jack and Stanley Jeyaraja Tambiah. 1973. *Bridewealth and Dowry*. Cambridge University Press.

Greene, Margaret E. and Vijayendra Rao. 1995. "The Marriage Squeeze and the Rise in Informal Marriage in Brazil," *Social Biology* (Spring) 42:65-82.

Haddad, Lawrence and Ahmed A. Akhter. 2000. "Poverty Dynamics in Egypt: 1997-1999." International Food Policy Institute (September).

Hoodfar, Homa. 1997. *Between Marriage and the Market: Intimate Politics and Survival in Cairo*. Berkeley: University of California Press.

Ibrahim, Barbara. 1980. "*Social Change and the Industrial Experience.*" PhD dissertation. Indiana University.

Ibrahim, Barbara et. al. 2000. *Transitions to Adulthood: A National Survey of Egyptian Adolescents*, 2nd Edition. New York: The Population Council.

Ibrahim, Barbara and Hind Wassef. 2000. "Caught between two worlds: Youth in the Egyptian hinterland," in Roel Meijer, ed., *Alienation or Integration of Arab Youth: Between Family, State and Street*. London: Curzon Press.

International Bank for Reconstruction and Development and The World Bank. 2000. *World Bank's World Development Indicators*. Washington, D.C.

Joseph, Suad. 1996. "Gender and Family in the Arab World" in Suha Sabbagh, ed., *Arab Women: Between Defiance and Restraint*, pp. 194-202. New York: Olive Branch Press.

Lampard, R. 1993. "Availability of Marriage Partners in England and Wales: A Comparison of Three Measures," *Journal of Biosocial Science* (July) 25: 333-350.

Leila, Reem. 2000. "The Terms of Engagement," *al-Ahram Weekly* 484 (June 1-7).

Lloyd, Cynthia B. and Nora Guhl Naguib. 1994. "Gender Inequalities and Demographic Behavior." The Population Council. New York.

Lundberg, Shelly and Robert A. Pollak. 1997. "Separate-Spheres Bargaining and the Marriage Market," in .Lawrence Haddad, John Hoddinott, and Harold Alderman, eds., *Intrahousehold Resource Allocation in Developing Countries, Models, Methods, and Policies*, pp. 75-94. Baltimore, MD: The Johns Hopkins University Press.

McClamroch, Kristi. 1996. "Total Fertility Rate, Women's Education, and Women's Work--What are the Relationships?," *Population and Environment* 18:175-186.

Ministry of Agriculture and Land Reclamation and Ministry of Trade and Supply. 1997. "Egypt Integrated Household Survey." (June 16). Cairo.

Ministry of Agriculture and Land Reclamation and Ministry of Trade and Supply. 1999. "Egypt Household Expenditure Survey." (January 14). Cairo.

Mir-Hosseini, Ziba. 1999. *Islam and Gender: The Religious Debate in Contemporary Iran.* Princeton: Princeton University Press.

_____. 1993. *Marriage on Trial: A Study of Islamic Family Law Iran and Morocco Compared.* London: I.B. Tauris.

Moghadam, Valentine. 1993. *Modernizing Women: Gender & Social Change in the Middle East.* Boulder: Lynne Rienner Publishers.

Nagi, Saad Z. 2001. *Poverty in Egypt: Human Needs and Institutional Capacities.* Lanham: Lexington Books.

Osman, Magued and Laila Shahd. 2000. "Who Marries Whom in Egypt: A Response to Marriage Constraints." Paper presented at Ninth Annual Symposium, Cairo Papers in Social Science Conference, "The New Arab Family." 6-7 May, Cairo.

Rao, Vijayendra and Francis Bloch. 2000. "Terror as a Bargaining Instrument: A Case Study of Dowry Violence in Rural India." World Bank Policy Research Working Paper 2347, The World Bank (May).

Rao, Vijayendra. 2001. "Poverty and Public Celebrations in Rural India," *Annals of the American Academy of Political and Social Science* 573: 85-104.

Rashad, Hoda and Magued Osman. 2000. "The Nuptiality Transition in the Arab World and its Implications." Paper presented at Ninth Annual Symposium, Cairo Papers in Social Science Conference, "The New Arab Family." 6-7 May, Cairo.

Rashad, Hoda and Zeinab Khadr. 1998. "The Demography of the Arab Region: New Challenges and Opportunities." Unpublished paper presented at the "Conference on Population Challenges in the Middle East and North Africa: Towards the Twenty-First Century." Arab Fund for Economic and Social Development and the Economic Research Forum for the Arab Countries, Iran and Turkey. 2-4 November, Cairo.

Rugh, Andrea. 1984. *Family in Contemporary Egypt.* New York: Syracuse University Press.

Schlegel, Alice. 1993. "Dowry: Who Competes for What?," *American Anthropologist* 95:155-157.

Schlegel, Alice and Rohn Eloul. 1988. "Marriage Transactions: Labor, Property, Status," *American Anthropologist* 90:291-309.

Shafey, Halla E. 1998. "Adolescence and State Policy in Egypt." The Population Council, Cairo.

Shahine, Gihan. 1998. "The Double Bind," al-*Ahram Weekly* 397 (1-7 October).

Shukri, Shirin J.A.. 1999. *Social Changes and Women in the Middle East: State Policy, Education, Economics and Development.* Brookfield, VT: Ashgate.

Singerman, Diane. 1995. *Avenues of Participation: Family, Politics, and Networks in Urban Quarters of Cairo.* Princeton: Princeton University Press.

Singerman, Diane and Homa Hoodfar, eds. 1997. *Gender, Development and Change in Cairo: A View from the Household.* Bloomington: Indiana University Press.

Singh, Susheela and Renee Samara. 1996. "Early Marriage Among Women in Developing Countries," *International Family Planing Perspectives* 22:148-157.

Sonbol, Amira El Azhary, ed. 1996. *Women, the Family, and Divorce Laws in Islamic History.* Syracuse: Syracuse University Press.

Tapper, Nancy. 1991. *Bartered Brides: Politics, Gender, and Marriage in an Afghan Tribal Society.* London: Cambridge University Press.

Tove, Stang Dahl. 1997. *The Muslim Family: A Study of Women's Rights in Islam.* Trans. Ronald Walford. Oslo: Scandinavian University Press.

United Nations Development Programme. 1997. *Human Development Report.* New York: Oxford University Press.

United States. Department of State. 2000. "1999 Country Report on Economic Policy and Trade Practices--Egypt." Bureau of Economic and Business Affairs (March).

Van der Veen, Klaas W. 1972. *I Give Thee My Daughter: A Study of Marriage and Hierarchy Among the Anavil Brahmans of South Gujarat.* Assen: Van Gorcum.

Wiktorowicz, Quintain and Suha Taji Farouki. 2000. "Islamic Non-Governmental Organizations and Muslim Politics: A Case from Jordan," *Third World Quarterly* 21: 685-699.

Women & Law in the Muslim World Programme. 1996. *Special Dossier: Shifting Boundaries in Marriage and Divorce in Muslim Communities.* (Fall) 1.

Zhang, Junsen and William Chang. 1999. "Dowry and Wife's Welfare: A Theoretical and Empirical Analysis," *Journal of Political Economy* 107:786-808.

FROM SEXUAL SUBMISSION TO VOLUNTARY COMMITMENT: THE TRANSFORMATION OF FAMILY TIES IN CONTEMPORARY TUNISIA

LILIA LABIDI

Over the past several decades, since a Personal Status Code (PSC) promulgated in 1956 outlawed repudiation and polygamy and made divorce judicial, the Tunisian family has undergone a significant transformation in the content of some of the values that constitute the foundation of relationships between its members.[1] The new generations of couples, belonging to a middle class that constitutes 35 percent of the total population, elaborated a culture that broke away from their traditional imaginary but did not abandon the basis of their moral values. We will focus in this paper on analyzing the notion of "shame", to illustrate the change in relations between men and women, formerly founded on the woman's sexual subjection through defloration, now becoming relations that have their basis in fidelity, a symbolic pact where one's word is given freely. To analyze this change, we will treat three different phenomena: the privatization of the wedding night and the fact that families do not express opposition to this; women's work outside the home, which no longer puts the honor of the men in danger; the presence of the men in private space, without disturbing their

---

[1] The 1956 PSC is often considered the veritable constitution of the Tunisian state. With regard to the reforms introduced in the Personal Status Code even before the Tunisian constitution was adopted, Y. Ben Achour says (2000:60; my translation), "Conceptually and juridically, it [the Personal Status Code] is the nation's true constitution." In addition to the provisions cited in the text, the Code also transformed women's lives by establishing a minimum age for a girl to marry, specifying that schools would be co-educational, stipulating that women would receive salaries equal to men's. Many of these provisions contributed to strengthening the role of women in public space. Reforms introduced in 1993 dealt with matters such as the reciprocal obligations of husband and wife, the marriage of minors, acquisition of nationality through the mother, and domestic violence.

sexual identity.[2]

We will see that this new culture in process, while continuing to give virginity a role in sexual life (as a freely made choice), no longer consecrates maintaining a separation of the sexes, a separation which betrayed men's fear with regard to women. We will see how these transformations lead to a new paradigm where the man, no longer dreading being weakened by the woman, takes the initiative to carry out *Lailat al-dukhla/Lailat al-'umr* with his spouse, far from family and clan;[3] where the man is not ashamed when he is no longer the sole provider of domestic financial needs; where the man does not fear contamination by femininity if he spends time in private space (Zouilai 1990:100). All happens as if, in distinguishing the material danger from the psychic danger, the man distinguishes what is real from what is imaginary. In the woman's case, her archaic reaction of hostility (to take vengeance for her defloration), projected onto the oppressive reality around her, has been put to the service of constructing a new ethics where the speaking subject is no longer solitary--transformations that answer the ambitions of an intellectual and moral life to which reformers, feminists and thinkers of the Arab world contributed (Haddad 1978).

From *Lailat al-dukhla* to *Lailat al-'Umr*

Wassila: "As for me, I spent my wedding night hiding in the toilet."

Nabiha, a secondary school student, was 16 years old during the 1930s when she married a physician. After the defloration, she said, "Is that all there is to it?" Her husband answered, "Why? did you want me to slaughter you!"

Olfa's husband tells his wife on the night of her defloration (which could only take place one week after the marriage because the bride was so frightened), "Here's the proof of the crime!".

---

[2] Unlike some other countries of the region, neither the right of women to vote, nor their driving a vehicle, nor the trips abroad they make alone, are any longer topics of controversy.

[3] *Lailat al-dukhla* (the night of entrance) has two meanings: the entrance of the bride into her new home and sexual penetration; *Lailat al-'umr* (the night of life) focuses on the positive aspects of this night which will play a role in determining the rest of one's life (Labidi 1989).

We have chosen to relate these fragments because they show how defloration was experienced both by women and by men as a "significant" moment--the former faced it with fear and the latter with a consciousness of the violence men were visiting on the women's body. This pushes us to ask: what is the status of virginity in society? We will here look at two sorts of answers, one cultural, the other artistic. The first comes from the prophet's *sira*--the acts and behavior of the Prophet Muhammad, of his wives and companions--a privileged site for the construction of symbols that contribute in a major way to the formation of the ideals of Muslim subjects. The second comes from a Persian painting of the fourteenth century, showing the feelings of that society towards virginity.

The first *hadith* concerns the Prophet Muhammad, the second his wife Aisha.

1) *Jabir Ben Abdallah says that when he was about to marry a woman as his second wife, the prophet asked him:*

- *"Why are you in such a hurry?"*
- *I am, I answered, about to celebrate my marriage.*
- *"With a virgin or an already married woman?" asked the prophet.*
- *An already married woman, I answered.*
- *"Why didn't you marry a girl whom you would caress and who would caress you, he countered?"*

A second version of this same *hadith* emphasizes virginity more. Here, the prophet is reported to have said: "Why not marry a virgin? She would amuse you and you would amuse her."

2) The second *hadith*, concerning Aisha, is important because Aisha was the only one of the Prophet's wives who was a virgin when he married her. Married when she was six years old according to some sources and at seven according to others, the marriage was not consummated until she was nine. The *hadith* puts the accent on her virginity and on the prophet's preferences, confirming the previous *hadith*.

"Oh, Messenger of God, if you were camped in a valley where on one *side there was a plant that had been browsed and on the other a plant that had not been browsed, to which side would you graze your camel?"*

"On the side that had not been browsed", he answered.

God's messenger meant by this that he had not married any other virgin, says Aisha.

Aisha gained some benefits from this status: among the qualities that made her the favorite among the prophet's wives, she mentions virginity. Ibn Saad notes how, when she told of the qualities that distinguished her, she put virginity in first position. She said: Muhammad married no other virgin woman than me. Al-Tabari places this value fourth in rank. According to him, she said: I was virgin, so he did not share me with another man (El Bokhari 1914).

This highly valued characteristic gave great advantages to those that married virgins. An Iranian painting by Janayd, dated 1396, titled "After the consumption of the marriage," shows the bride alone, crying, while other women examine the stained sheet. Her spouse, on the other hand, collects homage from the men: some give him money, others kiss his feet (Grabar 1955, fig. 6-18).

Tunisian traditions up until the mid-1970s in the cities and throughout the 1970s in rural areas prescribed marriage festivities that were to last seven days and seven nights. The proof of the wife's virginity and the spouse's virility--the bloodied *souria* (nightgown)--had to be exposed. Flight before the first sexual intercourse was a frequent occurrence as brides tried to defend themselves, traumatized as they were by the spectacle to which they were subject where blood, the basis of life, carries with it sadistic connotations. The absence of virginity, perhaps a result of rape or a sexual relation outside marriage, quickly turned to drama. When not a virgin on the eve of her marriage, the bride was often killed by her brother or father. He who killed to save the family's honor was not punished; the act was not considered a crime.

One *hadith* was cited at the time of the enactment of the PSC in Tunisia, which concerns the relationship between lailat *al-dukhla* (wedding night), *mahr* (the sum paid before the consumption of marriage) and *diya* (the sum paid in case of rape to commute the crime of honor), is essential to understanding what is not explicitly formulated.

The *mahr* has a regulating function. To understand how this works, we need to make a short detour via the Grand Tradition, where we learn, regarding the *mahr*: "And give the women (on marriage) their dower as a free gift" (Quran, IV *sura*, verse 3[4]). The PSC (1966 version[5]) refers to a *hadith* related by a Muslim who says that the Prophet addressed a man in these terms:

- *Do you possess something?.*
- *No.*
- *Did you learn some verses of the Quran?*
- *Yes, I know by heart such and such* suras.
- *Do you know them by heart?*
- *Yes.*
- *Go, I give her to you in marriage.*

The Tunisian legislator, in referring to this *hadith*, draws a parallel between the *mahr* and "knowledge." What is there to know? What do we need to know? We know that the *mahr* is or can be paid in two parts: the *mu'ajjil* is the part paid before the consummation of marriage and the *mu`akhar* is the part paid subsequently. Sexual relations were prohibited if the *mu`akhar* had not been paid by the end of a specified period indicated in the *sadaq* (contract of marriage). Article 12 of the 1957 PSC declares that: "The dowry can be made up of any licit good that has a money value;" article 13 mentions that: "The husband cannot, if he has not fully paid the dowry, force the woman to consummate the marriage. After consummation the woman, creditor of her dowry, can only ask for the payment of it. The failure of the husband to pay does not constitute reason for divorce."

What do we learn from the enactment of the PSC in 1957 and the reforms of 1993? The woman who doesn't receive the *mu`akhar* is only a creditor (Code du Statut Personnel 1998:7-8). Habib Bourguiba, first president of the Tunisian republic, and his wife Wassila Ben Ammar,

---

[4] *The Holy Qur`an*. Text, translation and commentary by A. Yusuf Ali. Washington DC: The American International Printing Company, 1946 (1932):179. The parenthetical phrase is the translator's.
[5] Cited by Es-Snoussi, E.T. 1970:15-16.

introduced on the occasion of their marriage in 1962 the practice of the symbolic *dinar*, breaking with the custom that formerly required the payment of a substantial *mahr*. The law of 1993 restates the legislator's position that the *mahr* belongs only to the woman.

Starting in the 1960s, Tunisian families practiced more and more frequently the *mahr* in the form of the symbolic *dinar*, thus making the distinction between fantasy and trauma. Relations within the couple are no longer grounded in the "murderous" encounter between opposites. Both members of the couple, knowing one another before the marriage, often for a long time, conceive of this union on the basis of the love that each has for the other. Two other elements follow from this change in values affecting the *mahr*--changes in *lailat al-dukhla* and in notions related to crimes of honor.

Up until the 1960s, *Lailat al-dukhla*, the night of the first sexual encounter between the couple, led to the display of the blooded sheet, proof of the bride's virginity. This custom, which had existed for centuries and of which we can see traces of in old Persian paintings, was about to undergo a significant change. The notion of virginity will still be in force but the role that it plays will change. The bloodied sheet that had to be displayed--not to do so meant admitting that the bride was not a virgin and this might lead to a life being taken; or was an indication that the groom was impotent and this too led to a drama, to shame on his family.

With the 1970s the couple, more and more educated, no longer wished to follow this practice. The bloodied sheet came to connote trauma and violence. Educated women no longer gained much benefit in declaring themselves virgin at marriage and the men no longer prided themselves on deflowering a virgin bride. Did the families follow the preferences of this younger generation? The wedding night, *lailat al-'umr*, became a private affair. The young couples, no longer able to finance the costly marriage ceremony (the difficult economic context contributed here, an indication of the failure of theories of development, of social and economic crisis, and so on), began more and more frequently to have a civil and religious ceremony for relatives and friends, and a small celebration for the close family.[6] At the

---

[6] Several Arab countries hold collective marriage ceremonies as an aid to young couples. The Tunisian media regularly run campaigns deploring the high costs of weddings. Whereas during the 1960s the *mahr* was often criticized, today the

same time, the expanding hotel infrastructure, at the outset aimed strictly at tourists, began to target young couples in its advertisements. "Honeymoon" stays at competitive prices became possible for the young couple. Tunis Air also began to offer special reductions for couples. The trip, which used to begin only after the display of the bloodied sheet, was now gradually becoming the occasion for young couples to establish their intimacy. This practice became institutionalized very quickly and the *lailat al-'umr* became a private matter. The blood of deflowering which, formerly, one had to display or suffer shame, now became shameful to display, as this change of values continued.

Do girls and women make complaints to the authorities when they are victims of rape? Do the police record such complaints in appropriate categories? Whereas the former seem to prefer to keep silent about a matter the community sees as shameful, the latter tend to minimize the violence visited on the bodies of women. Although Islamic law deals with the matter of rape victims, putting into place a system of recognition of the crime and a system of compensation, the culture of *sitr* (the protection of privacy) gave rise to various machinations so that the exercise of vengeance and crimes of honor might be averted. Law 72 of 12/7/1993 criminalizes crimes of honor and abrogates article 207 which punished the author of a crime of honor with 5 years' imprisonment, usually not fully served because of "good behavior."

We follow with a case that illustrates very well that what society formerly accepted as the norm now, in this new context, has become psychopathological. An inspector of the criminal police in the northwest of Tunisia gained permission, in 1988, to exhume the body of a girl eight months after burial. Under interrogation, the father and brother of the girl admitted having rained blows on her, leading to her death. The reason: she had kept in her closet the photograph of a young man of the region, in a

> photographic union ... without risk, more symbolic than anything else .... While going through his sister's possessions, the brother had found the two photos. After summoning her to explain herself, (the brother) grabbed the chain from his motorbike and attacked his sister with it. He stopped only when he realized she had lost consciousness.... With the father's arrival, the beating took up again

---

great expense involved in equipping a home is the object of criticism. See Bergaoui (1990), El-Bour, 1990, Ben Bassine and Hanachi 1999).

(with a stick), especially on the head, and the irreparable ensued. (Hamdi 1988)

Conscious of the horror of their crime, they brandished neither the notion of crime of honor nor defense of family honor, but sought to disguise as illness the murder they had committed.[7]

It is evident that the criminalization of crimes of honor is in accord with the wishes of Tunisian families, who increasingly prefer that the rapist be punished rather than marry the victim (even though he would not be allowed to divorce her for two years). A study of judicial proceedings in Tunis concerning crimes of honor show that these crimes are decreasing in importance: they constituted 8.84 percent of all crimes committed between 1964 and 1974, 3.75 percent of those committed between 1975 and 1985 and 2.58 percent for the period from 1986 to 1996.[8] Another study, involving 850 people chosen at random in metropolitan Tunis in January 1998, shows that 50 percent of people questioned were no longer in favor of marriage between the rapist and his victim. Respondents of both sexes stated that they

---

[7] To what extent can the brother's and father's acts be attributed to their socio-cultural environment? Although this environment certainly cannot explain everything, some figures here may help us understand the objective living conditions of youth who attack women as a way of expressing their own frustrations. Socio-economic indicators from the 1994 census portray a mediocre situation in the Northwest region, where this crime took place. The unemployed are 49.8 percent of men and 16.8 percent of women. The proportion of families possessing certain goods is equally revelatory: in 1994 9.2 percent owned an automobile whereas the national rate is 15.7 percent; 0.6 percent had access to satellite television whereas the national rate is 2.1 percent; 37 percent owned a refrigerator compared to 55 percent nationally; 63 percent have cooking appliances without ovens, whereas nationally the rate is 55.4 percent; 5.5 percent use a washing machine whereas the rate is three times as high nationally. The region is also characterized by a dispersed residence pattern which has a significant impact on education: in 1994, 33.8 percent of households were farther than 2 km from a primary school, whereas this is true for only 17.6 percent of households nationally; 50 percent were farther than 4 km from a secondary school. More than half the population of this region must travel more than 2 km to reach a health care center, and more than one-third of these must travel more than 4 km. The illiteracy rate is high: 9.6 percent for those between 10-14 years old, 14 percent for those between 15-19, 23 percent between 20-24, and 34.5 percent for those between 25-29 (Institut National de Statistique (1994).

[8] Crimes of honor include, in addition to offenses committed for loss of virginity, those committed by a husband against an adulterous couple (Yousri 2000).

did not consider such a marriage necessary to safeguard the girl's honor and that they favored criminalization of rape instead.

In this way, the new Tunisian family was adopting new ethical behavior (Labidi 2001). Women adopted the symbolic *dinar* for the *mahr*[9] upon signing the marriage contract, and were no longer willing to accept marriage with the rapist as reparation. The honor of the victim and that of families is no longer tied to the girl's hymen.

These facts illustrate how the restructuring of feelings, taking place over several decades, contributed to establishing a new ethics. Legislation based itself on a *hadith* which privileged knowledge--the opening up of the unconscious. The *mahr* must be paid on each occasion where there is ignorance of this 'knowledge'. This construction of a new ethics supports the movement toward salaried women's work that will no longer be experienced as shameful by the husband, as well as toward the growing presence of the husband in private space, no longer constituting a danger for his sexual identity.

New Couples

At independence, Bourguiba asked Khadija Rebah, a woman from Metouia in southern Tunisia and an active participant in the struggle for liberation, to continue her struggle for development and emancipation (Labidi 1990:45-55). Development would then consist of encouraging women to follow Khadija's path. Whereas Khadija had sewn shirts at home to help her husband, she had not yet thought that working outside the home was a way to continue the struggle. Khadija was hired as a laundry worker in one of the hospitals in the capital city. Many women admired Khadija's success, although they themselves had been unable to make the leap. Gaining autonomy and independence are the terms that are common to the two struggles--on the one hand for her country and on the other for herself. To

---

[9] Although the Great Tradition focuses on the *mahr*, it does not require an object of money value where such an object cannot be paid. For example, freeing a slave is considered the equivalent of a dowry, and a man who possesses nothing--not even an iron ring--but who knows verses from the Quran can marry. The notion that dominates since the enactment of the PSC is that, whatever the material condition of the couple may be, the *mahr* should amount to the symbolic dinar that the groom gives to his bride upon signing the marriage contract.

understand the significance of this, we will turn to two examples, one taken from literature, the other from a daily event.

Rachid Boujedra in *The Repudiation* (1969), a novel written during the 1960s, introduces us to the experience of women facing polygamy and repudiation. The feelings of "Ma" (the mother of the main character) constitute in themselves a psychological treatise. She analyzes very accurately the status of the repudiated women who remains "financially and morally dependent on her father," for in this universe "a woman is never an adult." It is clear that without financial autonomy women would remain dependent. So the discourse which counsels that men provide for women, treat them *bi-ma'rouf* (in all fairness), continue to support them even after repudiation, is only there to force the man to conform, suggesting that these kinds of behavior were not common practice. Judicial divorce, the right of women to seek divorce, and the economic independence of women, contributed to a reorganization of relationships within the family.

During the 1960s, requests for divorce came more frequently from men. This trend only changed in the 1980s, when we begin to hear the term "uniformization" with men and women seeking divorce at similar rates (Hermassi et al 1983:29). It is important to note that divorce rates in Tunisia, where the woman has the right to seek divorce, are lower than other Arab and than European countries (See Table 1). The percentage of divorced persons in advanced countries is about 10 times the divorce rates in the same countries, while in Tunisia the percentage of divorced persons is only 5 times the crude divorce rate (Ouni 1976:12).

What are the reasons that women invoke in seeking divorce? Three kinds of reasons, in three different periods, appear.

- "Assurance of food support" ranked first starting with the early 1960s.[10]

- "Irreconcilable marital difficulties" emerges as the most frequent reason towards the end of the 1960s (see Table 2). Twenty years after the enactment of the PSC, women dare to invoked ill-treatment whereas men invoke moral conduct (Hermassi et al 1983:55). Women white-collar workers questioned during the 1990s invoke sexual incompatibility and role conflict as the most

---

[10] Of 13,188 divorces, 3,540 were at the request of the husband with no reasons given. Only 6 divorces were upon the request of the wife, also with no reasons given. See De La Grange (1968:1109-1112).

frequent reason (Ben Rjeb 1986:316).

- "Domestic violence" appears during the second half of the 1980s, when it was denounced by women who drew a parallel between physical and symbolic violence and were angered at the "usurpation" of their liberty by "those who are nostalgic for women's oppression and for male power, whether they base this on religious interpretation or something else." (Omrane 1985:24). A study carried out in 1998 in greater Tunis involving a thousand women victims of violence shows that the face is the part of the body most often subject to blows. Does the man attack the face because a woman's aspirations are mirrored there?

Table 1

Divorce Rate in Various Countries

A. Countries and percentage of divorced persons out of total population
Tunisia: 0.57 in 1966; 0.45 in 1975
Algeria: 0.03 in 1966
Egypt: 2.23 in 1960
Kuwait: 0.56 in 1970

B. Percentage of divorced persons out of married population:
Tunisia: 1.64 in 1966; 1.35 in1975.
Algeria: 2.85
Egypt: 2.50
Kuwait: 1.53

C. Percentage of divorced persons in the total population of Tunisia and Advanced Countries
Tunisia (1966)   0.57% divorced persons
England & Wales (1966)   0.68
Japan (1965   0.98
Australia (1965)   0.81
Bulgaria (1965)   1.01

Source: Ouni 1976

Two-thirds of women who were victims of violence did not make a complaint to the police. Whereas the level of education does not appear to determine whether a woman will address a complaint to the police, economic independence seems to free her from her husband's domination. Their list of reasons for violence contains, in descending order, psychological reasons (jealousy, alcoholism), authority (the woman's disobedience); and lastly economic reasons such as food support.[11]

Table 2

Reasons for Divorce in Tunisia about 1970

Reasons for divorce	Urban	Rural
Irreconcilable marital difficulties	61.3	84.3
Husband's abandonment of household	6.0	4.0
Brutality of husband	2.4	2.0
Husband doesn't assume conjugal responsibilities	1.0	0.3
Husband in prison	0.0	0.3
Husband refuses to continue marriage	5.0	1.0
Behavior of the fiancée	2.2	0.0
Virginity	1.0	0.0
Behavior of the wife	3.0	0.3
Wife's abandonment of the household	8.0	4.9
Wife refuses to continue marriage	4.0	1.0
Expected conjugal life is seen to be impossible before marriage	6.1	1.9

Source: Camilleri 1973:115

Women working outside the home is not a phenomenon restricted to urban areas. In rural areas as well, young women also choose to work, be it only until marriage.[12] According to the census of 1984, households counted 1.68 active workers. The rate of women with an outside job climbed from 18.7 percent in 1975 to 23.6 percent in 1994. The proportion of women who declared themselves to be unemployed was 20.9 percent in 1989 and

---

[11] These results come from an unpublished survey of battered women in Tunis entitled, "Ech-hadou", carried out by psychology courses at the Faculté des sciences humaines et sociales, University of Tunis, March 1999, under the direction of the author. Over a year later (2 August 2000), the Tunisian President and the Minister of Women's and Family Affairs discussed violence committed against women and proposed assessing the importance of this phenomenon and putting into place programs and measures to combat it. Tunis: La Presse de Tunisie (3 August 2000).

[12] Ben Salem (1990). Ben Bassine, O., in "Destins d'argile," reports the words of young women ceramics workers in Sejnane, who dream of "going to work in a factory in Mateur." For these young women, the ideal remains marriage and going to live in the city. Tunis: La Presse de Tunisie, 21 May 2000.

17.2 percent in 1994. Among working women, only 25 percent had part-time employment in 1994. Naturally, work for women is not experienced in the same way everywhere and by everyone. During the 1980s, the sociologist Naima Karoui pointed out that the "submission-passivity" of women with regard to men had become transformed into a "power-authority" aggression and a sense of responsibility, growing from the fact that women were working and supporting families. The husband, preferring to wait for salaried work rather than working the land, rebelled "in silence against this new situation which escaped his control" (Karoui 1989). Today, women's work has taken on such value that young men prefer to seek marriage to working women.[13]

The woman's salary raises living standards. The proportion of households which have only one room has been decreasing, going from 32.2 percent in 1984 to 20.6 percent ten years later, whereas the proportion of homes with 3 or 4 rooms increased by 11 percentage points. Housing could often be acquired only with the help of the woman's salary.[14] Also in 1994, 80 percent of households owned their homes. These rising living standards also obtain as far as household equipment is concerned (see Table 3). The proportions of those owning a television set and those owning their homes are practically the same. We also note that the proportion of those owning a washing machine has been increasing, with 16.9 percent of families owning one in 1994 (Chebbi 1988:20). Although the price of such an appliance is high--between US$1000 and 1500--buying on credit allows many families to obtain one, with positive effects on women's health and enabling them to be available to satisfy other family needs, such as supervising the children's homework and leisure time, caring for the old, giving more time to communal life, and so on.

A half-century after the enactment of the PSC--the judicial framework which provides for equal pay to both sexes for equal work--men are no

---

[13] In Egypt, where unemployment rates are very high, the cartoonist Nagui Kamel provided an illustration of men's preferences for women with money: a cartoon published in *al-Ahram* on 24 April 1999 and again on 13 February 2000 shows a marriage broker offering photos of young women to a man who smiles approvingly at the photo of a woman whose arms are filled with gold bracelets.
[14] See Fakhfakh (1973:166-167, 167-199). In 1982, Ali Abid drew a cartoon showing a "modern" woman carrying a two-story villa in her arms (presented at a round-table discussion on "The Arab family in cartoons", Tunis 6 March 2000).

longer ashamed to admit they do not have sole responsibility for meeting the family's needs, and a woman's economic independence appears to provide her with an effective protective mechanism. The need for bread gives way to the need for psychological security, leading to solidarity between the couple, where each partner is responsible to the other. This change only became conceivable when mechanisms of social solidarity began to be taken over by the state through the creation of centers for abandoned children and orphans and others for the aged. Here and there some generous souls were at first offended at the intrusion of the state into the private domain, while others were ashamed to admit they could no longer assume such responsibilities without the assistance of a third party. Now both groups, "relieved" that these burdens are not theirs alone, are able to develop new interests.

Table 3

Increase of Equipment in Tunisian Households (percent)

Equipment	1984	1994
Radio	56.5	68.2
T.V.	57.4	79.0
Washing machine	0	16.9

Source: Institut national de statistique (1994)

Perfumes of the "gardens": Private and Public

Men, excluded from private space after their circumcision, normally only returned to it in order to supervise it. However, among the consequences of the movement of girls and women into public space--consequences insufficiently examined by the social and human sciences of the region--is that of the growing presence of the husband in private space. While it is true that women were in public space before, it was only possible in those areas that were strictly reserved for them unless they were under the protection of a male. Starting from the beginning of the 20th century several secondary schools in the main Tunisian cities and in the capital[15] were reserved for girls who came largely from the upper classes. The democratized schools

---

[15] The "Lycée de jeunes filles de la rue du Pacha" in Tunis is now 100 years old.

established upon independence were from that moment on mixed sex schools, in accord with the morality of the new republic.

In order to understand and see the significance of this mini-revolution-- the movement of women into public space and mixed sex schools--we should cast a glance at the sexual behavior of men. Here we will put forth three examples: one from the Tunisian historian Hichem Djaït; another from the press of the 1960s which treats the behavior of men around the girls' secondary schools; and the third a scene from the film "Omar Gatlato", by the Algerian director Merzak Allouache.

In his study "Personality and Arab-Muslim Development," Djaït depicts male sexual behavior as a "an alimentary or animal representation of male sexual aggression," which dresses this behavior with a vertiginous attractive power whose other side is a strong feeling of purity. Djait (1974:206) evokes homosexuality as being, in this context, "a fundamental element of the basic personality" in so far as it is "a secondary institution resulting from the reaction of this basic personality to sexual repression and frustration," with a "clear preponderance of active homosexual tendencies over passive attitudes, resulting from the strong condemnation and contempt for any feminization of the male."

If recourse to homosexuality prior to marriage functioned as a reaction to the dichotomy of space, to sexual repression and frustration, with marriage men must reestablish heterosexual desire--which helps explain the anxiety of families as they wait for the evidence of deflowering. A study carried out during the early 1970s corroborates this behavior. Workers, peasants, and students were shown to be more indulgent towards masculine homosexuality than were housewives and white-collar workers. Workers, students, and housewives strongly condemned clandestine feminine prostitution (Bouhdiba 1971:161, 165).

On another level, two phenomena were often discussed in the press of the 1960s. The first relates to the presence of young men lingering in front of girls' secondary schools at times when the students were leaving. The second refers to how men in cars--an object of consumption still rare at that time--constituted an attraction for young women. Families, although certainly upset at such behavior, were nonetheless not ready to withdraw their daughters from school for this reason. On their side the young women, raised in the earlier traditions, maintained the image of the body as social capital and also negotiated their sexuality as family planning policies were introduced in 1963.[16]

The passage from space marked by dichotomy to space that the two sexes occupied together was not a passage secured without shocks. The film "Omar Gatlato" illustrates this key moment. Omar has fallen in love with a woman's voice he has heard on a cassette. He manages to discover who the woman is and finally speaks to her on the telephone, and they agree to meet. But, when the time to meet arrives, Omar cannot bring himself to cross the street to greet her, and returns home to resume his former pattern of life. This film, often cited as an important one in the corpus of Maghrebi cinema (Armes 1999), portrays how the language of sexuality, the enterprising behavior of men toward women, the anonymity favored by the voice, served as outlets for the "alimentary or animal representations" which today have been restructured by mixed sex schools and the presence of men in private space, thus reworking sexual notions and behavior.

Images of young men spending hours outside schools waiting for the girls to appear, or of drivers at the steering wheel keeping watch are, today, outdated. Work habits and leisure habits have undergone significant transformations. The café maintained its role as a place of masculine socialization until the 1970s. Television was introduced in an effort to retain the clientèle, but this measure failed. These spaces now had to adapt to the social changes underway: some became known for gambling or alcoholic beverages, others adopted a 'cafeteria' mode where clients stood at the counter. Men now watch soccer matches at home more often than at the café, and the importance of television at home has become a favorite motif of cartoonists, with one cartoon depicting each member of the family watching his own television program.[17]

---

[16] Family planning, introduced into Tunisia in 1963, targets married women of reproductive age. Sex education, introduced into school texts in the 1970s, targets students taking the baccalaureate exam. Health clubs, starting in the mid-1980s, began to provide sessions for secondary school students. None of these structures reaches girls who are not within the school system and who thus remain vulnerable to unwanted pregnancies.

[17] In Tunisia, a cartoon drawn by A. Abid shows a man watching television alone, having muzzled his cat and dog and ignoring his children who leave the room unhappily; in Egypt, Nagui Kamel published a cartoon where each of four family members watches her/her own television program on a set that has four screens (in Al-Ahram, 1 September 1999).

The psychological security generated by the new situation of women in public space and men in private space has led to new primary institutions and has restructured sexuality. A psychology determined by the failure of the other and the breakdown of objects of desire (Labidi 1986:65-76), and by the dichotomy of space which generated an 'elastic sexuality' (homosexuality prior to marriage, reestablishing heterosexual desire upon marriage) on the basis of inter-masculine promiscuity, has become modified. We will present here three scenes which would have been impossible to imagine just a few decades ago.

- Public opinion reacted strongly when, towards the end of the 1980s, it was discovered that the administration wanted to hold the baccalaureate exams in single sex rooms. When this measure was reported by the media, public opinion opposed it, and it was withdrawn.

- It is now no longer in good taste for a family man to spend much time away from home in the café.[18]

- Where formerly it was not appropriate for a father to take his child on his knees in the presence of his own father, or even to play with the child in public, he now is comfortable in such activities and feels no need to hide them (Zitouni 2000).

Today, the education that children and youth receive in this new environment greatly depends on this recent restructuring, a new introjection of good and bad, of new moral rules as consequences of developmental processes, consequences favored by the care provided by adults and by the adults themselves (Winnicott 1974:55-70). The restructuring of the Tunisian family is a consequence of the outlawing of polygamy and the instituting of judicial divorce, of the privatization of sexuality, of a new-found psychological security and solidarity within the couple, and of the mixed sex nature of space (greater in urban than in rural areas) where meetings between the two sexes (in school, at work, in hospitals, etc) are no longer based on fear of the other. This has contributed to changing the images that each gender has of the other.[19]

---

[18] This trend became even more pronounced during the 1990s.

[19] Although mixed-sex public space is omnipresent, for some people this still constitutes a problem. The presence of both sexes in the same space often calls for a reinterpretation of certain cultural themes, for although the changes in public space do not challenge the basic relationship between the sexes, we still find people showing symptoms of anxiety and stress when they are not able to

In conclusion, we can say that whereas the notion of shame continues to play an important role, its content has changed. If we look at the three complexes--virginity, salaried women's work, and the sexual segregation of space--attitudes have changed significantly, as summarized in Table 4.

Table 4

The Culture of Shame

Themes	Past	Present
Virginity	The shame of not displaying the blood	The shame of displaying the blood
Salaried women's Work	Humiliating for the man	Humiliating for the man that the woman has no job
Space	Shameful for man to spend time in private space	Shameful for man to spend time in the cafés

The outlawing of polygamy and the institution of judicial divorce, as enacted in the PSC, had significant implications for the forming of new kinds of bonds between the couple and within the family. Among the most important of these are:

- The privatization of sexuality. This reveals that ceremonies like propitiatory rites (involving precautionary measures) carried with them disquieting predispositions (Freud 1969:66), violently revealed through the 'alimentary' and 'animal' behavior occurring at the woman's deflowering during the wedding night.

- The discovery by men that the economic security and marital commitment that they offered were not sufficient to ensure the woman's love and desire (Dolto 1982:242).

- Mixed sex space showed that the practice of male homosexuality prior to marriage, a fundamental element of the basic male personality before the

---

verbalize the imbalance between the sexes--tensions that often are not easy to control (Belgacem 1999 and Labidi 2000).

1960s and going together with the obligation to reestablish heterosexual desire upon marriage, was encouraged by sexual frustration and repression. The preponderance of active homosexual attitudes as opposed to passive ones was a sign of the condemnation of any "feminization of the male" (Djait 1974:209-208).

These changes have led to a new representation of the couple, where the reorganization of conjugal ties has encouraged the passage from the woman's sexual submission--epitomized in her deflowering, paradigm of the earlier model--to fidelity (Lacan 1978:303), via a freely contracted agreement. In love and the encounter of desires, the women's access to public space and to salaried labor put an end to the request for divorce for 'alimentary' reasons, and enabled women to develop a commitment to their children beyond that of satisfying their primary needs, and now including a responsibility toward their future.

References Cited

Armes, Roy. 1999. *Omar Gatlato de Merzak Allouache: un regard nouveau sur l'Algérie*. Paris: L'Harmattan.

Belgacem, Imen. 1999. "Sciences et enjeux de la mixité, approche psychologique. Etude conduite en milieu hospitalier tunisien". Masters thesis. Tunis: Faculté des sciences humaines et sociales. Mémoire de maitrise.

Ben Achour, Yadh. 2000. "Pour un parti bourguibien," *Jeune Afrique/L'Intelligent* No. 2049 (18-24 April), p. 60.

Ben Bassine, O. 2000. "Destins d'argile," *La Presse de Tunisie*, 21 May.

Ben Bassine, O. and H. Hanachi. 1999. "Mariage: combien ça coute?," *Magazine la Presse* No. 610 (20 June).

Ben Rjeb, Souad. 1986. "Le divorce d'après le vécu des femmes tunisiennes cadres," *Revue tunisienne des sciences sociales* 84/87:277-344.

Ben Salem, Lilia. 1990. "Structures familiales et changement social en Tunisie," *Revue tunisienne des sciences sociales* 100:165-181.

Bergaoui, Med. 1990. "Mariage, la facture," *L'Economiste Maghrébin* (8 August) 8:23-25.

El-Bokhari. 1914. *Les traditions islamiques*. Tome V. Présenté par Marçais, W. Publications de l'école des langues orientales. Paris: Ernest Leroux.

Bouhdiba, Abdelwahhab. 1971. *Public et justice: Une étude pilote en Tunisie*. Rome: Institut de recherche des Nations Unis sur la défense sociale. Publication No. 4..

Boujedra, R. 1969. *La répudiation*. Paris: Denoel.

El-Bour, Hamida. 1990. "Très cher le mariage," *Le Temps* (22 June).

Camilleri, Carmel. 1973. *Jeunesse, famille et développement: Essai sur le changement socio-culturel dans un pays du tiers monde (Tunisie)*. Paris: CNRS.

Chebbi, M. 1988. "La politique de l'habitat en Tunisie depuis l'indépendance" in P. Robert Baduel, ed., *Habitat, état, société au Maghreb*. Paris: CNRS. Pp.17-35.

Le Code de Statut Personnel. 1998. Tunis: Publication de l'Imprimerie Officielle de la République Tunisienne.

De Gaudin de la Grange, E. 1968. "Cause du divorce en Tunisie,". *Revue Algérienne des sciences juridiques, économiques et politiques* 5(4):1109-1112.

Djaït, H. 1974. *La personnalité et le devenir arabo-musulman*. Paris: Seuil.

Dolto, F. 1982. *La sexualité féminine*. Paris: Scarabée & Co/A.M. Metailie.

Fakhfakh, Françoise. 1973. "Deux types d'immigration: le déterminisme migratoire: Carnoy, Cité Populaire," *Revue tunisienne des sciences sociales* 32/35:161-199.

Freud, S. 1969. *Contribution à la psychologie de la vie sexuelle*. Paris: P.U.F.

Grabar, Oleg. 1955. "Toward an aesthetic of Persian painting" in *The Art of Interpreting*. University Park PA: Pennsylvania State University Press.

Haddad, Tahar. 1978. *Notre femme, la législation islamique et la société*. Tunis: MTE.

Hamdi, N. 1988. "L'affaire et le cadavre enterrés ... trop rapidement!," *Tunis Hebdo* (4 April).

Hermassi, A. et al. 1983. "Le divorce dans la région de Tunis. Evolution et aspects psychosociologiques". Tunis: UNFT/Institut Laamouri.

Institut National de Statistique. Recensement 1994. Tunis.

Karoui, Naima. 1989. "Le couple en Tunisie: du discours à la réalité," *Revue tunisienne des sciences sociales* 98/99:59-80.

Labidi, Lilia. 1986. "Le passé ou le pouvoir de l'abject" in *Psychologie différentielle*. Tunis: CERES.

------------. 1989. *Çabra Hachma: tradition et sexualité*. Tunis: Dar Ennawras.

------------. 1990). Les origines du mouvement féministe en Tunisie. Tunis: Imprimerie Tunis Carthage. 2nd edition.

Labidi, Lilia, et al. 2000. "Mixité, technologie au Maghreb: quelles images?" Paper presented to the colloquium "Image, Images et société", Tunis (6-7 March).

Labidi, Lilia. 2001. "Tradition et pluralisme: participation des femmes dans le monde arabe—la cas de la Tunisie" in Marie-Hélène, ed., *Pluralisme, Modernité, Monde Arabe*. Québec: Presses de l'Université Laval. Pp. 287-293.

Lacan, J. 1978. *Le moi dans la théorie de Freud et dans la technique de la psychanalyse*. Le séminaire. Livre II. Paris: Seuil.

Omrane, Nadia. 1985. "Le désamour, petit état du divorce en Tunisie," *Réalités*, 25 January, p. 24.

Ouni, Ali Ben Tahar. 1976. "Divorce in Tunisia: 1963-1972." Demographic Center. Seminar on marriage and family in some Arab and African countries. Cairo. 18-23 December 1976. (unpublished).

The Holy Qur'an. 1946/1932. Text, translation and commentary by A. Yusuf Ali. Washington DC: The American International Printing Company.

Es-Snoussi, E.T. 1970. *Le Code du Statut Personnel, annoté, mis à jour au premier juillet 1966.* Tunis: S.T.A.G.

Winnicott, W. 1974. "Morale et éducation" in *Processus de maturation chez l'enfant.* Paris: PBP.

Yousri, Daly. 2000. "Crimes d'honneur." DEA project in psychology. Tunis: Faculté des Sciences Humaines et Sociales de Tunis.

Zitouni, Insaf. 2000. "L'esprit maternel dans la famille tunisienne moderne, approche inter-culturelle." DEA project in psychology. Tunis: Faculté des Sciences Humaines et Sociales de Tunis.

Zouilai, Kaddour. 1990. *Des voiles et des serrures: de la fermeture en Islam.* Paris: L'Harmattan.

FAMILIES AND HOUSEHOLDS: HEADSHIP AND CO-RESIDENCE

ZEINAB KHADR AND LAILA O. EL-ZEINI

INTRODUCTION

The family, the foremost social institution in the Arab region, is currently experiencing dramatic changes. Recent socio-economic and demographic changes, redefinition of cultural norms and traditions and the emergence of new value systems within the Arab region are disturbing the solid ground upon which the family has been rooted. Some of these changes can be effortlessly observed in many societies in the Arab region, for example the increase in female-headed families and solitary living persons, which were rare events in Arab societies in the past. Monitoring these changes and their impact on the social life of the population is of extreme importance in highlighting the main guidelines for future policies. However, the study of changes in the family implies a detailed comprehensive research that calls for interdisciplinary collaboration and cannot be addressed in this brief paper.

In this paper, we are mainly concerned with only two important issues in this regard. In the first part, we revisit some of the definitional issues concerning family and household and discuss the impact of the recent demographic changes on the structure of households in Arab countries. The second part discusses more specifically living arrangements and residence patterns of the Egyptian population. In particular, we focus on some social groups such as women in the headship position, individuals living alone, and the older population, in order to highlight the need for policies to improve their quality of life.

Family and Household: Issues of Definition

"The family is the basic unit of society," it has always been said. No one, however, could provide a universally applicable definition for that unit--the family. Failing to derive an appropriate functional definition of the family, anthropologists and other social scientists are currently using structure definitions (Seymour-Smith 1986). These structures are based mainly on some assumed basics of kinship relations. For example, Goodenough (1970) considers a woman with her dependent children as the universal nuclear family. Although broader definitions of the nuclear family are more popular, they also assume the superiority or primacy of specific kin ties and functions (Yanagisako 1979).

For demographers, the family has always been a focal point, mainly because it is assumed to be the reproduction unit as well as the decision-making unit. Family systems are considered, hence, among the main factors in demographic processes. The term 'family demography' is used to distinguish a branch of demography that is concerned with the family or the household as the unit of analysis (Burch 1979). Less interested in theorizing than in collecting quantitative information, demographers have been satisfied with operational definitions of the term. For them, a 'family' is defined as the group of kin who share the same dwelling unit or the same household (Levy, 1965).

The term "household" proved to be no less problematic than the related term "family". In their introduction to an edited volume on households, Netting and his co-editors aptly state that:

> The household is a fundamental social unit. Households are more than groups of dyadic pairs. They have an emergent character that makes them more than the sum of their parts. They are a primary arena for the expression of age and sex roles, kinship, socialization, and economic cooperation where the very stuff of culture is mediated and transformed into action (1984: xxii).

Confronting such a challenging concept, demographers have limited themselves to their own operational definition of the household that is based on two distinct features: co-residence and sharing a common budget. These definitions are mainly functional and, as pointed out by Bender (1967), not appropriate for comparative purposes. Therefore, anthropologists employ the term 'domestic group' as a more appropriate term. However, there are also problems in distinguishing these groups and defining what is meant by domestic. In demography, the household is considered the basic unit for data collection in censuses and surveys, where the common decision-making or "housekeeping" characteristic of households is stressed. Social demographers and other social scientists, however, have indicated their disenchantment with the concept and recognition of the limitations in its measurement (Modell and Modell 1985; McDonald 1992; Goody 1996).

Two aspects of the household are of special interest, namely, headship and co-residence. For census purposes, the head of the household is mainly a reference person. In a single-person household, the head is the only resident in the household. In other types of households, the head is forming a household unit with other co-residents through pooling their resources. Those co-residents can be either relatives or non-relatives. The group of relatives residing in a household, according to the census guidelines, forms the family within the household. Households consisting of married couples with no children or of parents (or one of them) with their children are considered nuclear-family households. Non-nuclear-family households can be either extended-family households where other relatives reside with the nuclear family or composite households including non-relatives in addition to family members. (United Nations 1998a).

For population enumeration purposes, the member designated as the head of the household can be any person residing in it. However, in order to serve other purposes, the designated head is assumed to play specific social roles. It is noted in the United Nations universal guidelines for census taking that

> [t]he notion of head of household assumes that most households are family households (in other words, that they consist entirely, except possibly for domestic servants, of persons related by blood, marriage or adoption) and that one person in such family households has primary authority and responsibility for household affairs and is, in the majority of cases, its chief economic support. This person is then designated as the head of the household. (1998a: 66)

Implicit in this assumption is that the head is assumed to be the household member who is "the principal governor of the family" and "its sole representative to the larger world beyond the household" (Smith 1992: 430).

The fact that this assumption is unrealistic in many cases is not lost on the writers of the United Nations guidelines, and hence they require that each country specifies and publishes the criteria used in identifying the heads. It is also noted that even in situations where the conventional picture of the head, which is mainly sex-biased, is valid, there are still circumstances where the declared head of the household is different from the member actually assuming the main responsibilities. This difference between the *de jure* and the *de facto* head is usually noted in studies on female-headed households (e.g. Khadr and Farid 1999).

Diverting the interest from the head to other family members residing in the same household with the head, other definitional problems arise. It is a common practice in censuses and surveys to record for every household member a specific relation to the head. Ignoring non-relatives, the head with his co-resident kin form the total household family. For family households, then, household structure is equivalent to the structure of the family within the household. A major issue in characterizing possible different structures is the identification of a basic familial unit. The current census approach in defining the nuclear family puts special emphasis on conjugal ties and on the family function as a childbearing and child-rearing unit. It is worth noting that this choice of a basic or minimal family unit is based on two main assumptions. The first is that the basic characteristic feature of a household or a family unit is making decisions in common. The second assumption is that married couples are most likely to make joint decisions and that parents living with dependent children make decisions on behalf of their children (Ermisch and Overton 1985).

Although the notion of the nuclear family seems to be taken for granted, the underlying assumptions are far from being indisputable. One clear practical problem arises from the ambiguity of the term 'dependent children'. A possible criterion is being under the legal age of majority. But it is clear that children do not attain autonomy just by turning eighteen or twenty-one. Being unmarried is another criterion, and in fact it is the one usually used in practice unless the unmarried child was designated as the head of the household. This practice could result in confusion, especially when the criteria used in identifying the head are unclear--as is usually the case. For example, a household containing a group of unmarried siblings living with their mother may be classified as a nuclear-family household if the mother is declared as the head of the household, and as an extended-family household if the oldest brother is classified as the head. Another instance of a confusing case is the classification as an extended-family household of a group of children living with their grandparents who have complete judicial and social authority over them. It should be noted that such confusion results from the application of a functional definition of the nuclear family when dealing with household data that only provide relational information.

In order to overcome that inherent problem of the conventional definition of the nuclear family, in this study a structural definition is adopted. A basic family unit is defined as individuals residing in the same household who are either married, or are blood related up to the second degree within a maximum of two generations. This co-residing kin group is called a "basic family unit." The nuclear-family household is then defined as a family household containing only one basic family unit. Households containing more than one basic family unit are classified as extended-family households. Each basic family unit in an extended-family household is called a "subfamily". According to this definition, some members of an extended-family household can belong to more than one subfamily. For instance, a married man residing with his wife and children in addition to his mother and an unmarried brother belongs to the two subfamilies within that household. Such relational approach to characterizing household types has the advantage of not assuming superiority of specific kinship ties over other ties of the same degree. It also avoids the dependence on the declared head in classifying different households.

Household Structure in Changing Demography

With the changes taking place in the demographic picture, one is forced to consider their potential consequences. One such consequence that can greatly affect people's lives is the impact of the demographic transition on kinship structure. With a typical transition, individuals tend to marry later, have fewer children, and live longer. Among other manifestations, these changes are reflected in the prospects of having specific kin ties during different stages in one's life. The potential effects of demographic changes on kinship structure have been studied extensively (e.g. Burch 1970; Watkins et al. 1987; Casterline 1999). As expected, changes in mortality and fertility schedules have been shown to affect the availability of kin of different types.

But the family is more than a kinship unit. The decision for a kin group to co-reside has more to it than the availability of members belonging to such group. This capricious feature of the household structure or family living arrangement precludes its subjugating to formal demography. Like individuals, the residential unit has a life-course. But the structure of families within households is not only determined by marriages, births and deaths, but also by fission and fusion. These latter processes add great complexities to the attempts to study the dynamics of household structure. This challenge is summed up eloquently by Norman Ryder,

> Demographic analysis of residential redistribution is exceedingly difficult. ... These changes in household composition represent a further level of complexity superimposed upon the already burdened depiction of the family life course; they are resistant to demographic skills. Residential redistribution of personnel is implicit in the dual character of the family. Because it is a descent unit, it is exposed to the vagaries of demographic processes; because it is a residence unit, its cross-sectional composition must make economic sense day to day. (1992: 169)

Notwithstanding such insuperable challenges both in defining the household and in analyzing its dynamics, it is plausible to assume that household structure and family living arrangements cannot help being affected by the demographic forces as well as by the economic, social, and cultural changes. Considering the Arab family, one potential factor is the higher age at marriage and the increasing prevalence of celibacy. Another is the decline in fertility and mortality and the resulting aging population (Rashad and Khadr 1998). These demographic changes, accompanied with socio-economic transformations, result in larger pressure on the policy arena from emerging vulnerable social groups that overburden the conventional family support. Clear examples are the rise in the proportion of never-married women, single-parent families, and the elderly. In focusing on such groups, it is of great significance to investigate not only their characteristics but also the types of households they are most likely to reside in since these households embody the locus of care for those vulnerable groups.

One of the main dimensions in the study of household structure, either as an outcome or a determinant of other demographic and social processes, is the dichotomy of nuclear/extended households. For a long period, it was believed that with industrialization extended family tended to be a less desirable mode of residence, and hence it became less prevalent. Although evidence accumulated by social historians have proved the invalidity of that assumption (e.g. Laslett 1977; Ruggles 1987), it has been noted that household structure has not been stable due to demographic, social, economic, as well as ideological reasons (Angel and Tienda 1982; Cherlin 1983; Goody 1996).

Evidence from the literature on the Arab family indicates that although extended-family households have been considered as an ideal living arrangement, the extended-family model was not a universal reality in the region (e.g. Goode 1963; Prothro and Diab 1974). Of course demographic forces have occasionally prevented reaching the ideal of an extended multiple-generation household, but other economic and social forces have also worked at breaking up joint families. On the other hand, although the extended-family arrangement seems to be less in favor in the modern Arab societies, many newlywed couples are forced by economic pressures to start their family lives in extended-family households (Rashad and Osman 2000). The culture heritage that endorses large and composite households seems to facilitate the adoption of such temporary arrangements (Al-Thakeb 1985).

Household Structure and Vulnerable Social Groups:
The Case of Egypt

Data. The data set used in this part is adopted from the household module of the 1995 Egyptian Demographic and Health Survey, EDHS 1995. This survey was designed to provide key estimates of population, health and women's status indicators for the country as a whole and for the six major administrative regions: urban governorates, urban Lower Egypt, rural Lower Egypt, urban Upper Egypt, rural Upper Egypt, and the Frontier governorates (El-Zanaty et al. 1996). The sample yielded 15,555 households with a response rate of 99.2 percent. A total of 89,014 individuals occupied these households out of which 2 percent were visitors yielding a total of 87,086 *de jure* members of these households.

In the original data set, the relationship to the designated head of the household was the only variable that reflects the structure of the household. This variable has been recoded to reflect the relation to an objectively chosen reference person. In order to facilitate the identification of different household types, the reference person was chosen as the oldest member in the family to which the majority of household members belong. Table 1 explains the main definitions used in identifying the different types of households.

Table 1

Definitions Used in the Classification of Households

Type of household / family	Definition
Single-person household	Household occupied by only one person
Basic family unit	Married couple/at least one parent with children / siblings
Nuclear-family household	Household occupied by one basic family unit (married couples / at least one parent and children / unmarried siblings)
Extended-family household	Household occupied by more than one basic family unit.
Composite household	Household occupied by two or more persons who are not related by blood relation or marriage
Subfamily	A basic family unit residing within an extended household (e.g. a household that consists of two parents and their married child includes two subfamilies, the married child and his family constitute a subfamily while the parents and the child constitute another subfamily.)

According to these definitions, Table 2 shows that three fourths of Egyptian households are nuclear-family households with two thirds of the household population residing in them. It also shows that extended living arrangements come second in prevalence. Only one out of every five households is an extended-family household. However, extended-family households accommodate almost one third of all the household population.

The least prevalent living arrangement is the single-person household. Only one out of twenty households is a single-person household, with less than one percent of all household populations living alone.

Table 2

Distribution of Households and of Population by Type of Households (EDHS 1995)

Type of household	% of households	% of household members (household population)
Single-person household	5.4	0.9
Nuclear-family household	75.1	66.5
Extended-family household	19.5	32.6
Composite household	< 0.05	< 0.05

Since only an insignificant minority of the Egyptian household population lives in composite households, such households are excluded from the subsequent exposition. We start with a brief comparison between the different types of households and their population, followed by a focus on only three segments of the household population that we perceive as requiring special emphasis. These segments include a) women in headship position, b) solitary living individuals, and c) older persons.

Living arrangements of the Egyptian household population. To shed some light on the different living arrangements among the Egyptian household population, Table 3 presents some of the important characteristics of these living arrangements and the population residing in them. It shows that single-person households are slightly more prevalent in urban areas than in rural areas. They are mostly occupied by females and have the lowest standard of living compared with other living arrangements. Their population is mostly old (56 percent aged 60+), previously married (72 percent), females (63 percent), uneducated (57 percent), and not working (69 percent).

Table 3 also shows that nuclear-family households exhibit almost the same pattern of place of residence as single-person households, in which they are slightly more prevalent in urban areas. In contrast, nuclear-family and extended-family households share many characteristics that differ markedly from those of single-person households. Both nuclear-family and extended-family households are mainly headed by males, and have almost the same standard of living. Their populations are equally divided by sex and are mostly youth (40 percent of their populations are less than 15 years of age). However, as expected, extended-family households accommodate more older persons than nuclear-family households, which in return affects some of the other characteristics. While nuclear-family households' population is mostly currently married (60 percent), extended-family households' population includes a high percentage of previously married persons. Furthermore, illiteracy and unemployment are more prevalent among the extended-family household population.

Women in headship position. In recent years, traditional gender roles have been challenged by the emergence of many demographic and socio-economic forces. The increase in the incidence of divorce, widespread male out-migration, and raising women status and participation in public spheres have redefined many aspects of women's roles in and out of their households. One marked shift in this regard is the rise in the proportion of women assuming duties and responsibilities for their households or the rise in female-headed households.

Table 3
Characteristics of Households and Their Population by Type of Household (EDHS 1995)

Characteristics	Type of Household		
	Single person	Nuclear	Extended
Characteristics of households			
Place of residence			
% urban	57.8	55.9	29.5
Household headship			
% male headed	38.2	90.7	88.2
Household size (mean)	1.0	4.9	8.1
(std)	(0.0)	(2.0)	(3.8)
Standard of living* (mean)	7.7	10.4	9.3
(std)	(4.7)	(4.3)	(3.9)
No. of households	840	11,689	3,018
Characteristics of household members			
% aged <15	0.0	40.7	38.5
% aged 60+	55.8	4.0	9.3
% female	63.0	48.1	50.3
% previously married	72.2	4.4	12.3
% currently married	7.6	59.3	60.8
% never married	20.2	36.4	27.0
% illiterate	57.3	33.8	49.8
% currently working	30.9	31.0	28.7
No. of household members	884	57,912	28,390

A standard of living index is calculated for each household based on the household possession of 16 consumer durable goods and 4 housing conditions. It has a range of 0 to 20.

However, the definition and identification of female heads have created a major controversy in the literature. A wide range of criteria is proposed in an attempt to identify female heads (for a discussion of these criteria see Khadr and Farid 1999). However, the simplest criterion that has been used by the majority of the early female headship literature is the one built on self-reporting or other members' acknowledgement of headship. Although this criterion has been heavily criticized, the simplicity of its data requirement and the availability of such data have overridden its shortcomings.

Using this criterion, the 1995 EDHS data show that 12.6 percent of all households in Egypt are headed by females. These households accommodate more than 7.8 percent of the total household population. Table 4 shows some characteristics of these households, their heads and other resident population. It shows that female-headed households are almost equally as urban as the male-headed households. It also shows that single-person households are more prevalent among female-headed households than male-headed households. One out of every four female-headed households is a single-person household compared with one out of every forty in male-headed households. This high concentration in single-person households is reflected in a two-person difference in the average household size between female and male-headed households. Table 4 also shows that female-headed households exhibit a lower standard of living than that of male-headed households.

Table 4 also indicates that female heads are more likely to be older than male heads. As expected, the majority of female heads are previously married, widowed or divorced (87 percent). However, one out of every ten female heads is currently married. An examination of households headed by married females shows that only 8.3 percent of them have resident husbands at home. Those resident husbands tend to be older than their wives. Among this group, more than two thirds of the husbands are aged 60 years or older, while the group of wives is aged less than 44 years. This might be a reason for those men to decline their headship status to their wives. Furthermore, female heads are more likely to be illiterate and less likely to be working compared with male heads.

Table 4

Characteristics of Households and Their Population by Household Headship (EDHS 1995)

Characteristics	Female-headed households	Male-headed households
Characteristics of household		
Type of household		
Single-person	26.4	2.4
Nuclear-family	55.2	78.0
Extended-family	18.2	19.6
Place of residence		
% urban	48.9	49.2
Size of household (mean)	3.5	5.6
(std)	(2.7)	(2.8)
Standard of living (mean)	8.9	10.2
(std)	(4.6)	(4.2)
Characteristics of head		
Age (mean)	53.2	45.2
(std)	(13.1)	(13.3)
% previously married	87.3	2.6
% currently married	10.4	93.7
% never married	2.3	3.7
% illiterate	63.6	31.9
% working	17.6	87.5
No. of households	1966	13589
Characteristics of household members (excluding the head)		
% aged <15	40.3	48.3
% aged 60+	1.9	3.1
Characteristics	**Female-headed**	**Male-headed**

	households	households
% female	44.2	58.4
% previously married	6.4	5.8
% currently married	18.4	51.2
% never married	75.3	43.1
% illiterate	27.7	38.6
% currently working	27.2	17.1
No. of household members	6,817	80,268

With all these social, economic and cultural vulnerable characteristics of female heads compared with male heads, those female heads shoulder a burden that is only slightly lower than that carried by their male counterparts. Other coresident household members in female-headed households are more likely to be unmarried male adults with higher levels of education and participation in the labor market than their counterparts in male-headed households. In other words, although the burden on both male and female heads is almost equal, the vulnerability of female heads dictates adopting various coping strategies by household members. These include postponement of marriage, more participation in the labor force and aspiration through higher educational attainment that would secure a better quality of life.

One of the major criticisms of the self-reporting criterion in defining female headed households is its bias in only identifying 'survivor' households or households that overcome the economic, social and cultural challenges faced by women in heading their households through a variety of coping strategies. Those who could not endure these challenges chose other coping strategies, including rejoining related households or remarrying. Widows and divorced women, in particular young women with dependent children, face the greatest challenge since they are bound culturally to be absorbed by their kin rather than to maintain separate households. These women, although co-residing within their kin's households, maintain in most cases their headship to their subfamilies and in other cases they might contribute in providing for their new households (Khadr and Farid 1999).

We chose to refer to these cases of female headship as implicit female heads.

Among households in Egypt, we estimate that 99,000 households have at least one resident basic family unit headed by a divorced woman or a widow who cares for at least one child. Table 5 presents some characteristics of those implicit heads and their living conditions. It shows that those female heads tend to be young with an average age of 31 years, and they are more likely to be divorced (63 percent). Due to the cultural norms that disapprove of separate living arrangements for young, previously married women, four out of five of implicit female heads are daughters returning to their parental household and almost one eighth of them are daughters-in-law co-residing with their ex-husbands' family. Implicit heads also tend to be uneducated and are less likely to work (less than one out of four of them are currently working). Table 5 also shows that those heads have on average 1.6 children. The average age of those children is slightly under 10 years.

Implicit female heads co-reside in households that are relatively smaller and poorer than the average extended-family households (compare with corresponding figures in Table 3). These households are mainly concentrated in rural areas where cultural norms are more strictly observed. It is worth noting that slightly less than one third of those implicit heads and their subfamilies live in female-headed households, which increases their vulnerability to harsh living arrangements and lower quality of life.

Solitary living individuals. In our discussion of single-person households, we observed that the majority of these households are occupied by women (63 percent)--a fact that revealed itself again in having 26.4 percent of female-headed households classified as single-person households. This over-representation of females in single-person households, combined with the relatively old age of the population residing in single-person households, signals a crucial gender dimension in the establishment of these households. This signal challenges one of our strongly held cultural views in which women are protected from birth to death by their male family members.

Table 5: Characteristics of Implicit Female Heads and Their Households (EDHS 1995)

Characteristics	%
Characteristics of implicit heads	
Age (mean)	31.4
(std)	(7.0)
Marital status	
Divorced	63.6
Widow	36.4
Relation to head of household	
Daughter	80.0
Daughter-in-law	12.5
Sister	7.5
% Uneducated	53.3
% Working	23.2
Number of children (mean)	1.7
(std)	(1.0)
Age of children (mean)	9.4
(std)	(5.5)
Characteristics of households	
Size of household (mean)	7.6
(std)	(3.7)
Standard of living	8.1
(std)	(3.8)
% urban	35.3
Household headship	
Male	71.3
Female	28.7
No. of cases	**134**

Table 6 provides a portrait of the residents of single-person households by gender. It shows that men in single-person households are relatively young, educated, working and living at a reasonably good standard. Solitary living males are more concentrated in urban areas, which reflects the exodus of adult males from rural areas to urban centers in search of better living chances. In sharp contrast, women living in single-person households are obviously the most underprivileged group among household populations in Egypt. They are old (aged 62.3 years on average), widowed or divorced, illiterate, not working and live mainly in rural areas in households with far lower living standard than other households.

Table 6

Characteristics of Single-Person Households by Gender (EDHS 1995)

Characteristics	Male	Female
Age (mean)	45.7	62.3
(std)	19.2	10.8
percent 60 + years of age	30.1	69.8
percent previously married	41.9	89.2
percent currently married	13.5	2.7
percent never married	47.9	5.1
percent illiterate	28.3	71.1
percent working	70.1	9.2
Standard of living (mean)	8.7	7.0
(std)	4.4	4.7
percent urban	73.5	48.2
No. of households	337	547

Older population. Although population aging and the aged population have not yet emerged as a critical demographic and social issue in Egypt, recent declines in fertility combined with the continuing declines in mortality are expected to result in a rapid pace of aging of the Egyptian population. By the year 2020, it is projected that almost 10 percent of the population will be 60 years of age and older (United Nations 1998b). Presently, the responsibility and care provided for older persons, according to our cultural norms and traditions, are shouldered by their family members (Khadr 1997). However, with the projected increase in the proportion of older persons in the population, the burden on other family members is expected to grow and to call for policy intervention.

Table 7 presents a picture of the older household population by gender. No significant difference can be observed between the mean age of older males and females. However, while the majority of older males are currently married, older females tend to be previously married, in particular widows, which can be partially attributed to higher rates of remarriage among men compared with women. A long history of favoring male over female education is reflected in the great difference between the proportions of uneducated by gender. While almost one out of every two older males is educated, the comparable percentage for the female population is only one out of every four. Older males also continue to participate in the labor market in large proportion (48.4 percent), which might be attributed in part to the limited resources available to this segment of population and their need to provide for their families. On the other hand, only 3 percent of older females are currently working, reflecting in part their low level of labor force participation throughout their lives as well as the cultural constraints opposing women's work in old age.

The vast majority of older males are the heads of their households (92 percent) and those who are fathers of the household head or his/her spouse are only a small minority (6 percent). In contrast, older females are mainly mothers of the heads (40 percent) followed by being heads (29 percent) or wives of the heads (26 percent). Older women are also more likely than their male counterparts to live with their extended relatives. These relations are mirrored in the living arrangement of the older population by gender. Almost one out of every two older women resides with her married children, compared with one out of every three older men. Older women are also more likely to live alone or to live with relatives other than their children compared with older men.

Table 7: Characteristics of Older Persons and Their Households by Gender (EDHS 1995)

Characteristics	Male	Female
Older persons characteristics		
Age (mean)	67.5	66.5
(std)	(6.9)	(7.0)
% previously married	12.6	69.1
% currently married	86.9	30.0
% never married	0.5	0.9
% illiterate	58.5	75.9
% working	48.4	3.0
Relation to head		
Head	92.4	28.9
Spouse of head	0.1	25.9
Parent/ parent in law	6.2	39.9
Brother/ sister	0.5	1.7
Other	0.8	3.6
Standard of living (mean)	9.9	9.2
(std)	(4.3)	(4.4)
% urban	46.1	42.8
Living arrangement		
Alone	3.9	14.3
With spouse	14.2	7.7
With unmarried children	43.7	19.4
With married children	36.8	53.4
With others	1.4	5.3
No. of members	2,640	2,677

Conclusion

The study of the impact of socio-economic and demographic changes on families and households is a long-standing subject for research. Western historians, anthropologists, and social scientists have contributed significantly to this venture, in particular through studying the Western family. In the Arab region, efforts in this endeavor are rather limited, particularly within the demographic discipline. Family demography has not yet seized the due attention with all the recent changes in the context of the family. This paper is a small contribution in this regard.

The paper starts by discussing some of the conventional definitions implemented in the literature regarding the family and household. With the inability of these conventional definitions to grasp clearly the structure of the family household and to mend some of their many drawbacks, we proposed a new unit of analysis, namely the basic family unit. A basic family unit was defined as individuals residing in the same household who are either married or are blood related up to the second degree within a maximum of two generations. Based on this proposed unit, a nuclear-family household is defined as a household containing only one basic family unit. The practicality of the proposed basic family unit concept is underlined in the case of extended-family households. According to our proposed definition, and similar to earlier ones, an extended-family household constitutes multiple basic family units. However, the new proposed definition allows for multiple classification of an individual within the same household, e.g. an individual can be a son/daughter in one basic unit and a head of the other.

The paper continues to examine the living arrangements of the Egyptian household population according to the newly proposed criteria. It further extends to discuss special segments of this population. One of the most striking findings is the consistency of identifying older unmarried women as the most vulnerable group in this population. They have the lowest socio-economic characteristics and living standards. They either live alone or depend on others for their support. Even when they shoulder the responsibility, their resources do not match their burden. The paper also highlights the susceptible status of female heads, whether living in separate residence or absorbed by their kin, and their needs for policies that better their chances in life. The aged also call for special attention, with the majority of them continuing to shoulder heavy responsibilities that drive them to work in their advanced age. Our paper, through bringing those groups under the spotlight, calls for policy makers to reconsider their future plans and re-evaluate their policies since we expect the continuing growth of the size of these vulnerable groups.

References

Al-Thakeb, F. T. 1985. "The Arab Family and Modernity: Evidence from Kuwait," *Current Anthropology* 26(5):575-580.

Angel, R. and M. Tienda. 1982. "Determinants of Extended Household Structure: Culture Pattern or Economic Need?" *American Journal of Sociology* 87(6):1360-1383.

Bender, D. R. 1967. "A Refinement of the Concept of Household: Families, Co-residence, and Domestic Function," *American Anthropologist* 69(5):493-504.

Burch, T. K. 1970. "Some Demographic Determinants of Average Household Size: An Analytic Approach," *Demography* 7(1):61-69.

Burch, T. K. 1979. "Household and Family Demography: A Bibliographic Essay," *Population Index* 45(2): 173-195.

Casterline, J. B. 1999. "Longer Lives, Fewer Children: Demographic Transition and the Demography of the Egyptian Family." Oral presentation, Cairo Demographic Center, Cairo (1 December).

Cherlin, A. 1983. "Changing Family and Household: Contemporary Lessons from Historical Research," *Annual Review of Sociology* 9:51-66.

El-Zanaty, F., I. Hussein, G. Shawky, A. Way, and S. Kishor.. 1996. *Egypt Demographic and Health Survey 1995*. Cairo: National Population Council and Calverton, Maryland: Macro International Inc.

Ermisch, J. F. and E. Overton.. 1985. "Minimal Household Units: A New Approach to the Analysis of Household Formation," *Population Studies* 39(1):33-54.

Goode, W. 1963. *World Revolution and Family Patterns*. New York: Free Press of Glencoe.

Goodenough, W. H. 1970. *Description and Comparison in Cultural Anthropology.* Chicago: Aldine.

Goody, J. 1996. "Comparing Family Systems in Europe and Asia: Are There Different Sets of Rules?" *Population and Development Review* 22(1):1-20.

Khadr, Z. 1997. "Living Arrangements and Social Support Systems among Older Population in Egypt." Ph.D. Dissertation, University of Michigan, Michigan.

Khadr, Z. and I. Farid. 1999. "Who is the Head? An Anthropo-demographic Perspective on Female headed households." Paper presented at the IUSSP Committee on Anthropological Demography, seminar on Social Categories, Cairo (September 5-18).

Laslett, P. 1977. "Characteristics of the Western Family Considered over Time," *Journal of Family History* 2:89-115.

Levy, M. J. Jr. 1965. "Aspects of the Analysis of Family Structures" in A. J. Coale, L. A. Fallers, M. J. Levy, Jr. D. M. Schneider, and S. S. Tomkins, eds., *Aspects of the Analysis of Family Structure.* Princeton: Princeton University Press.

McDonald, P. 1992. "Convergence or Compromise in Historical Family Change?" in E. Barquo and P. Xenos, eds., *Family Systems and Culture Change.* IUSSP International Studies in Demography. Oxford: Oxford University Press.

Modell, J. and J. Modell. 1985. "The Household: Problems of Redefinition," *Contemporary Sociology* 14(3):318-320.

Netting, R. McC., R. R. Wilk, and E. J. Arnould, eds. 1984. *Households: Comparative and Historical Studies of the Domestic Group.* Berkeley: University of California Press.

Prothro, E. T. and L. N. Diab. 1974. *Changing Family Pattern in the Arab East*. Beirut: American University of Beirut Press.

Rashad, H. and Z. Khadr. 1998. "The Demography of the Arab Region: New Challenges and Opportunities." Presented at the Economic Research Forum Conference, Cairo, November 2-4.

Rashad, H. and M. Osman. 2000. "Nuptiality Transition and Its Implications." Presented at Cairo Papers in Social Science Symposium on the New Arab Family, Cairo, May 6-7.

Ruggles, S. 1987. *Prolonged Connections: The Rise of the Extended Family in Nineteenth-Century England and America*. Madison: University of Wisconsin Press.

Ryder, N. B. 1992. "The Centrality of Time in the Study of the Family" in E. Barquo and P. Xenos, eds., *Family Systems and Culture Change*. IUSSP International Studies in Demography. Oxford: Oxford University Press.

Seymour-Smith, C. 1986. *Macmillan Dictionary of Anthropology*. Macmillan Press Ltd.

Smith, D. S. 1992. "The Meanings of Family and Household: Change and Continuity in the Mirror of the American Census," *Population and Development Review* 18(3):421-456.

United Nations. 1998a. *Principles and Recommendations for Population and Housing Censuses,* Revision 1. United Nations Department of Economic and Social Affairs, Statistics Division. ST/ESA/STAT/SER.M/67/Rev.1

United Nations. 1998b. *World Population Prospects*, the 1996 Revision. United Nations Department of Economic and Social Affairs, Population Division. ST/ESA/SER.A/167.

Watkins, S. C., J. A. Menken, and J. Bongaarts. 1987. "Demographic Foundation of Family Change," *American Sociological Review* 52:346-358.

Yanagisako, S. J. 1979. "Family and Household: the Analysis of Domestic Groups," *Annual Review of Anthropology* 8:161-205.

AMONG BROTHERS: PATRIARCHAL CONNECTIVE MIRRORING AND BROTHERLY DEFERENCE IN LEBANON

SUAD JOSEPH

The Brother-Patriarch

Hanna is the eldest son of a family of five brothers and two sisters in which the five brothers follow each other in succession with the two girls being the youngest. When I met them in 1971, they were a very modest working class Lebanese/Palestinian Christian family living in a small two room apartment in the Greater Beirut municipality of Borj Hammoud. I have been living next door to Hanna's family from 1971-73 and repeatedly visited with him and his family over the past thirty years and have made one consistent observation: all his siblings, especially his brothers, have deferred to him since I came to know him when he was still only 17 years old and both his parents were living.

Now in his late forties, and with his father dead, he has consolidated his position as the brother-patriarch. In his increasingly successful shop, selling and installing air-conditioners and household appliances, he employs one brother and his niece and sometimes his nephew, he has helped another brother start an independent business, managed the rent for two and at one point three small apartments for three of his brothers (including one brother married and with children) and his mother, and continually offers to micromanage the personal and work lives of his siblings. At one point, one of his brothers appeared to be more financially successful than Hanna. Two of his brothers are taller than he. One brother is more educated and has become more white collar (the only brother that continues to live outside the country and away from the family). Both sisters have married, moved away, and had children. One of them (living in a nearby neighborhood of Greater Beirut), remains closely under Hanna's purview and influence. The other sister remains Hanna's highest ideal of womanly beauty. For all of the siblings, Hanna has been, from his teens, the authority figure in the family.

His current position as brother-patriarch, therefore, seemed predictable from my observations of family dynamics in the 1970s.

Another Lebanese family I have observed since the 1960s is upper middle class, highly educated, with four boys and one girl who were raised by relatively progressive and liberally-minded parents. The parents seemed to support the individuality and autonomy of each of their children. In the 1970s, the brothers and sister all seemed headed for success along quite different paths. Their relationships seemed relatively egalitarian, with what seemed to be only the slightest deference to the eldest son. Now all the siblings are married and the brothers all have children. In this case, the second brother (who is actually the third in birth order) is the wealthiest. He has invited the youngest brother into his business as a partner and has done more to support his siblings financially than any of the others. Yet all the brothers defer to the eldest, Habib, who, at times, has been the least financially able of the siblings. All the brothers appear to relish the deference to the eldest brother. The eldest brother, with the aging and death of the father, increasingly consolidated his position as brother-patriarch. While the brothers have frequently helped each other financially, they are now all well established and do not need to depend on each other's resources. Though Habib was assertive as a young man, so were all his siblings. The apparent democratic family relationships of the early 1970s, which I was able to observe in depth, would not necessarily have allowed me to predict the kind of extended domestic patriarchy that has taken hold with Habib as the brother-patriarch.

These two apparently different cases, and many others covering a range of classes, educational levels, religions, and regions in Lebanon, raise the question: why are one or more brothers (and sisters) willing to defer to another brother? I try to examine the basis of brotherly deference in this paper. I want to make clear, as a caveat, that I do not argue that all brothers in Lebanon defer to a senior brother. Brotherly relations, like all social relations, are highly contested and variable. Nor do I suggest that the argument I offer here explains all brother relations. They are certainly far too diverse to theorize easily in a short paper.

Rather, I focus on one set of relationships, brother to brother, and specifically those relationships in which one or more brothers defer to a senior brother (leaving aside brother/sister relations which I have discussed in Joseph 1994). I suggest a relationship between the psychodynamics of deference and the structure of a social organization that, I argue, is based on the civic myth of what I call the "kin contract". My paper tries to offer a set of vocabularies or some conceptual bridges between the dynamics of culture and psychology, between structure and self, between the complex determinations of cultural norms and the complex range of choices that describe agency. The brotherly relationship is a point of departure, in this exercise, for unraveling the dynamics of domination, the link between family and political culture, and the psychosocial underpinnings of a society in which kinship relationalities, moralities, and idioms weave themselves throughout the fabric of social life. The analysis of the brotherly relationship is part of a larger project of understanding the interlinking notions of self, family, citizenship, and the state in Lebanon (Joseph 1999a, b, c, d).

Conceptual Bridges

"I against my brother; my brother and I against my cousin; my cousin and I against the world." This is probably the most commonly cited adage about the relationship between brothers in Arab societies. The proverb appears to characterize brotherly relationships as fundamentally competitive, each man standing on his own, for himself, against his closest of kin--his brother. The call for solidarity in the face of increasingly distant sets of relationships seems to ascribe brotherly connection/loyalty under circumstances of danger from external relationships, but brotherly distance/mistrust when external threats are absent. Appearing very Western in its succinct summary of human self-interest, the proverb became an anchor for Western scholars who sought to theorize Arab society as competitive and individualistic--most clearly in the influential early work of Clifford Geertz (Geertz, Geertz, and Rosen 1979). Perhaps no Arab country has appeared to fit that competitive, individualist Western trope more fully than Lebanon, where I base the ethnographic research for this paper.

Given that patriarchy, patrilineality, and patrilocality have been privileged in Arab cultural norms, the centrality of brother-brother relationships to the reproduction of Arab family systems seems self-evident. Yet relatively little work, beyond recitation of proverbs and summary ethnographic descriptions, has theorized the psychosocial dynamics of brother-brother relationships in Arab communities. Nor has there been much work problematizing the assumptions of the staged sequencing of brotherly competition, giving way to brotherly solidarity. This paper is not so much concerned with the question of whether brothers are competitive or cooperative (both are true at various times). Rather, I query the nature of the identification of brothers with each other which undergirds the psychosocial dynamics of their relationships. In particular, I ask: why would one or more brothers be willing to become considered "junior" to another brother who is considered "senior"?

Although junior and senior most often correspond to age-based relations, here I use "junior" and "senior" refer to status and authority rather than age, since younger brothers can and do, at times, achieve higher status and authority in the family to become the "senior" brother. The senior brother, for reasons discussed below, occupies the position of the "brother-patriarch". The junior brother(s) occupy the position of "deferring-brother".

I focus in answering the above questions in this paper on the culturally idealized structure of the Arab family. Here, I investigate the culturally idealized structure of Arab family relations to extrapolate the institutional substructure which underwrites patriarchal psychosocial dynamics in their culturally mythologized form. The relationship between cultural structures and myths and social practices is complex and central to this project. However, for the purpose of the brief intervention this paper permits, I will focus on the structural underpinnings which subsidize the authority structure of brotherly relations rather than the concrete range of lived brotherly relations. Lived brotherly relationships expand a range of realities that can not be accommodated in a short paper. My purpose, rather, is to unravel a knotty thread linking the institutions of authority as prescribed in cultural norms and social structures and the psychodynamics which translate the rules of cultures/structures into motivations for behavior--keeping in mind that cultures, structures, and motivations never fully correspond.

To enter this inquiry, I start by rethinking terms key to Arab family systems as they have been theorized--patriarchy, patrilineality, and patrilocality. I then introduce concepts critical to the rethinking of brother/brother relationships which I have coined and theorized elsewhere--"kin contract" (Joseph 2000), "care/control paradigm" (Joseph 2000), and "connectivity" (Joseph 1993). A newly theorized construct, "patriarchal mirroring", is introduced here to build the repertory of conceptual tools to understand family relationships in Lebanon. I then argue that the deference of one or more brothers to another brother in Lebanon may be understood in part, as a result of patriarchal mirroring, underwritten by a connective notion of self and authorized by the social myth of the kin contract which is mediated through the care/control paradigm.

Patriarchy, Patrilineality, Patrilocality

I define patriarchy as the privileging of males and seniors (including senior women) and the justification of male and senior privilege in the idioms and moralities of kinship, sanctified by religion (Joseph 1993). Kin groups in Lebanon have been seen as organized along gendered and aged structures of authority, legitimated by religious authority.

This notion of patriarchy differs from the definition commonly used by Western feminists, who tend to see patriarchy as the privileging of males as males over females as females (Pateman 1988). I suggest this definition, while perhaps suited to parts of some Western countries, fails to capture two important aspects of patriarchy as practiced in Lebanon and many other Arab countries. The first aspect is that patriarchy in Lebanon is kin based. Men come to have authority, in the first instance, as fathers, brothers, uncles, husbands. Their authority is experienced by women, in the first instance, as daughters, sisters, nieces, wives. Secondly, patriarchy in Lebanon is characterized by the empowerment of women as elders. Elder women often have authority over junior males and females and their authority may increase as they age.

This kin-based gendered and aged authority is codified in law, sanctified by religion, and reinforced continually in the political and economic arenas through the use of real and idiomatic kin relationships. Family law and citizenship law in particular codify the authority of kin males over kin females (Joseph 2000). In Lebanon, as in most Arab countries, family law is in the domain of religion. In addition political, economic, and religious leaders continually reinforce patriarchal authority through their use of kinship as a means of recruitment of political leaders, followers, workers, and for constructing their relationships with them in the public arena.

Patrilineality is the reckoning of descent through the male line. Membership in kin groups is passed from fathers to children. Given this masculine genealogy, brothers become the key to holding the genealogy together in the short term (though in the long term, even lateral male kin give way to the vertical charting of father/son/father/son descent). In the genealogical memories of most kin members, women as mothers, sisters, wives, and daughters often drop out of the patrilineage chronology. Patrilineality assures the continuity of masculine identity and identification. It works to intensify the relationship among brothers, in particular, but extends to lateral and vertical male kin as well.

Patrilocality is the cultural preference for married couples to live near the parents of the husband. While residence practices are quite variable and often more dependent on economic and other circumstances than rarified cultural values in Lebanon, patrilocality (if possible for the couple) remains, to some degree, a value for many individuals. Patrilocality, however, is often not only overridden by economic pressures, but when it is practiced may be unarticulated as a motivating force when the marriage is kin-endogamous (a still highly valued practice in village Lebanon) and both sets of families live relatively close to each other. Patrilocality, when it is practiced, further charges the intensity of brother/brother relationships.

Kin Contract, Care/Control Paradigm

The long Western political tradition based on the idea of the social contract is well represented in the literature. Carole Pateman's (1988) feminist critique argued that the social contract was historically based upon the hidden sexual contract: the cultural understanding that only adult men operated in the civil/public domain as citizens and that the women, domestic relations, and the family were under the authority of men (as husbands) and subject to natural law rather than civil law. Pateman argued that the sexual contract was the basis of the emergence of Western patriarchy--the privileging of men as men (rather than as fathers) over women as women.

I link Pateman's notion of the sexual contract to Rogers M. Smith's (1997) notion of civic myth to develop the idea of the kin contract. "A civic myth," Smith notes (1997:33) "is a myth used to explain why persons form a people, usually indicating how a political community originated, who is eligible for membership, who is not and why, and what the community's values and aims are." For Smith, civic myths, though riddled with contradictions, are constitutive of the nature of the political community and the relationships within it. The kin contract, as I have discussed elsewhere (Joseph 1999c, 2000), is a civic myth which conceptualizes the nature of social organization in Lebanon. The civic myth of the kin contract which has undergirded the Lebanese social order, has contributed critically to the psychosocial dynamics of brotherly relations through the complex and paradoxical operations of a care/control (Joseph 2000) paradigm, supported by the state and religious sects.

The reality is that kinship has been very diverse in Lebanon. Patriarchy, like all aspects of kinship, has always been a struggled-for and struggled-against institution (by both women and men, juniors and seniors). The lived kinship system has always been complex and contested. Kin have not always taken care of their own. They can be very competitive and hostile to each other. Contrary to the famous proverb, kin have often allied with strangers against each other. Though the reality of kinship has been full of contradictions, kinship and the kin contract have remained the center of social and political action in Lebanon.

The "kin contract" in Lebanon has been about the ideal of family love organized within a patriarchal structure of rights and responsibilities. The kin contract has romanticized the ideals of family love, mothers' and fathers' sacrifices for their children, children's respect for their parents, the love and care of brothers, grandparents, uncles, aunts, and cousins many steps removed. The kin contract extols the love of siblings for each other (Joseph 1994). The persuasiveness of the kin contract has been grounded in the material realities of Lebanese social life. Kin relations have been the core of social identity, economic stability, political security, and religious affiliation. Kin often are the first (or last) line of security--emotionally, socially, economically, and politically. The kin are expected to care and largely do care. Rights, in Lebanon, have been grounded in kin relationships for it has been kin against whom one has had irrevocable rights and towards whom one has had morally mandated (at times legally prescribed) responsibilities. In the long run of life, the kin who have had the most irrevocable rights and moral responsibilities toward each other are brothers. Kin identity and loyalty, for the Lebanese, has been seen as superseding national identity and loyalty to the state and competing only with religion. Again, no relationship has been more centrally an anchor point in these cultural genealogies than that of brothers.

In Lebanon, the strength of extended kin relationships (particularly brother/brother relationships) has been coterminous with relatively weak conjugal relationships. Natal kin have continued to demand the loyalty and allegiance of their relatives long after marriage. Brother/brother, sister/brother, mother/son, father/son, grandparents, uncles, aunts, and other natal relationships often have been seen to compete with husband/wife relationships (Joseph 1994, Barakat 1985). Men of the patrilineage have been seen to be responsible for their patrilineal kin regardless of later affinal relationships (Meeker 1976).

The kin contract has been reinforced by marriage practices favoring kin endogamy. The marriage preference for Muslims in Lebanon has been patrilineal kin endogamy. While Christian churches technically forbid close kin endogamy, it has been widely practiced among Christians as well. For both Muslims and Christians, kin endogamy in practice has been both patrilineal and matrilineal. Kin endogamy has tended to reinscribe the power of kinship in the lives of kin members. Even when endogamy has been village or neighborhood (rather than kin) based, it has strengthened the authority of resident kin. Given the tendency toward patrilocality (residence following the groom's father), endogamy has contributed to generationally reconstituting kin group in the sites which empower patrilineal patriarchy, reinforcing the centrality of kin relationships. Endogamy has been seen as a particularly powerful way of preserving patrilineal solidarity and property. I would suggest that the key structural connection between endogamy and patrilineality is the relationships of brothers. Structurally, it is brothers who exchange sisters. In the cultural ideal, it is cousins as brothers, exchanging sisters, as wives. As such, structurally, males, as brothers, act to preserve genealogically condoned masculine authority (even though in practice endogamy is often matrilineal.

Kin groups have been crucial to the economic security of kin members. In much of rural Lebanon, land, handed down through generations, often has remained undivided. The result has been to wed descending generations of siblings and cousins to their kin as common property holders. Women, even when they are entitled, often have not (or are not permitted) formally to inherit land. The rationale has been that since men of their patrilines, especially their brothers, remain responsible for them, leaving their land in the hands of their brothers repays the patrilineage for the protection they offer their women.

Men also often have not subdivided property inherited from fathers/grandfathers. Indeed, male kin often further invest with each other in businesses. Brothers often jointly build multiple storied buildings in which each may occupy an apartment on marriage. Lebanese have turned regularly to kin in times of need for loans, networking, *wasta* (brokerage), references, jobs, housing, and other financial assistance. Lebanese have relied upon kin, rather than the state, for protection and security. And political élites have recruited their following through the mobilization of kin networks, including their own. In addition, success to political leadership has been, and remains critically, through kin ties.

The care of kin has been conjoined with the control of kin. Kinship has entailed both accepting the structures of patriarchal authority and the demands of kin responsibilities as well as receiving the benefits of kin nurturance. Social control has been achieved in Lebanon largely through the discipline of extended patriarchal kinship.

The Lebanese state has relied upon and mobilized extended kin groups on behalf of the political order it has been attempting to construct. The state has assimilated the logic of kinship as an institution of governance. For the sake of political order, it has been kin groups that have had to be kept together. Pivotal kin institutions have mobilized to solidify the loyalty of kin and authority of kin males and seniors over kin members. *Wasta*, mediation by brokers (usually kin elders, male and female), has put moral pressure on kin members to resolve disputes and maintain kin civility. Kin patriarchs often have been able to strengthen their personal and kin positions vis-a-vis political leaders by disciplining kin members to vote, in local and national elections, in a block for the same leader. *Zu'ama`* (political leaders), for their part, have courted kin patriarchs and attempted to funnel resources from the state to their clientèle through kin elders. In this manner, the interests and actions of political leaders and kin elders often have coincided to reinforce the political advantages of kin solidarity.

Public order requires keeping men (as well as women) in their place. While patriarchs have had control over females and juniors, they also have had responsibilities for them. The kinship system, by tying males and seniors to their responsibilities to females and juniors, have acted as a form of discipline over those it has empowered. The kinship system has constrained the males and seniors it has privileged. It has cared for the females and juniors it has controlled. The kin contract and the care/control paradigm intimately link love and power in Lebanon. The love of kin for each other is genuine and the experience of being cared for is profound. The domination and at times crushing by kin is as real and pervasive as the love and caring. Love acts to recruit persons into systems in which they may thrive and they may be disciplined.

Connectivity, Patriarchal Connectivity, and Patriarchal Mirroring

Connectivity, as I have developed elsewhere (1993, 1999d), is a structure of self which is organized around fluid boundaries. The person sees her/himself inside significant other. Unlike the autonomous, bounded, separative, individualist, possessive self theorized in Western classical liberal political economy, the connective self's psychosocial investment is less in identifying and maintaining boundaries and separateness and more in making connection. Patriarchal connectivity is the production of selves with fluid boundaries who are psychodynamically organized for relationships of gendered and aged hierarchy based in kinship values and moralities.

Mirroring is a psychodynamic process in which the self is reflected by the other. The person is able and allowed to "see" herself/himself by "bouncing off" the other, or by recognizing the components of the self that are similar to the components of the other, thus allowing for a "reflection" of the self to mirror back to the self. In the psychodynamic literature, healthy mirroring is part of the process of creating and maintaining the boundary between the self and the other (Mahler, Pine, and Bergman 1975:223 n.1). In mirroring, the self is not "merged" with the other. The self identifies with like components of the other. Mirroring is considered, particularly in object relations psychodynamic theory, important to the process of healthy child development.

The concept of **patriarchal connective mirroring** builds on and adapts this notion of mirroring to critical dynamics which I observed, particularly in brotherly relations, in Lebanon. First I add, to the idea of mirroring, the idea of connectivity. In **connective mirroring**, the boundary between the self and the other is more fluid, so that components of the self are experienced as being "in" the other. As such, it is the "self in the other" that is being reflected back to the self. Second, I add the idea of patriarchy. In **patriarchal mirroring** the other reflects back the gendered and aged status and authority that the self might have, or wishes to have in other relations or at other times. It is the "self that will be" that is experienced and identified with.

Patriarchal connective mirroring is the process by which the person experiences components of the self "in" the other which reflect back the self's alternating capacities for gendered and aged deference and authority. Patriarchal connective mirroring reflects to the self those aspects of the self that have assimilated the gendered and aged system of hierarchy. It absorbs the emotionalities and intentionalities of domination into complementary and constitutive components of subordination. The subordinate person comes to see components of the self in the patriarchal other. The patriarchal other is or comes to represent the authority the self has or will have in other relations. At a more removed level of analysis or experience, the patriarchal other comes to represent, to the subordinate self, the system of relations which underwrite the psychodynamic expectations of what the self is or can be. The patriarchal other comes to represent to the subordinate self, the system of kin relations which underwrite gendered and aged hierarchy and which evokes the care/control paradigm embedded in the kin contract.

The kin contract, for this psychodynamic process of patriarchal connective mirroring, rationalizes the need for subordination and domination. It supports the structural conditions which help to reproduce, in daily life, the realities affirming the need for family, family elders, and the social political system in which family anchors the self's identity, status, security and social mooring. The brotherly relation is the epicenter of the kin contract. It is the heart of patriarchy--both its weakest link and its strongest bond.

For brothers, patriarchal connective mirroring organizes a psychosocial dynamic which helps the subordinate brother to see his brother-patriarch as himself. There is an identification of the inferior with the superior--and identification of the superior with the inferior. There is mutual mirroring and identification that is gendered and aged. The inferior hopes and has reason to believe that he too will be a patriarch. Deferring to the brother-patriarch helps reproduce the system which promises the deferring brother that he will become a patriarch himself, or has already authorized his status as patriarch in relation to his wife, children, mother, sisters, and other female kin and junior male relatives.

In some sense, the deferring brother needs his own deference to help reproduce the family system which supports his authority elsewhere. By deferring to the brother-patriarch, the junior brother reinforces the structures which give him authority over his wife, children, sisters, mother, and other women and juniors. His deference to his senior brother's authority, for example, helps teach and model his children's deference to his own patriarchal authority.

For the junior brother, the part of his self that is or yearns to be a patriarch yearns for family (it has absorbed the myth of the kin contract), needs solidarity, sees the brother-patriarch as a symbol of that self, that system, that set of psychosocial relationships and arrangements which make his sense of self possible. This is the part of the junior brother that is willing to defer to the senior brother. The junior brother defers because his patriarchal self is "in" the patriarchal brother. He defers because the patriarchal brother *enables* the self. He defers because the patriarchal brother *animates* the self. The patriarchal brother becomes the symbol of the kin contract. He comes to embody the self as patriarch, self as power, self as authority. The br(other) becomes self and other.

Identification with authority may be universal and probably is an important component of the dynamics of hegemony. The interesting aspect of the brother/brother identification with authority is that the deferring brother can and probably will become a patriarch himself when he establishes his own family. He can expect to have a position of authority vis-a-vis women and juniors. By identifying with the authority of the patriarchal brother, he supports the system which gives him his patriarchal authority.

Connectivity and mirroring facilitate the psychodynamics which allow the subordinate brother to partake of the authority of the patriarchal brother. In doing so, the deferring brother enacts his part of the kin contract. And despite conflictual experiences, the deferring brother is daily reminded of the merits of the kin contract in a range of social and institutional realities in Lebanon--from the law, to religion, to patron-client relationships, to the market place, to the neighborhood.

Conclusions

To summarize the conceptual intervention of this paper: the focused question I have been examining is why one or more brothers are willing to defer to the authority of another brother in Lebanon. Cultural norms seem to indicate the possibility of brotherly competition in close proximity and the admonition for brotherly solidarity when relations of distance are at play. Family structure and social, political, economic, and religious institutions seem not only to make kinship sacrosanct but vitally necessary for survival and success in Lebanon. Given the centrality of the brotherly relationships to the patriarchal, patrilineal, patrilocal culture and social structure, these forces would seem adequate to explain brotherly hierarchies and brotherly deference.

I explore, in this paper, an additional dimension of brotherly deference, not developed in the anthropological literature on brotherly relations. Lebanon is a society in which kinship is central to the state, politics, economics, religion, social organization, and the law; in which the underlying civic myth is more organized around the kin contract than the social contract; in which social institutions reinforce patriarchy and patrilineality in multiple domains. Yet it is also a society in which competing social, economic, political, and religious forces offer citizens choices which can and do pull them in contradictory directions. What motivates men to become " junior" to "senior" brothers under these circumstances?

I suggest a series of conceptual bridges linking structure, culture, psychosocial dynamics, and the self. Patriarchy, patrilineality, connectivity, the kin contract, the care/control paradigm, patriarchal connective mirroring each, and together, offer conceptual steps to articulate motivationalities with actions, agency with structure, psychology with culture.

References Cited

Barakat, Halim. 1985. "The Arab Family and the Challenge of Social Transformation" in Elizabeth W. Fernea, ed., *Women and the Family in the Middle East: New Voices of Change*, pp. 27-48. Austin: University of Texas Press.

Geertz, Clifford, Hildred Geertz and Lawrence Rosen. 1979. *Order in Moroccan Society*. New York: Cambridge University Press.

Joseph, Suad. 1993. "Connectivity and Patriarchy Among Working Class Arab Families in Lebanon," *Ethos* 21(4):452-484.

---------------. 1994. "Brother/Sister Relationships: Connectivity, Love, and Power in the Reproduction of Arab Patriarchy," *American Ethnologist* 21(1):50-73.

---------------. 1999a. "Citizenship Responsibility and Children: Dilemmas of Patriarchal Relational Responsibility in Lebanon" in Walid Moubarak, Antoine Messarra, and Suad Joseph, eds., *Building Citizenship in Lebanon*, pp. 175-194. Beirut: Lebanese American University Press (in Arabic.

---------------. 1999b. "Children's and Women's Rights: Gender, Relationality, and Patriarchy in Rights Practices in Lebanon" in .Najla Hamadeh, Jean Said Makdisi, Suad Joseph, eds., *Gender and Citizenship in* Lebano, pp. 325-341. Beirut: Dar al Jadid Press (in Arabic).

---------------. 1999c. "Descent of the Nation: Kinship and Citizenship in Lebanon," *Citizenship Studies* 3(3):293-318.

---------------. 2000. "Civic Myths, Citizenship, and Gender in Lebanon. Gender and Citizenship in the Middle East" in Suad Joseph, ed., *Gender and Citizenship in the Middle East*, pp. 107-136. Syracuse: Syracuse University Press.

Joseph, Suad, ed. 1999d. *Intimate Selving in Arab Families: Gender, Self and Family*. Syracuse: Syracuse University Press.

Mahler, Margaret, Fred Pine, and Anni Bergman. 1975. *The Psychological Birth of the Human Infant: Symbiosis and Individuation*. New York: Basic Books.

Meeker, Michael E. 1975. "Meaning and Society in the Near East: Examples from the Black Sea Turks and the Levantine Arabs," *International Journal of Middle East Studies* 7:383-422.

Pateman, Carole. 1988. *The Sexual Contract*. Stanford: Stanford University Press.

Smith, Rogers M. 1997. *Civic Ideals: Conflicting Visions of Citizenship in U.S. History*. New Haven: Yale University Press.

SISTERHOOD AND STEWARDSHIP IN SISTER-BROTHER RELATIONS IN SAUDI ARABIA

SORAYA ALTORKI

Although attention in the scholarly literature on the organization of family in Saudi Arabia has gradually increased, thus far no study has focused on sibling relations, including those of sister and brother. One likely reason for this is that scholars of the Saudi family have felt it necessary to study what they consider to be the "primary" relationships, including those between parents and children, spouses and their in-laws, and spouses with one another, before examining the "secondary" dyads of sisters and brothers. Yet, upon further consideration, it seems that in many respects sister-brother dyads are extremely important. This is especially so as the father typically predeceases his sons, and the latter then become responsible for their sisters' conduct. Even after their sisters' marriage, the brothers continue to retain a residual degree of investment in and responsibility for their sisters' behavior. And, in the event of unmarried sisters, if the father is absent, brothers not only are responsible for the conduct of their sisters but also their care. Even if the father is alive, his absence from the household during long hours of the day while on the job, and even for weeks, months, or years when they take jobs in distant geographic locations, means that the brother plays a more central role than one might normally think.

In this paper I will describe sister-brother relations in Saudi Arabia based on field research with 13 élite families in Jeddah in the 1970s and 1980s. Generational differences are evident in the behavior of siblings toward one another. In the older generation families, brothers conducted themselves in relation to their unmarried sisters as a second father, as it were. It did not seem to matter whether there was only one or several sons in the family-- although the younger brothers did defer to their older sibling with regard to the rights and obligation of the younger unmarried sisters. Among the middle and newer generation families, sisters secured wider leeway for themselves than was the case in the older generation.[1] However, in all cases the relationship between brother and sister was asymmetrical, with power and status honor vested in the former. Sisters were not powerless, although generally they showed deference to an older brother. Beyond this, the bond in all cases was suffused with love. Sisters endorsed their brothers' image as strong male role models and desirable potential husbands. Unmarried sisters also envied the mobility and freedom of their brothers, and they knew and sometimes resented the fact that their elder brothers could censor them in the absence of their fathers. This made for tension and some conflict between sisters and brothers, even though sisters often did what they wanted, sometimes with their mothers' consent and help. Altogether, love and friendship overwhelmed the power dynamic.

In the discussion that follows, the cases will illustrate the following themes: (1) unmarried sister-brother relations; (2) married sister-brother relations; (3) sister-brother relations following the father's death; (4) sister-brother relations in the context of inheritance matters; and (5) older sister confrontation with younger brother over inheritance. In the last part of the paper I theorize brother-sister relations in the context of structuralism as elaborated by Bourdieu and Giddens, and in the light of Scott's work on domination and resistance.

Unmarried Sister-Brother Relations

Samiha was the youngest unmarried daughter in a middle generation family headed by a prosperous merchant who had several sons and daughters. The age difference between Samiha and her eldest brother, 'Umar, was 10 years. Another sister, 'A`isha, was the eldest sibling in the family. Samiha and 'Umar had particularly close ties, with 'Umar running interference for Samiha and standing up for her during quarrels between her and 'A`isha. This support was due in part to the fact that he did not agree with 'A`isha's views.

The patriarch of the family, 'Abdallah, was relatively enlightened and encouraged his daughters to be educated, and in the case of Samiha he was willing to allow her to receive the equivalent of college training. In his

---

[1] On this distinction among generations, see Altorki, (1986:13).

relations with his daughters, 'Abdallah took 'A`isha as his confidant and gave her responsibility to allocate the family's daily expenses, while he indulged Samiha in ways that were consistent with her younger age. It is fair to say that Samiha was the patriarch's pet. 'Umar, as well, adopted his father's favoritism toward Samiha, ratifying many of her choices, approving of her hair style, and bringing her gifts that seemed more substantial relative to the presents he brought for 'A`isha. For her part, Samiha showed great respect for 'Umar and promoted his self-image in ways that bordered on doting upon him.

The relationship was subjected to a severe test when Samiha, who was 19, sought to go on an outing with friends at a time when her father was out of the country. Given the relative latitude that she enjoyed, her brother's objection came as a surprise. The idea was to visit with her friends and stay at one of their homes overnight. 'Umar objected that a good friend of his was a son of the family in that home, and he did not want his sister to give the appearance of allowing the opportunity of an encounter with someone she could possibly marry. Samiha sought her mother's intercession, but she agreed with 'Umar. The episode caused a major strain between sister and brother, and words were exchanged. Other women in the family supported 'Umar and urged Samiha to make up with her brother. Although she told me that she resented having to do so, in fact she did approach 'Umar and tried to break the ice between them. 'Umar, never relishing the idea of acting as an autocrat toward her, made it easy for her to apologize by telling her that he could understand her sense of hurt. He explained his reservations and reasserted his concern that this outing might lead people to talk critically of Samiha, since she was young and of marriageable age. For her part, Samiha insisted that many of her friends of comparable standing engaged in similar behavior, and asked why she should be prevented from doing so. She later told me that things were really changing in relations within other families known to her, and she could not understand her brother's obstinacy in making matters difficult for her. Afterwards, the relationship between Samiha and 'Umar was gradually restored. Interestingly, the ties seem to have emerged strengthened from this episode.

Because this incident involved sleeping out, it had special significance, and consequently Samiha had less room to negotiate her way through her brother's and mother's restrictions on her movements. She did not question her brother's concern that her freedom of movement could lead to a comprising incident, but she argued that the methods she would use (being driven to her friend's house in a car and remaining veiled whenever in the presence of men) were sufficient to prevent this. Unmarried women of Samiha's age go out in public more often than those of the older generation. Brothers may learn of these outings by chance or by receiving information in their father's absence. Daughters seek the cooperation and approval of their mothers and try to negotiate an expansion of their rights by focusing on procedures and logistics more than on the merits of the issue.

Married Sister-Brother Relations

Maha was the only daughter and oldest sibling in an older generation family with several brothers. She was a dutiful daughter who delayed marriage, and as the years passed, her prospects for marriage dwindled. The reluctance of her father, Hamza, to approve offers of marriage by presentable suitors had led Maha almost to abandon any further hopes. When I inquired why Hamza had opposed these offers, I was told that he did not want to lose her services in the family--in particular assistance with raising the sons, but also because he wanted Maha to attend to him and his wife in their advancing years. The fact that Maha was an only daughter facilitated Hamza in his conduct, for in a family of several daughters, it is customary for the oldest to marry first; and were she delayed in this, marriage plans for the younger daughters would accordingly also need to be deferred, causing them to feel resentful of the situation.

Amina, Maha's mother, informed me that she often had pleaded with Hamza to relent, but her oldest son, Walid, fortified Hamza's resolve when he strongly supported him in the matter. The middle and younger sons sided with Maha and Amina, but they were unwilling to press hard for their sister's position. I learned that relations between Maha and Walid were tense, despite the fact that Maha was quite deferential to the authority of the men in the family. Maha spoke quite plainly about what she felt were Walid's exaggerated claims to the deference and respect owed him. They had quarreled over the years about the limits of his prerogatives, and even though he was her brother, she was, after all, older than he. Also, it was commonly accepted in the family that Walid had been rather spoiled by the attention that had been lavished upon him by his parents.

Amina and Maha frequently talked to the female relatives about the situation, but opinion was divided as to what to do. Most advised patience, although this was tempered by the realistic calculation that time would soon run out for Maha, who was approaching 30. At length, Amina decided to appeal to Na'if, who was Hamza's older brother, to intercede on behalf of his niece. Na'if's status in the community was higher than Hamza's and his reputation as a "weighty" person was well-established. He had a strong personality, adopted a no-nonsense and direct approach to matters, and spoke frankly and bluntly. Na'if informed Hamza that he was wrong to reject marriage proposals for his daughter, invoking religious and cultural traditions about the seemliness of timely marriage for well-born daughters. After some resistance, Hamza agreed. This forced Walid's hand, and Maha's parents soon after this intervention accepted a proposal from a man considerably older than Maha but who had made a favorable impression on the family and relatives.

After the marriage, relations between Maha and Walid had remained tense. He somehow believed that her marriage amounted to a defeat for him and a derogation of his authority, even though his own father had accepted this marriage. This was probably magnified by Walid's sense of injury and insult that his uncle's intervention had fostered in him. Na'if, in his characteristically blunt manner, had espoused Maha's cause and rather cavalierly equated Walid's attitude to his immaturity and being spoiled. But Maha was a very resourceful woman. At family encounters, she relied on the excellent rapport she had with Walid's children to overcome the strains in their relationship. In fact, her good nature made it difficult for anyone to find fault with her, and she knew that she could rely on this resource to accumulate good will all around. Thus, Walid basically found himself isolated and eventually came to the conclusion that it was unreasonable for him to persist in his course of sullen resistance. I concluded that Maha's success in winning her brother over was by no means a foregone conclusion but that it indeed required a great deal of patience, planning, and marshaling of resources on her part to bring about the reconciliation that she so ardently desired. In their subsequent relationship, Maha endeavored as much as she could to lead Walid to believe that his affection was critical to her own happiness. In this, she was rewarded by a major change in his behavior toward her. His earlier exaggerated sense of himself in his relations with her did not disappear, but neither did he allow his conduct toward her to be consistently dominated by it.

Sister-Brother Relations Following the Father's Death

Yusuf, the father of a middle generation family of four sons and three daughters, fell ill and, after a prolonged illness and died at the young age of fifty eight. He had been a benevolent father and somewhat of a social lion whose reputation for hospitality was widely appreciated by relatives, neighbors, and friends. At the same time, it had been commonly-held opinion that his wife, Salwa, had been not only his equal in terms of family authority but indeed also in the larger social world. For example, she had substantial property and had invested in the family business. Thus, her prominence manifested itself not only in terms of parent-child relations--where it would be expected that the mother of a younger generation family would have a very important influence in her children's lives, such as decisions as to their schooling and career choices--but even outside the domestic scene.

Salwa's relations with her daughters were extremely strong. She prided herself on the thought that they always came to her to share their innermost thoughts and feelings, although, as I learned from these daughters, this consultation may not have been as comprehensive as she believed. Still, mother-daughter ties in this family were secure and based on maternal-filial affection. The two older sisters married well, but the younger one, Latifa, had long wished to have a career and was not sure whether a future husband would regard this prospect with equanimity.

Upon Yusuf's death, the oldest son, Amin, took over responsibility for the well-being of his mother and his youngest sister, Latifa. Amin was a successful engineer who had married and moved his wife into his own separate home prior to his father's death. He was a more assertive personality than his father had been and often intervened in domestic matters. Even after he had left his father's household, he continued to have a major say in matters affecting the lives of his two married sisters and even more in

Latifa's. Upon Yusuf's death, Amin brought Salwa and Latifa into his own home.

Relations between Latifa and Nahid, Amin's wife, were tense. Latifa was a professional woman who had gone on to university and was a pediatrician with her own practice. Her career gave her a certain tactical leverage which she used to carve out a significance degree of autonomy in her life. But as an unmarried woman she simultaneously had to respect social conventions, which held that the brother's wife was to be respected in her own home. Latifa was not only a medical doctor, but she had been educated at a prestigious foreign university, a rare development even for a member of a younger generation family. Try as she might, she could not bestow upon her sister-in-law the deference that was her due and wondered to herself why her brother had settled for a conventional, uneducated wife. Meanwhile, Nahid was jealous of Latifa, especially since Amin clearly supported his sister on many issues and was extremely proud of her professional achievements. Latifa wanted very much to play the role of the good aunt with her nieces, but she had to acknowledge that her relations with them were inevitably influenced by the tension that characterized her conduct toward Nahid and Nahid's toward her. It seemed to Latifa that whenever Nahid perceived Latifa drawing close to these nieces, she would make an effort to subvert this. Once, Latifa was encouraging them to think of a career in teaching or science and the discussion was warming up, the nieces were evidently interested and asking many probing and interesting questions. Nahid, at an inopportune moment--or so it seemed to Latifa--broke into the conversation and "bribed" her daughters away by announcing that she wanted to take them shopping. Enough such incidents had occurred to lead Latifa to believe that Nahid was determined to deny her the role of beloved aunt in the family. Nahid, at the same time, was convinced that Latifa disrespected her, which Latifa not only admitted to me was true, but which I could observe in her conduct toward Nahid.

Amin was clearly aware of the tension between his wife and sister but was not sure how to deal with it. On the one hand, he hoped that his daughters would follow Latifa's precedent to receive an advanced education and have the opportunity to live fulfilled lives outside the confines of the household. At the same time, he was not sure how committed he really was to this view, as his own choice of a more traditional, less educated spouse indicated. He therefore tried to compromise by welcoming Latifa's interactions with his daughters but at the same time not interfering in his wife's practice of socializing them in very traditional ways. For example, Nahid was in the habit of criticizing "modern" ways of thinking that she attributed to some of her daughters' friends, including delaying marriage into the late twenties.

Latifa decided to confront Amin about Nahid's behavior toward her. Although Amin was a "modern" husband and brother, he did not take well to his sister's comments. He informed her that she was being unfair and that he disagreed. Although taking care not to reveal his sentiments in Nahid's presence, he reproved Latifa. For her part, she perceived this incident as a litmus test of her brother's real feelings about not only her relations with Nahid but more generally about her style of life and career orientation. When I spoke with Latifa about this incident, I suggested to her that he was bound to defend his wife from her accusations because she had placed her brother in an awkward position. Latifa expressed hurt and related the old adage about how a sibling is more valuable than a spouse, because spouses might pass from the scene and be replaced, whereas one could not replace a sister or brother. In my last contacts with them, I was given to understand that the breach had not been healed completely between Latifa and Amin, and that Latifa had come away from the episode somewhat chastened and wiser about the limits of the possible in her ties with him. Despite the fact that her education and career privileged Latifa in the eyes of her family and relatives, this episode shows that limits beyond which a sister may not go in her relations with her brother, and, as well, beyond which a brother does not care to go in valorizing traditional ways.

Sister-Brother Relations in the Context of Inheritance Matters

Madiha was the youngest daughter of a younger generation family, with three sisters and an older brother. The only son, her brother Kamal, was closer to her than to the other three sisters. Their rapport was so strong that it served as a source of comment on the part of family members and relatives. Despite their age separation of 15 years, they could be described as close friends, as well as close siblings. Their father had been an important official in the office of the provincial governor, as well as a wealthy land owner in his own right. Upon his death, the relationship between Kamal and Madiha became even closer than before. Madiha had not thought twice about leaving to her brother the job of supervising her portion of the estate, which was not insubstantial.

Educated abroad, with a degree in business administration, Madiha was a manager in an firm in Riyadh. Although Kamal had agreed to this arrangement for his unmarried sister, he was uncomfortable with it. Madiha's job was not a high paying one, but her salary was enough to enable her to live within her means and have some left over for incidental expenses. She had remained single because, among other reasons, she did not want to be tied down to a domestic life, which the typical prospective spouse would have insisted upon as a condition of their marriage. Although this was not the most secure arrangement, she felt comfortable in the knowledge that her share of the inheritance could provide her with a cushion should her financial situation somehow suddenly worsen.

For a number of years, whenever she needed supplementary funds for travel or vacations, she called upon her brother to withdraw funds from the accumulated interest in her savings account. However, Kamal's own business prospects worsened as a consequence of the downturn in the economy in the 1980s. A successful businessman, he soon faced sharp cutbacks in his work and took ruinous losses in the stock market. As his own expenses mounted, including those related to the education of his children, the range of his options became increasingly narrow, and he fell significantly into debt.

Finally, his prospects became so dire that he found it necessary to use the power of attorney that Madiha had given to him to supervise her assets by exhausting these to liquidate some loans. He never notified Madiha of this, thinking that he could recoup the money and replace it without her realizing it. Unhappily for them both, this did not happen. Planning to make a sizable investment herself in a condominium, she requested a large transfer of funds from Kamal. At that point, he told Madiha that he could not do this, but without providing an explanation. Madiha was stunned but did not know how to respond. She felt profoundly the cultural norms mandating a younger sister's love, respect and deference for an older brother, and given her solidarity and love for her brother she did not finally confront him directly. Instead, she found it necessary to play the role of sympathetic supporter, only dropping hints from time to time that she hoped he would sense her astonishment at this betrayal of her father's legacy to her. Madiha also told me that she hated the idea of trying to recruit other family members to her cause. This was something between her and her brother, and she believed deeply that trying to bring others in would deal a fatal blow to a relationship that she desperately wanted to restore.

Madiha told me that she felt bitterly toward her brother's action. It was not so much his clear infringement of her rights that distressed her--though that was a serious breach of norms relating to the property of women, and especially serious coming from an individual who had strongly upheld the rights of women. Rather, it was his failure to consult her about the matter that she found distressing. Could it be that her brother, deep down, was a traditional man, willing to act in a highhanded manner when it came to the legacy she had inherited from her father?

At the time of conclusion of my fieldwork, the situation remained unresolved. My guess is that although the incident undermined Madiha's entitlement and hence her status, it could paradoxically contribute eventually to her empowerment. While her prospects have been diminished materially, her brother's conduct may be interpreted by some as empowering her in an ethical sense that could have implications for further increasing her autonomy from her brother. The dynamic by which this could operate is that the episode shows that women can establish their credentials in a "man's world" in ways that lessen their dependence on men; and men, on the contrary, can overstep their bounds and reveal themselves to be unreliable in protecting their womenfolk's entitlements--a clear violation of social norms and values. The implications of this argument could be that women may be expected to secure their interests directly, circumventing male intervention and control of these, without that appearing an unseemly breach of social conventions.

Older Sister-Younger Brother Confrontation over Inheritance

Amal was the oldest child in a middle generation family of five children-- four daughters and one son, whose name was Hamid. The age difference between Amal and Hamid was two years, she being 40 and he 38 at the time of field work. Their father had recently died and left a considerable estate, which Hamid believed it was his duty to oversee on behalf of his four sisters. Amal had married a prominent member of Jiddah society. At the time of the crisis over her father's bequest, Amal was already a well-established lady of a prominent household in the community. Possessing a strong personality and a high degree of self-confidence, she also was unusual in her exceptional ability to organize the affairs of her family.

Hamid was educated abroad and was a construction engineer. He was a liberal-minded individual but also keenly felt his obligations as the head of the family upon his father's passing. The other sisters were willing to leave their share of the inheritance in his custody for the time being and did not press Hamid to furnish them with their share. Amal, however, was determined to secure her share. This determination was not, as far as I could tell, generated by Amal's sense of economic insecurity. Her husband was very wealthy and devoted to her. It is possible that she may have wished to hedge against the eventuality of being thrown upon her own devices were something untoward to happen.

Amal had always been her own "boss" as an eldest daughter in the household. Her father had encouraged her as the senior sibling to "take charge" in making important domestic decisions, even if this meant taking on some of the functions normally reserved for the mother. This goes a long way to explaining her self-confidence. At the same time, however, the father had remained emotionally somewhat distant from her and, in fact, every one was aware that his favorite was his youngest daughter. Amal, perhaps to compensate, found she could regulate her relationships with her brother and sisters efficiently, serenely, and confidently. She was not afraid of her brother and was quite prepared to cross him in the defense of her own rights.

Accordingly, not long after her father's death, she boldly asked Hamid for a cash settlement of her portion of their father's estate. He was taken aback by the forthright manner with which she approached the matter and demurred. That Amal was making this demand in the presence of her mother was somewhat shocking. Actually, her mother had witnessed other altercations between the two before, so the fact of a falling out between them was not new. But this time, the subject of the dispute was financial and related to her father's property. Hamid's reaction not to comply was due in part to his sense that what Amal was doing was morally wrong and approached scandalous behavior. Additionally, complying with Amal's request was not a simple matter. It required legal procedures, the disentangling of parcels of property, and the sale of such property, since none of the other members of the family were seeking their own separate shares, and the inheritance was not desegregated in any neat way.

Eventually, Hamid gave in and provided Amal with her share. However, the consequence of this episode was the estrangement of sister and brother. This estrangement has continued over the decades. The death of their mother did not alter the fact of their alienation from one another. It is of interest that Amal was not a career woman nor particularly highly educated. She did, however, have three advantages that she put to good use in making her claims to her entitlement: (1) she had a strong personality; (2) her father had encouraged her to stand up for herself and to act as a "younger mother" in relation to her sisters; and (3) she was married to a very prominent and wealthy individual who was devoted to her, a fact that gave her great security to demand her rights in an open breach with her brother.

Analysis

A number of scholars argue that patriarchal relations are the basis of the Arab family, maintaining that older men exercise control over women (and younger men) by using institutional and organizational resources to maintain their power. Perhaps so, but the nature of patriarchy is not fixed as a universal category. It is in fact a historical outcome. Many variables affect it, including the role of the state, ethnicity, religion, class affiliation, socialization patterns, educational achievement, social mobility, cultural values, and the personality of the actors. In short, patriarchy is subject to change over time and space. Consequently, it is best to situate the concept of patriarchy in everyday practice by recognizing that actual arrangements of relationships are subject to strategic negotiation and the adoption of what post-structuralist theorists call "subject positions." (Moore 1994:4, 118, 120)

Patriarchy is a form of structure of power, but individuals and roles within this structure are not fixed. Persons who are involved have options to accede to or oppose the power that is exerted upon them, and there are many shadings of compliance and resistance. Outright opposition to customary norms is extremely rare. But abject obedience is hardly the rule. It is always an empirical question as to where on the spectrum of compliance and resistance one might expect to find family members. Influencing this, as has been mentioned, are a series of external and internal factors impinging on the particular family in question. Accomplices, for example a mother or a spouse, may play a role. A feisty personality, combined with a power base, offers a sister a certain flexibility vis-a-vis her brother, for example, that a more demure temperament cannot as readily lay claim to.

Much of the discussion in this paper may be contextualized by reference to structural theory. It is a characteristic of structuralism to seek the integration of theory, practice, and history, as the work of Bourdieu[2] and Giddens[3] suggests. By this, I suggest that explanations of behavior among those who have greater empowerment and those who have less can only make sense if we examine not simply the formal requirements of the roles that people fill, but also their daily, practical conduct in actual historical contexts. To these theorists, as well as others, structuralism stresses, among other things, the importance of language and cognition. Superordinates and subordinates will utilize language and reflection, including self-reflection, as an "art" of domination and resistance, as Scott (1990) puts it. In the context of the cases studies provided here, the brothers are dominant and the sisters subordinate. To be a brother or sister is to be an incumbent of a role, and these roles have their formal obligations and prerogatives. But whether or not particular individuals behave according to such role expectations is a contingent, empirical question.

These considerations allow us to focus on the phenomenon of performance. In our context of sisters and brothers, these individuals are actors playing roles. These roles, as mentioned, are associated with certain expectations. To be a brother, then, carries with it the expectation that one will behave in a certain way, and similarly for sisters. They are engaged in what Scott would call enactments of public and hidden "transcripts". In a word, human behavior throughout history involves acting and performance

---

[2] Of Bourdieu's many works, the most important for present purposes are Bourdieu 1977, 1990, 1991, and 1998.
[3] Giddens's preferred term is "structuration". See Giddens, 1984, 1981-1985, 1990, and 1991.

according to scripts. Public transcripts "are systematically skewed in the direction of the libretto, the discourse represented by the dominant" (Scott 1990:4). The public performances that the actors engage in mainly conform to expectations established by superordinates. Subordinates, for their part, will more or less conform to what the script mandates from them, but whether or not they mean what they say or signal is another question. They will minimize confrontations that they know in advance are not winnable by publicly acceding to do those things required of them. In our cases, the public transcript is spelled out by reference to patriarchy.

Subordinates, however, also have and are influenced by hidden transcripts. Such hidden transcripts contain a plot line that varies dramatically from that of the public transcript. The subordinate desires as much as possible to effectuate the plot of his or her hidden transcript, all the while fully aware that discretion requires him/her to appear to be conforming to the plot line of the public transcript. In the case of Scott's peasant, his ability to negotiate from a position of weakness has much to do with how he uses language ("speech acts") as well as passivity, non- or substandard performance, evasiveness, deceit, or subversion, to signal where he stands. But it is dangerous for him to try in some direct way to substitute his hidden transcript for the public one in which he is enmeshed and which is controlled by the landlord. It takes a great deal of skill to negotiate one's way between the demands of the public and one's own private transcripts. In the case of the sisters in our case studies, it is a question of speech acts, as well as a repertoire of behavior that may variously include manipulation, insinuation, suggestion, ruse, and artifice. Disguise is, of course, the instrument of the subordinate, whereas, except for the most gullible superordinates, surveillance--for the purpose of breaking through the disguise to learn what the subordinate truly believes--is the weapon of dominants.[4]

But, superordinates also have their hidden transcripts. In the case of Scott's élites, these entail speech acts or such behavior as theft, arrogation of luxuries and privileges, bribery, extortion, slander, tampering (Scott 1990:14). In the context of our discussion of brothers, their hidden transcripts might involve various forms of verbal and non-verbal

---

[4] This leads Scott (1990:4) to talk of "the dialectic of disguise and surveillance that pervades relations between the weak and the strong [which] will help us, I think, to understand the cultural patterns of domination and subordination."

communication, including efforts to make their sisters feel guilty or ashamed or incompetent, or, on the positive side, efforts to project their own manliness, efficacy, rationality, farsightedness, and the like.

Of course, actors are conscious of the public transcript and their own particular hidden transcripts. But they are usually unable to know the hidden transcripts of others "because the hidden transcripts of dominant and subordinate are, in most circumstances, *never in direct contact*" (Scott 1990:15; emphasis in original). However, the analyst may be able to access the missing information. Thus, our knowledge, as observers, of what is going on "can be advanced by research that can compare the hidden transcript of subordinate groups with the hidden transcript of the powerful and both hidden transcripts with the public transcript they share" (Scott 1990:15).

In the cases that I have reviewed in their varying ways exemplify these considerations. The sisters all attempted to reduce the sphere of control that brothers and fathers sought to maintain. How they negotiated their way in this effort varied, but in each situation these women demonstrated that family relationships are malleable. Even in the cases (1, 3, 4) where things did not finally go their way, the actions of these sisters secured for them a degree of tactical leverage to widen the space within which they could operate.

In the first case, we saw that a sister's desire to go on an outing was blocked by a normally empathic brother who customarily not only supported her decisions but valorized them more than those of her older sister. Seeking to overcome this, she tried to enlist her mother's backing, but this ultimately failed. Not to be stymied, she resorted to the device of invidious comparison with families whose status in society was similar to their own and arguing that if those families could accept actions of the sort she was contemplating, then her brother was "behind the times" to object.

Additionally, we can note that her brother did not relish the idea of acting as an autocrat toward her, but he actually did do so in conformity with the requirements of power and control that the community's public transcript mandated. This sister's identity, moreover, had been formed to a significant degree by the closeness that she experienced toward her brother--who, recall, had stood up for her interests in the face of the older sister's quarrels with her. In other words, not only was he lenient towards her, but she used this leniency as she was growing up to form a surer sense of her own identity.

However, it must be noted that although the younger sister's hidden transcript did involve some manipulation of the males in her family to get her way, there were limits to this manipulation, as she ruefully discovered. So her brother's impact on her as a "connective patriarch" had ambiguous outcomes for her. Generally speaking, she enjoyed unusual latitude in her actions, but sometimes, as with the specific case of the outing, she would be ruled by her brother's edict.

In the second case, an older brother who had correct but not especially friendly relations with his sister tried to hinder her marriage plans, even though time was running out for her. Securing her mother's validation of her plans and then calling upon a respected relative to intercede, this sister got her way and then used the leverage of her relations with her brother's children to get him to overcome his sense of injured self-esteem--a strategy that effectively worked. One might say that the public transcript that governed the conduct of sister and brother in this instance included terms of reference that allowed her to overcome her brother's explicit enjoinment of her to engage in a particular action. Public transcripts are supposed to create the appearance of unanimity (Scott 1990:55ff), but in this case this proved impossible, as enough "wiggle room" existed--including the availability of a powerful male intercessor--to overcome restrictions. Thus she could overcome his resistance because the norms allowed her to use (1) the mother; (2) a senior male relative; and (3) the brother's children. All these norms are basic elements of the public transcript of the community.

Our third case featured a sister-brother relationship that was based on very strong bonds of love and respect, in which the sister was a career woman who had conflicts with her more traditional-minded sister-in-law. As in case number one, connectivity in this situation would appear to be an important factor in the sister-brother relationship. As Joseph (1994) maintains, connectivity rests on a bifurcation of love and power. In this case, the sister expected understanding from her brother but was surprised to learn that he reproved her for criticizing his wife to his face in a private encounter. In this episode, the sister tried to mobilize the resource of her own paradigm as a successful professional woman--a paradigm she knew her brother was proud of--to carry the day. And although the strategy was quite rational, the results were substantially less than she thought she could achieve, leading her to question whether her brother's overall endorsement of the example she set for women in general was merely superficial.

In the fourth example, another career woman who had such confidence in her brother's stewardship of her inheritance that she never bothered talking about financial arrangements with him was devastated to learn that he repaid her badly for that trust. Although his action in breach of this trust was due to circumstances beyond his control, his failure to consult with her in advance about his plans to use her money to pay his debts was directly at odds with the whole record of their open relationship dating to their early years as children in the family. Not able to confront him directly, nor wishing to recruit others to her cause because she knew that this would finally wreck any chances of restoring the relationship, she resorted instead to insinuations to him of his wrongful behavior.

The public transcript clearly entitled this brother to manage her portion of the estate as he best saw fit, as long as he believed he was administering it in the best interests of the family, which included her individual interests. His hidden transcript stressed that he could access her assets in the defense of his own personal interests, on the condition that this would not entail a permanent appropriation. Her hidden transcript, once she learned what had transpired, consisted of a sense of anger and betrayal, but the expression of this was limited to imputations and insinuations whose maximum cumulative effect might be to cause him to feel guilt for what he had done. The love that she had felt in this connective relationship to her brother was too powerful to allow her to openly rebuke him, much less resort to even stronger sanction. Note that this sister realized that it would have been very difficult to resort to legal action to restore her rights. Neither could she readily have sought the mediation of male (or any other) members of the family. Moreover, she was conflicted over the idea of exposing him, since that would have caused him great hurt, markedly diminishing his stature in the community. A countervailing point, however, is that her abandonment of the notion of exposing him would lead to the ultimate result of placing him in her debt, thus obligating him to her in ways she could later use to her advantage. Yet she felt a sense of loss and inadequacy and questioned why she could not resort to more confrontational conduct. As a career woman, her autonomy was bounded in ways that she perhaps had deluded herself into thinking could not be summoned against her.

The fifth case is one that seems to suggest that the power of a brother can be directly challenged. While patriarchal connectivity involving sister and brother in this instance does not seem to be evident explicitly, we may perhaps conjecture that nevertheless it was a factor. For consider the situation. The older sister was an assertive, self-confident woman who had become used to getting her way in matters of family organization. It can hardly be supposed that this resulted from the force of her personality. Since the brother had from early years had, at best, a correct relationship with this sister and, at worst, a conflictual one, one might conclude that he was not a factor in the formation of her identity. But in a negative way, perhaps he was after all. That is, perhaps she constructed her identity partly in reaction to him and what he stood for as the heir apparent of the family. Moreover, structurally within this family her father had encouraged her by various actions of his to assume a powerful role on the organizational side of family matters--deciding or helping to decide such things as expenditures, the holding of parties, the exchange of visits, and the like. This encouragement no doubt contributed to the evolution of her self-perception and identity.

Then, at a critical moment, she mobilized her resources to demand her assets from the estate of her father when the public transcript held that she should not. Her hidden transcript, which was almost overt and public, was that she was as eligible to dispose of the business of the family as any sibling, including a brother. Her marriage to a powerful individual in the society gave her additional tactical leverage to get her way. If she experienced doubts or a sense of "*'ayb*" (shame)--that what she was doing simply was not done--she did not show this. Meanwhile, the connectivity that she had with her father, rather than with her brother, was the important factor in this case.

We may close the discussion by noting that sister-brother relations are similar to parent-children relations and different from wife-husband relations in the sense that they are characterized by the absence of a legal contract. The bargaining and negotiation that takes place in sister-brother dyads may nevertheless be said to occur within a contractual frame that may be termed normative understandings of roles and identities. Thus, how a sister interprets her role is obviously shaped by expectations that others have of these sisters. But it depends also on how such sisters view their own needs and rights, which are critical for defining themselves. Outcomes depend strongly upon how these sisters and their brothers interpret the public transcript in which they are embedded and then deploy their own hidden transcripts to advance their causes.

The different outcomes in our five cases should by themselves tell us that a simplistic invocation of the concept of patriarchy by way of explaining the trajectories in these sister-brother relationships is basically useless. These outcomes instead are the product of contestation, dynamic interaction, and positive assertion of needs and rights. Connectivity is a mediating variable in this process. Finally, contesting and asserting identities, needs and rights does not necessarily bring about specific objectives--as we have seen, most of these stories show that the sisters fell short of their immediate ends. However, over the long term, as sisters seek to expand the sphere of their entitlements, they will contribute to the construction and reconstruction of sisterhood that, on the strength of the cases presented here, they hope will be less constrained and more empowered.

Referencess

Altorki, Soraya. 1986. *Women in Saudi Arabia: Ideology and Behavior Among the Elite.* New York: Columbia University Press.

Bourdieu, Pierre. 1977. *Outline of a Theory of Practice.* New York: Cambridge University Press.

---------------. 1990. *The Logic of Practice.* Stanford: Stanford University Press.

---------------. 1991. *Language and Symbolic Power.* Cambridge, Harvard University Press.

---------------. 1998. *Practical Reason: On the Theory of Action.* Stanford: Stanford University Press.

Giddens, Anthony. 1984. *The Constitution of Society: Outlines of a Theory of Structuration.* Berkeley: University of California Press.

---------------. 1981-85. *A Contemporary Critique of Historical Materialism,* 2 Vols. Berkeley: University of California Press.

---------------. 1990. *The Consequences of Modernity.* Stanford: Stanford University Press.

---------------. 1991. *Modernity and Self-Identity.* Stanford: Stanford University Press.

Joseph, Suad. 1994. "Brother/Sister Relationships: Connectivity, Love, and Power in the Reproduction of Patriarchy in Lebanon," *American Ethnologist* 21(1):50-73.

Moore, Henrietta. 1994. *A Passion for Difference.* Bloomington: Indiana University Press.

Scott, James C. 1990. *Domination and the Arts of Resistance: Hidden Transcripts*. New Haven: Yale University Press.

THE ABSENT FATHER

JOSETTE G. ABDALLA

Introduction

This research investigates whether father-deprived populations form a different father concept than that formed by children in father-present families; and how gender, socio-economic status, cause of father deprivation, and presence or absence of a father substitute impact on the father concept. Group 1 includes forty father-deprived five to seven-year-old boys and girls, group 2 forty non-father-deprived but otherwise comparable children, and group 3 twenty-five older siblings of the children in group 1. The Children's Apperception Test and the Thematic Apperception Test were the projective techniques used to identify the father concept among the children (groups 1 and 2), and the older siblings (group 3) respectively. Results demonstrate that the father concept is affected when the absence occurs during childhood. Social and economic factors influence the formation of the father concept. Females generally seem to be less affected by father absence than males, and greater impairment seems to be present when the father's absence is due to divorce, desertion, or separation than when it is due to death, The availability of father surrogates seems to be important for boys who are father-deprived.

Father Concept in Father-deprived Populations

Every interaction in a child's life has an impact on the child's social, psychological, moral, and cognitive development, and the family is considered a primary and dynamic forum that involves dynamic relationships in which familial patterns of interaction may play a significant role in forming the child's primary and personality traits and behavioral patterns (Mussen, Conger, Kagan, and Huston 1990; Snyder and Patterson 1987).

Investigation of the father's role, in particular, in the family dynamics, and the subsequent effect his active or passive interaction, presence, or absence have on the child's emotional, cognitive, personality, and other aspects of development, including the conceptualizing of the paternal concept, is of interest to applied psychologists. In traditional families, for example, where fathers play the expected idealized role, the child develops a certain concept of the father as representative of authority, protection, security, as influential in relationships with others, and as impacting sexual identification or gender identity (Sutton-Smith, Rosenberg, and Landy 1968). Deviation from the idealized family structure and dynamics may modify this father concept. Cause for deprivation, quality, and quantity of pre- and post- absence relationship and involvement with child and other family members, age of child at deprivation, gender of child, family context and dynamics, socio-economic status, or presence or absence of father substitute are among the variables impacting the child's father concept (Serbin and Sprafkin 1986).

The Egyptian society is a patriarchal one, and both religion and society endow the father with a significant sense of authority, power, security, and decision making. Consequently, a certain father concept is formed in the minds of Egyptians, and this concept is expected to be in line with the role the father is expected to play in the lives of the various family members. Therefore, when father absence occurs due to any of the traditional (divorce, separation, death) or untraditional (having more than one wife, working in other Arab countries, imprisonment) reasons, this absence is bound to impact on the father concept formed in the minds of the offspring of the absent father.

This research will attempt to identify the father concept formed by father-deprived populations and compare it with that of comparable father-present populations (see Abdalla 1988). Variables such as gender, socio-economic status (SES), cause of father deprivation, and presence or absence of a father substitute will be considered.

The hypotheses investigated include:
1. The father concept among father-deprived children is different from that among father-present children.
2. The father concept among father-deprived children is affected by the gender of the child.
3. The father concept among father-deprived children is affected by the cause of the father absence.

4. The father concept among father-deprived children is affected by the presence or absence of a father substitute.

Participants in the Research

The sample is composed of three groups:

Group 1 includes forty father-deprived children, aged 5 to 7, to identify their father concept. Of these, 28 are boys and 22 girls. Fourteen are from a high SES, 15 average SES, and 11 low SES. Twenty-seven have father substitutes in the form of a step-father, uncle, grandfather, or older brother.

Group 2 includes forty non-father-deprived but otherwise comparable children, also to identify their father concept. This means that these participants also range between 5 and 7 years of age. Here too 28 are boys, and 22 girls. Fourteen are from a high SES, 15 average SES, and 11 low SES.

Group 3 includes older siblings of the father-deprived group of children in order to compare their father concept with that of their younger siblings in the same family, social context, and economic class. This group of participants at the time of conducting the research ranged between 14 and 18 years of age and had been deprived of their fathers after they had outgrown their early childhood (i.e. after they were 10 years old). Of these, 12 were male and 13 female. Seven were from a high SES, 8 average SES, and 10 a low SES.

Research Tools

The following tests were used:

1. The Children's Apperception Test (CAT). This is a projective technique that is used to elicit the themes operationally defined for the identification of the father concept. It involves administering 10 of the total pack of cards to the children in groups 1 and 2. Each participant is expected to recount a story for each of the cards exposed to the participant, and the test administrator is expected to make sure that the pictures are administered in a certain order and that the stories told by the participants are complete and appropriate for analysis. These cards are selected on the basis of their being the most appropriate in terms of time, gender, and content to elicit the underlying themes that implied in each of the pictures (Morgan and Murray, 1935).

2. The Thematic Apperception Test (TAT). This projective technique is similar to the CAT but is appropriate for use among the older participants (group 3). Ten pictures were also selected and administered to each of the subjects in this group, and as in the case of the CAT the choice of cards was based on their appropriateness for time, gender, and underlying themes (Morgan and Murray 1935).

Both the CAT and the TAT are well known and extensively used projective techniques. This means that these two measures are used to assess indirectly the traits or characteristics that the researcher wants to investigate. They are based on the idea that the subject is shown a series of pictures in a sequential order. Each picture elicits a certain theme based on the content of the picture. The subject then tells a story about the picture and the researcher analyzes the content of the pictures (both separately and as a whole) to formulate a certain profile of the themes being investigated. In both tests, the main themes identified were: the father as a source of authority and security, how he is viewed as influential in relationships with others, and his impact on moral development and sexual identification or gender identity. These two projective techniques are useful because they can be administered cross-culturally and, once the same analytic procedures are applied for comparison of responses, the results obtained can be considered reliable and valid.

3. The Socio-Economic Status Inventory for the Egyptian Family (Abdel-Ghaffar and Ashoush 1990). This inventory is typically used to identify the SES of the families of all the participants included in the sample. It gives a detailed analysis of four dimensions including aspects and level of education, housing conditions, and economic and social status, and gives the SES assessment in a numerical format.

4. The Structured Interview. School teachers, supervisors, and/or other persons who are familiar with the family background of the participants in the research were interviewed. The main goal of the interview is to identify the appropriate persons meeting the qualifications necessary for inclusion in each of the three groups included in the sample.

Research Method

1. The first task of the researcher was to gain access to schools representing different SESs, and to become familiar with teachers and supervisors of elementary forms 1 and 2 to identify the children who could fit into groups 1 and 2 of the sample.
2. With the help of the teachers and supervisors, the researcher conducted structured interviews to get the information necessary to identify :
    a. the SES of each child.
    b. the father-deprived and father-present children.
    c. the cause of father absence.
    d. the onset of father absence (i.e. to ensure that it occurred prior to the child's first birthday).
    e. whether any of the father-deprived children (i.e. those included in group 1) had older siblings who were not deprived of their fathers during the early childhood (to be included in group 3).
3. The researcher enlisted the help of the teachers and supervisors to allow her and/or her assistants to administer the CAT to the participants in groups 1 and 2, and to make contact with the older siblings (group 3) to administer the TAT
4. Official permission was obtained once the initial contacts had been made with the school officials to clarify the purpose of the research and to get school, teacher, and parental approval before administering any of the tests.
5. Selecting participants, obtaining permission, and administering the tests took about 5 months.
6. The contents of the CAT and TAT were analyzed, and based on this information, the hypotheses were investigated.

Results

Results of hypothesis # 1. The father concept among father-deprived children is different from that among father-present children.

Comparison of the responses made by the participants in groups 1 and 3 indicates that the father concept seems to be different when the absence occurs during early childhood than when it does so after the period of childhood. Several differences can be identified as the result of comparing groups 1, 2, and 3. For example, particularly in the cases of the younger children representing group 1 and who do not have a father substitute, it seems that the concept these children formulate regarding the father as representative of authority or security is not father-confined and is apparently more related to the current head of household who is actively involved in limit-setting, whether this is the mother or someone else. The pattern of interaction between this person and the other members in the household, including the child, is what the child digests and represents to himself or herself as being the concept of authority and security. Paternal involvement in limit-setting and providing of security also seems to be associated with self-esteem. Consequently, early father child relationships are particularly important for the child's self-esteem. Correspondingly, the responses from the older siblings' stories reveal that when the father had a presence during childhood, even if it was some time before, the result of this paternal interest and consistent participation contributed to the child's positive self confidence and self-esteem. The older siblings seem to have a more successful emotional and interpersonal adjustment, although the sex-role development appeared to be retarded or unfavorably affected in the cases in which the father was reported as having played what is considered a feminine role at home.

The younger father-deprived children produced significantly more father fantasies on the projective test than did either the control or the older siblings' groups. These fantasies either had an idealized or a punitive content, or both. The nature of the specific fantasy depended on the developmental phase of the child, on how the mother referred to the relationships at home during the father's presence, and on his impact on the family prior to his absence. Most of the children saw the father as an object of love and admiration (and thus important for identification), or as someone powerful and omnipotent (and therefore either as a protector or as a punishing, inhibiting, or castrating figure). They experienced greater inner anxiety on separation from their mothers, and more negative reactions to strangers than did the participants in either groups 2 or 3. Paternal deprivation also seems to interfere with the development of successful peer relationships. Father-deprived children reveal internal apprehensions of their being less popular and having less satisfying peer relationships than father-present children do.

Sex-appropriate behavior is very important in the formation of friendships among elementary school children, and the responses of some of the older siblings revealed that the presence of a warm father-child relationship established early in childhood was important in fostering well-adjusted development and, conversely, when the father was reported to have been hostile, rejecting, or maladjusted, the retarding influence took the form of less assertiveness. This could be because these children could not identify with the father, lacked a secure masculine orientation, and formed a father concept that was incongruous with that which usually depicts self-security, autonomy, and enhancement of peer and interpersonal relationships. Their peer relationships are not as satisfying as those that father-present children have.

Social class also seems to be affected or to be influential in the process of concept formation. Girls from a low SES in families in which the father is absent or ineffectual reveal a tendency to develop derogatory attitudes towards males. Father-present children and older siblings seem to have more ability to deal with differences of opinion and to consider more than one side of an argument or issue. Probing into the possible causes for this capability leads one to hypothesize that this is due to the presence of two adult authority figures with similar but different expectations and opinions regarding the child's behavior. Fathers are expected to serve as models and disciplinarians who contribute to the general family climate. Therefore, being father-deprived modifies this model and subsequently affects the child's behavior, as well as affective, social, and developmental adjustment.

Results of hypothesis # 2. The father concept among father-deprived children is affected by the gender of the child.

Females generally seem to be less affected by father absence than males, and have different father role expectations based on family and societal context, i.e. socio-economic class, gender of child, age, and other intervening variables. There is, however, some evidence supporting the conclusion that girls are at least as much influenced in their social and heterosexual development by father absence as are boys. The extent and direction of the differential impact of father absence on males and females probably varies with respect to which dimensions of personality are considered. Father absence seems to interfere with the girl's feminine development and her overall heterosexual adjustment.

Compared with the father-present boys, the father-absent boys are less aggressive and also demonstrate less sex-role differentiation. The father-separated children tend to produce an idealistic and feminine fantasy picture of the father when compared with the control children, who elaborate their father's aggressive tendencies. Consequently, their responses in the cards show that they tend to behave in an exaggerated masculine manner, or, conversely, at other times in a highly feminine manner. In addition, father-absent children tend to be less assertively aggressive and independent in their peer relations than the boys who have not been separated from their fathers. Father separation therefore seems to be associated with compensatory masculinity. That is, they manifest less projective sex role behavior, tend to be more dependent on their peers, and are less internally smooth and assertive.

Lower class father-absent boys demonstrate a tendency towards acting-out and antisocial behavior, and probably behave in this manner in an attempt to prove that they are masculine. Father-absent girls in this same socio-economic category do not seem to be unusually inhibited in their development of sex-typed interests or perceptions of the incentive value of the feminine role. The father absence seems to have more effect on the girl's ability to function in interpersonal and heterosexual relationships than it does on her sex-role preference.

The father-absent girls also seems to have some difficulty in coping with aggressive impulses. The expression of guilt following transgression, acceptance of blame, role conformity, and moral values seemed to be less prevalent among father-absent boys, but it did not appear that there were differences between boys and girls in the area of moral development.

The father-absence effects seem to be generally more pervasive for males than for females.

It may be that as the result of the formation of the father concept based on the previous circumstances, father-absent boys experience psychological difficulties in interacting with males. However, the notion that girls raised without fathers reject their femininity is controversial.

As for the group of older siblings who had not been deprived of their fathers during early childhood, the extent to which the father was viewed as head of the household appears to have been the influencing factor impacting on how the offspring conceives the father and thereby influences the sex-role development of the children.

Hypothesis # 3. The father concept among father-deprived children is affected by the cause of the father absence.

The reason the father is absent affects how the child views the role of the father in the family dynamics and how he is involved in the processes of implementing discipline, security, integrating the family members together and with other members in society. It also draws the picture of what is morally correct or wrong, and clarifies the sex role or gender identity of the offspring.

Responses of some of the older siblings who were deprived of their fathers after childhood because of divorce or separation revealed the formation of a father concept that included negative conceptualizations of the role of the father in terms of his importance and efficiency in providing stability, security, relaxed and clear relations among the family members. It also revealed a haziness as to what the role expectations of the various family members were, and when it appeared that there had been conflict or tension before the absence the father concept was less stereotyped. As for the younger children, it was clear from their responses that the current family dynamics had the greater impact on their psychological, emotional, and personality adjustment, and the role implications were in line with the societal and family expectations. If these were clear, then the adjustment was easier because it meant that the father concept they had formed individually was in line with the concept imposed by society. The responses to the cards that contained less anxiety, role confusion, or clear moral standards reflected that the adults in the family had handled the explanation for the father absence in a manner that downplayed shame, conflict, anxiety, social or economic upheaval, or rejection. Some of the responses from the subjects in groups 2 and 3 revealed that the presence of the father per se was no guarantee of adequate fathering, and that the quality of the father-child relationship was a more important variable than the mere physical presence of the father.

The reason for the father's absence and the ways in which the mother deals with the child also seem to influence moral development. Greater impairment seems to be found when the father absence is caused by divorce, desertion, or separation than when it is due to death. The interpretation for this is probably in line with the previous arguments which imply that when the mother and family of the child accept the absence (and in the case of death there is a fatalistic acceptance, and no personal implications or justifications can be introduced) it is easier to handle the situation. In the cases where there is divorce or separation, there are controversial points of view regarding who was involved in causing the absence, and different points of view are usually presented regarding possibilities in having handled the situation to have similar or different outcomes. All of these possible interpretations may impact negatively on the human context surrounding the child, which will, in turn, impact on the child and how he or she views the absent father, and consequently, how he or she adjusts to the father's absence.

Hypothesis # 4. The father concept among father-deprived children is affected by the presence or absence of a father substitute.

The analysis of the content of the cards reveals that boys raised without fathers or father substitutes tend to be either less masculine in their sex-role preferences and behavior, or else may exhibit compensatory masculinity. They seem to have what is normally referred to as feminine cognitive styles. Lack of opportunity to observe meaningful male-female relationships in childhood seems to make it more difficult for the father-absent female to develop the interpersonal skills necessary for adequate heterosexual adjustment.

The availability of a father surrogate seems to be important for children with absent fathers. Effective father surrogates can be salient or influential models, and positively influence the child's development.

Discussion

Although mothers are almost universally assigned primary responsibility for the care of the infant, the evidence reviewed indicates that most infants become attached to both parents in infancy. The important question relates to the nature of the mother- and father-infant relationships rather than to quibbles about their existence or relative importance. Although both fathers and mothers are traditionally assigned certain stereotyped roles, play appears to be a prominent characteristic of the father-infant interaction, whereas caretaking is more outstanding in the mother-infant interaction. The child constructs an expectation of its father as a person with whom interaction is pleasurable and stimulating. This enhances the child's desire to have commerce with the world in which the father immerses himself, and over which he exercises competence, and thus the child begins to explore the wider social system of which the father is the most accessible representative. As the more influential parent in this context, the father also serves as the medium through which the values and role demands of the social system are encountered and internalized.

An affectionate father-son relationship allows one to predict the son's masculinity. This may mean that the father's satisfaction with his gender role which is being observed by his child is not being tapped by the measures of masculinity, which, at best, employ a stereotyped definition of masculinity. The father also appears to play a major role in the sex role adoption of the young girl by encouraging feminine behavior and by providing a salient male figure whose behavior she learns to complement.

Absence of a father can have serious consequences for the sex-role, moral, and intellectual development, and personality adjustment of his children. Nurturing, competent, and available fathers positively influence their sons' and daughters' psychological functioning, whereas various forms of paternal deprivation are often related to difficulties in children's emotional, cognitive and interpersonal development. The length of the father absence and the age of onset of absence are important variables, and the results of this research are in line with those from previous studies that show that the longer the absence, and the younger the child at the onset of his absence, the more emotionally disturbed the personality is, and the more inadequate the moral development. When children do not have the opportunity to interact with adequate role models as represented by the father figure, father-daughter and father-son relationships may be affected.

The father's emotional support of other members of the child's social network--particularly the wife-mother--is another indirect effect of paternal parenting consequences. Consequently, his absence must leave an impact on the emotional stance of the family members, and how the family views and refers to his role prior to the absence and how this is seen as being affected by his absence are among the important intervening variables impacting on the children's social and emotional adjustment.

It is difficult to determine and understand the precise role of fathers because it is difficult to evaluate the consequences of father absence per se. There are far too many other variables that confound the findings, including reactions of other family members in his absence, his relationship to the mother and child before his departure, the economic conditions of the family, the child's age upon father deprivation, the reason for his leaving, and the support system available. Even the birth order of the children of each sex can influence the impact of the father's absence (Vandell, Wilson, and Whalen 1981).

The results of this research are clear and conclusive. The father concept of father-deprived children is different from that of father-present children. However, the extent of this difference depends on the surrounding variables and factors that have been highlighted in this research.

References

Abdalla, J.A. 1988. "Father absence: its effect on cognitive and personality development." PhD dissertation in Psychology, Ain Shams University.

Abdel-Ghaffar, A.S., and I. Ashoush. 1990. *The Socio-Economic Status Inventory for the Egyptian Family*. Cairo: Ain Shams University Press.

Morgan, C.D., and H.A. Murray. 1935. "The Thematic Apperception Test" in Davison, G.C., and J.M. Neale, *Abnormal Psychology* (7th ed.). New York: Wiley and Sons, Inc.

Mussen, P.H., J.J. Conger, J. Kagan, and A.C. Huston. 1990. *Child Development and Personality* (7th ed.). New York: Harper Collins.

Serbin, L.A., and C. Sprafkin. 1986. "The Salience of Gender and the Process of Sex Typing in Three-to-seven-year-old Children," *Child Development* 57:1188-1199.

Snyder, J., and G. Patterson. 1987. "Family Interaction and Delinquent Behavior" in H.C.Quay, ed., *Handbook of Juvenile Delinquency*, pp. 216-243. New York: Wiley.

Sutton-Smith, B., B.G. Rosenberg, and F. Landy. 1968. "The Interaction of Father Absence and Sibling Presence on Cognitive Abilities," *Child Development* 39:1213-1221.

Vandell, D.L., K.E. Wilson, K.E., and W.I. Whalen. 1981. "Birth Order and Social Experience Differences in Infant Peer Interaction," *Developmental Psychology* 17:438-445.

SOCIAL CHANGE AND ADOLESCENT-PARENT DYNAMICS IN EGYPT

SAHAR AL-TAWILA, BARBARA IBRAHIM, AND HIND WASSEF

Introduction

Generational differences in outlook and attitude appear to be a universal feature of human society, enshrined in folklore and native wisdom. Youth and their parents are expected to relate to each other in predictable ways based on their different positions along the life course. A distance or 'gap' between the generations is universally presumed, with youth less bound by tradition and more open to new ideas. When they grow to adulthood and eventually take up the parental position, these roles are then expected to shift in relation to a new generation of youth. While undoubtedly containing a partial truth, this approach does not give sufficient weight to the influence of unique historical features of any given era. Other research has posited a distinctive 'mark' on each new generation of youth, as their identities are shaped by the forces and ideas circulating during formative stages of their maturation (Neyzi 2000, Abdalla 2000). Rarely, however, has anyone tried to combine these perspectives, by looking at how young people relate to their parents in the context of profound societal changes at a given historical juncture.

In this paper we address the issue of generational differences between young Egyptians who are in late adolescence (ages 16 to 19) and their parents, most of whom are roughly between ages 40 and 50. We are interested in how the economic and social changes that are transforming Egypt affect parent-adolescent dynamics at the end of the 1990s. Is there a recognizable generation gap between adolescents and their parents, and if so, what types of families are most likely to experience it? Are different parent-adolescent communication styles related to greater distance in attitudes and behavior? Can we measure with any assurance the attitude gaps *within* as well as *between* generations? How does gender interact with age and generation to create distances in attitude and aspiration? These are important topics as Egypt grapples with its largest ever cohort of youth and attempts to integrate them into a rapidly changing social reality.

The availability of a unique data set, based on a 1997 household survey, enables us to explore some of these issues among a nationally representative sample of youth and their parents. Most studies have looked at these issues using clinical data or much smaller samples in one location (Ibrahim and Wassef 2000). We are interested in exploring the possibilities inherent in survey data to provide more rigorous analysis of changing generational dynamics.

Families As Intensive Arenas of Generational Interaction

In the Arab world, and Egypt is no exception, the family is still a central unit of society (Young and Shami 1997, Singerman and Hoodfar 1996). Individuals derive much of their identity and standing from familial associations. While nuclear families have increased in some areas, extended families persist and regardless of residential patterns take on important new roles, such as providing support for working mothers. Individuals almost never live alone in Egypt, and people come to define themselves in terms of and in relation to close family members (Joseph 1993). Members of a family or household also interact within power relationships and hierarchies that they consent to or redefine daily.

Social change and conflict is then intensified at the family level, since expectations of support and solidarity are high, as are norms of social control. Within the family setting, young people occupy a crucial position. They straddle and must accommodate two roles: that of conveying valued societal norms into the future, but also of opening the family to social change and new ideas from the outside. (Rosenmayr and Allerbeck 1979). Young people in Egypt are rarely able to live and function independently. They need the social, economic and emotional support of the family and their parents, but they are experiencing a youth that is radically different from that of their parents. How does this play itself out in parent-adolescent interaction?

We begin from the premise that 'generation gaps' are not universally the same across societies, communities, or time periods. In pre-modern societies, continuity of experience characterized the generations, minimizing differences and facilitating communication. At the other end of the spectrum, societies or communities which have reached a post-industrial stage have typically enshrined fast-paced change as part of the culture. They have already achieved large gains in education and standard of living for most of the population. We would expect, therefore, that a degree of similarity rather than extreme difference characterizes the two generations and allows them to accommodate to change and to each other with a relative lack of friction. In this respect, then, both pre- and post-change situations are somewhat similar with respect to generational continuity.

It is in societies or communities currently undergoing major transformation that we expect to find larger disparities of attitude and behavior between the generations. In those situations, young people will have markedly different experiences from their parents, as education replaces illiteracy and global ideas impinge on more localized worldviews. This potential for disjuncture between the experiences of the two generations is likely to be expressed in a divergence of attitudes and preferences. Those differences may in turn lead to conflicted relations within the family and/or the community.

Comparative data would be required in order to test these ideas across societies. However, within a society like Egypt it is possible to examine population groups that have experienced differential exposure to the rapid changes underway in the country. Differential exposure could result from many factors; those we expect to be most significant are socio-economic status, region of residence, and proximity to metropolitan centers. We can therefore think about three groupings of population (represented by categories of households) on which to test our propositions: those still relatively unexposed to change, through poverty and residence in more isolated settings governed by restrictive cultural norms; those experiencing heightened change by virtue of increased exposure to education, migration to urban centers, and transformation in economic roles; and those who have passed through these changes in an earlier era, represented by urban residence and high education and occupation levels.

What are the intervening factors that mediate between societal change and parent-adolescent dynamics? Of all the changes in Egypt during the past 40 years, exposure to education has perhaps had the most profound transformational effect. Education has moved from being a privilege of the urban minority to a nearly universal and taken-for-granted right. Net primary stage enrollment in 1994-96 was 98% for boys and 88% for girls in the ages of basic education.(World Bank 2000). Enrollment rates for the age group 8-11 in 1997 was found to be 90%, declining at age 14 to 73%, the age which signals the transition from the basic compulsory level to secondary non-compulsory level (El-Tawila, et al. 1999). With education comes exposure beyond the confines of the family, and tools to access a wider world through books and newspapers. As young people stay in school longer and jobs require longer skill preparation time, ages of marriage have also risen significantly. These and countless other related changes have created a more complex and longer period of adolescent transition today. So an illiterate woman who married at 16 in the late 1970s is more likely to have a daughter the same age today who is continuing in school, planning to work in a modern setting, and experiencing a world immeasurably different from that her mother inhabited as a teenager.

Education has long-term effects on the lives of men and women. Studies show that years of schooling have an impact on women's long-term fertility and age at marriage, decreasing the one and delaying the other. It also has an impact on attitudes toward a wide range of gender issues. Increased schooling was correlated with young people, but especially girls, being more likely to aspire to role sharing in their future marriages and more likely to oppose female circumcision (El-Tawila et al. 1999, Ibrahim et al. 2000).

Scholars have theorized that education exposes youth to peers and other adults on a mass scale, thus reducing the influence of parents and providing more opportunity for formation of youth sub-cultures (Mitterauer 1986 cited in Kiem 1994). By spatially separating young people from their families and providing an opportunity for young people to experience a different cognitive development from their parents, education is thought to widen the generation gap between youth and their parents. This hypothesis can readily be tested in developing countries where today youth are invariably better educated than their parents. Increased education also begins to reverse the social hierarchy within the household since young people see themselves, and older people may also see them, as superior based on their advanced education although their age should place them in an inferior and submissive position vis-à-vis their elders (Buchholt and Mai 1994).

Along with mass schooling, another important agent of change is the mass media (Berger et al. 1973). It exposes young and old to a world that can sometimes be alien to their immediate community. In Egypt the media are state sponsored, and so are a useful tool for instituting social change in the direction of government policies. Examples are introducing the idea of family planning in the 1980s, raising awareness about certain diseases or the need for child vaccinations, and encouraging citizens to vote. Television plays a powerful role in this process, particularly through evening drama serials. Lila Abu-Lughod (1998) discusses the ways in which rural villagers interact with the various images they see on television, ranging from westernized images and advertisements about certain commodities to representations of themselves as rural villagers via conceptions that are at times stereotyped and flawed.

A second basic proposition is that gender and generation are intricately entwined (Kandiyoti 1991). In a historically patriarchal society, men are presumed to have authority over women, but the young are also expected to show deference toward their elders. Boys can therefore expect to move from a position of relative subordination to one of relative dominance simply by virtue of the passage to adulthood. Girls, on the other hand, will transit from the subordinate status of youth to a similarly subordinate position in adulthood (Ibrahim et al. 1998). As one result, girls have more to gain from changes away from the 'traditional' gender arrangements, and therefore respond to those changes by embracing them to a greater degree than boys. We expect boys to display more entrenched gender role ideas, and be less likely to respond favorably to change, for the simple reason that they stand to lose power and authority in the process. For similar reasons, parents uphold traditional age and gender norms through authority vested in them by their senior positions in the hierarchy.

The within-generation differences between boys and girls during adolescence thus play themselves out by placing boys closer to the traditional attitudes of their parents' generation than girls. From the patriarchal and generational perspectives, girls experience their position in the family as one of low status and power. This may lead them to respond more readily to new ideas that hold a promise of more autonomy and to question traditional patterns. In doing so girls may find themselves alienated from the rest of the family to a greater extent than boys.

Specifically we put forward three related hypotheses for examination:

1. For both boys and girls, there is a significant inter-generational gap that reveals itself in the various ways members of the younger generation diverge by distancing themselves from their parents' experiences and views.

2. Within the young generation, girls show a higher level of divergence from their parents' views. They are more inclined toward 'modern' patterns of family formation and marriage relations. Boys and parents have more vested interests in maintaining the status quo in gender relations; thus boys display more similarity than girls to the gender role attitudes of the parents' generation.

3. Controlling for gender-based differentials, families experiencing heightened effects of social change will express more divergent attitudes between the generations; in turn, those differences will have a negative effect on family interaction.

Source of Data

The research program "Adolescence and Social Change in Egypt" (ASCE) had multiple objectives that cut across the socio-economic, cultural, and health dimensions of adolescent development. Given the lack of information available on this segment of the population in Egypt, the authors joined with a larger team of researchers to conduct a national survey that would provide comprehensive baseline data on adolescents.

In reality, adolescence has no clear-cut starting or ending point. The survey aimed at exploring various social and cultural understandings of this stage of life without imposing prior categories. A working definition of adolescence as the second decade of life, spanning the ages 10 to 19 was adopted. The survey design placed a strong emphasis on gender constructions of adolescent experiences. One major objective was to understand better how girls and boys experience adolescence differently, and how those patterns may translate into different attitudes, behaviors, and future opportunities.

The survey sample is a nationally representative, multi-stage, stratified, probability, cluster sample of adolescents. A total of 13,271 households were screened. The number of eligible households, defined as households with at least one member in the age range 10-19 years, amounts to 7,256 households. Using the Kish-grid, one adolescent from each sex was randomly selected from each eligible household. A total of 9,128 adolescents were successfully interviewed (4,354 boys and 4,774 girls)[1]. A quarter of the total randomly selected sample of adolescents was systematically sub-sampled for a second interview, focusing mainly on reproductive health and adolescents' gender-roles attitude (El-Tawila et al. 1999).

In this paper, the analysis is confined only to the group of adolescents who are 16-19 years old, never married and living in two-parent households. We chose this group because they have already passed the transitional phase of puberty and almost all have reached physical maturation. Education prospects are clearer for this group; some never attended school, others have already dropped out before reaching secondary education, some are continuing to secondary level, with the likelihood of continuing to university fairly predictable based on what type of secondary education track they followed[2]. This group is also legally recognized in the labor market, since the law in Egypt sets the minimum age of work at 15. It is thus plausible to expect that this group of young people have begun to have their own assessment of their social context and to formulate personal views in regard to future prospects and marriage. Most importantly for a study of generational dynamics, this group of young people are not affected by the complicating factors of single parenting or the remarriage of a parent, since they reside with both parents.

At the time of interview, 68 percent of 16-19 year old adolescents in the total national sample met these requirements, i.e. were not married and continued to live with both parents (2,162 adolescents representing 73

---

[1] The core instrument administered to selected adolescents had four main sections: educational history, prevalence and context of adolescent's economic participation, health perceptions and use of health services, and finally a detailed section on social integration and family relations.

[2] In Egypt, non-religious secondary education branches into two paths with very different prospects: 3-5 year vocational training programs with restricted access to higher education beyond this level, or, three years of general secondary program leading to university.

percent of boys and 63 percent of girls)[3]. Compared to all 16-19 year-olds in the sample, this selective group was slightly younger (more in the ages 16-17 than 18-19 among both sexes) and by definition more were never married, particularly among girls (100 percent of this group as opposed to 88 percent of all 16-19 year old girls). More of the selected girls were still in school (56 percent compared with 48 percent among all girls 16-19). Slightly fewer boys and girls in the selected sample were from Upper Egypt (25 percent compared with 28.5 percent overall) or from the lowest socio-economic status households (28 percent compared with 31 percent)[4].

Conceptual Framework

As we have framed this analysis, both intra- and inter-generation relations are seen as context-dependent outcomes. To assess the factors contributing to or decreasing a 'generation gap',we have constructed multivariate models that incorporate many standard background variables, but add other dimensions we believe are crucial to parent-adolescent relations. These include a measure of the socialization style at home--whether autocratic or more open to discussion and sharing of opinions--and a variable that measures where a particular family lies on the continuum of rapid social transformation that Egypt is experiencing. Figure 1 displays these relationships graphically.

---

[3] Out of 9,128 successfully interviewed adolescents in the age group 10-19, one-third (3,014 respondents) were 16-19 years old. This sub-sample includes 236 married adolescents and 616 cases 16-19, never married but not living with both parents. Excluding those two latter categories, the final sample size for the analysis presented here becomes 2,162 cases.

[4] In other words, our sub-sample only slightly under represents 16-19 year old adolescents from Upper Egypt and from the lowest socio-economic status households. A higher than average proportion of this group was not living with both parents because of marriage, work or study, or due to dissolution of parents' marriage. On the other hand, the sample over represents the attitudes of 16-19 year-old-girls who were still in school. Differences by work status and urban/rural type of residence were not pronounced.

Figure 1: Conceptual Framework of the Determinants and Dynamics of Intra and Inter-generation Gap

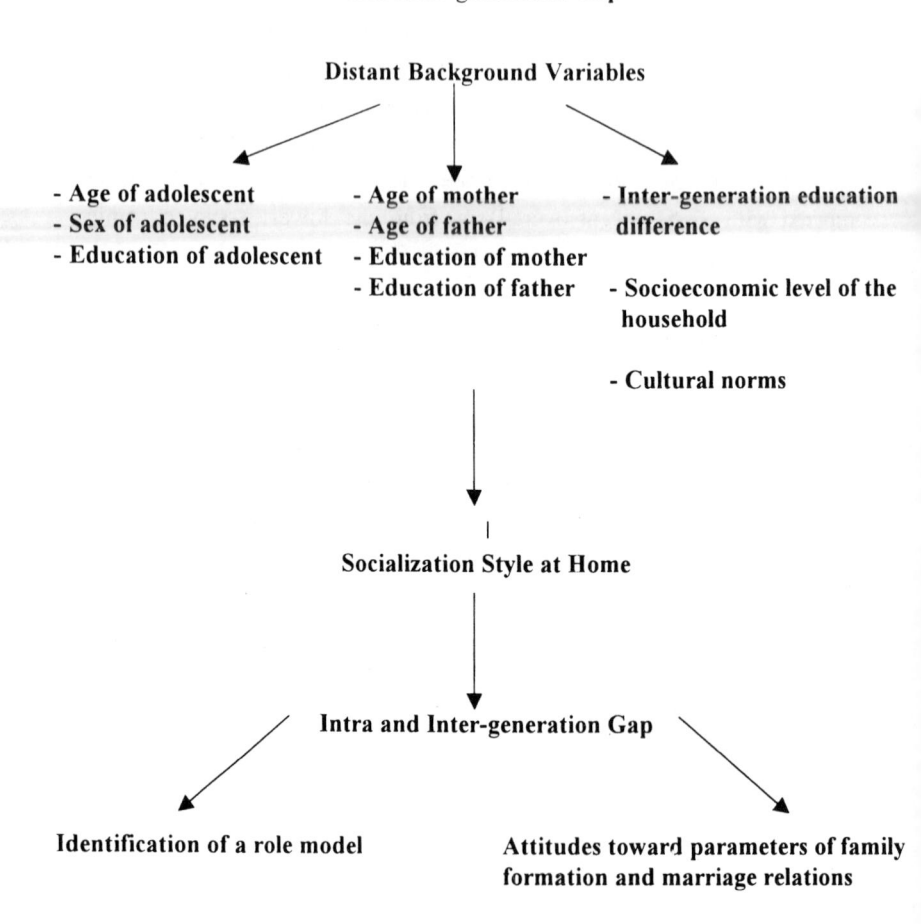

Distant Background Variables

- Age of adolescent
- Sex of adolescent
- Education of adolescent

- Age of mother
- Age of father
- Education of mother
- Education of father

- Inter-generation education difference
- Socioeconomic level of the household
- Cultural norms

↓

Socialization Style at Home

↓

Intra and Inter-generation Gap

Identification of a role model

Attitudes toward parameters of family formation and marriage relations

We propose that one way to measure the distance or 'gap' in intergenerational relations is to examine whether a parent figures in their child's repertoire of role models. Role model is defined as an individual the young person is attracted to and would most like to emulate; someone s/he admires for their attitudes, behavior or attributes. All adolescents interviewed in the ASCE survey were asked: "Who do you consider your role model (*namuthag igabi*), the person that you look up to and want to be like when you grow up?" Responses were then re-coded for purposes of this study into three categories--respondent identified either parent as a role model, respondent identified someone else as a role model, or respondent failed to identify any role model at all. Identification of either parent as a role model is taken as a proxy for convergence of ideas and goals with the parental generation. Among those diverging most from parents on this dimension are those who either have no role model or else seek models beyond the confines of the nuclear family by naming someone other than a parent as their role model.

The second indicator of inter-generation distance or gap is a construct that summarizes attitudes regarding the basic parameters of family formation and marriage relations. In the ASCE survey, older adolescents were asked questions regarding what they considered the best age and education difference (if any) between spouses. They were also asked their opinions concerning acceptable reasons for divorce. Another battery of questions measured gender-role attitudes regarding task sharing and decision-making between spouses[5]. These answers are then compared with attitudes or actual practices among the parents to assess the degree of convergence or divergence. Overall attitude distributions on items relating to the parental generation, when not available from the ASCE survey, are fortunately available in another national survey, the 1995 Egyptian Demographic and Health Survey (El-Zanaty et al. 1995). To the extent that responses of the younger generation diverge from the average experiences and attitudes of the parental generation, this is considered indicative of a distancing process between the two generations. We emphasize that this analysis compares the two generations at the aggregate level rather than creating comparisons of individual pairs of parents and adolescents.

---

[5] A more elaborate description of these dimensions among Egyptian adolescents is found in Ibrahim et al., 2000.

Table 1 lists the set of background (distant) explanatory variables that capture the individual characteristics of both adolescents and parents, as well as the socio-economic status of the household and surrounding culture of the community. For the younger generation, we expect that the effects of age and gender are crucial[6] as well as the effect of level of education attainment. We postulate that education will impact significantly on inter-generational dynamics by supporting the values inherent in social transformation. The impact should be positive if cultural norms in the family are already supportive of these values, or, if the experience of social transformation already led to more consistent 'high quality' attributes of family members. To the contrary, the postulated impact of education may become negative if prevalent conventions in the family are restrictive and the transformation resulting from increased education attainment among youth challenges the gender- and age-related power hierarchies within the family.

Region of residence is introduced as an indicator of the community culture around a family, with three sub-categories created, namely the urban governorates, Lower Egypt, and Upper Egypt. The three sub-categories are proxies for three different sets of cultural norms governing the attitudes and behaviors of both generations in each region. One dimension is varying degrees of cosmopolitanism, which is heightened in the urban governorates (mainly Cairo and Alexandria) and grossly depressed in Upper Egypt. The physical proximity of most of Lower Egypt to large metropolitan centers and its more rapid pace of development puts this region substantially ahead of Upper Egypt. That accelerated process of social change probably makes it easier to loosen conventional restrictive norms and adapt to contemporary ideas.

We believe that a third 'social transformation' variable may help to account for observed gaps between the generations in Egypt today. A new indicator was constructed that classifies families into three groups based on the stage they have reached in disengaging from a traditional social context and moving toward reintegrating into a more 'modern' context. The stage a

---

[6] Separate models are fitted for boys and girls to assess the gender differentials in responses within the younger generation and at the same time to control for these differentials later on in our appraisal of the inter-generation relations. Age of adolescents is already controlled since all adolescents included in this analysis are 16-19 years old.

family has reached in the social transformation process is measured by the difference in the education attainment of the adolescent and each parent. In the first group, both generations have little formal education; in the second group, the adolescent attainment is significantly higher than either parent; while in the third group both generations have achieved fairly high levels of education. This construct adds a relational dimension separate from the educational attainment of the adolescent and the parents individually. Our hypothesis is that, irrespective of gender differences, the inter-generation gap is significantly augmented among the middle group of families where the younger generation has acquired higher levels of education compared with their parents. We would also expect to find some signifcant differences in how group 1 and group 3 generations relate to one another.

We begin the analysis by examining how young people in Egypt select a role model to guide their passage to adulthood.

Table 1

Percent Distribution of Adolescents in the Sample by Distant Explanatory Variables Hypothesized to Impact Both Intra- and Inter-Generation Dynamics

Background variable	Boys	Girls
Education attainment of adolescent		
Never attended school	5.1	12.8
Dropped out before secondary*	29.2	23.2
Enrolled in/completed vocational secondary	42.4	37.6
Enrolled in/completed general secondary	23.4	26.5
Inter-generation education difference: father/adolescent		
Same low education	20.2	23.1
Adolescent's education is higher	68.1	61.5
Same high education**	11.6	15.5
Inter-generation education difference: mother/adolescent		
Same low education	12.4	19.2
Adolescent's education is higher	80.4	74.1
Same high education***	7.2	6.7
Mean age of mother	43.9	43.7
Mean age of father	51.2	51.3
Socio-economic status of the household		
Low	29.0	28.1
Middle	35.3	35.0
High	35.7	36.9
Region of residence		
Urban governorates	26.4	26.5
Lower Egypt	47.9	48.9
Upper Egypt	25.7	24.6
Total number of cases	1087	1075

* A small number of cases that dropped out after attending some but not all secondary schooling is included in this category.
** High education refers to secondary school level or higher.
*** See footnote 8.

Parents as a Role Model

In the national sample of adolescents 16-19 surveyed in 1997, when asked whom they admired and wanted to be like, fully one quarter failed to identify a role model at all. This suggests for a sizable number of young people a sadly limited horizon for relating to adults or envisioning their own futures. About 40 percent identified someone other than the parents, 11 percent reported an elder sibling, and 29 percent mentioned someone who was neither a parent nor a sibling. Among this latter group, a wide range of people were reported including well-known celebrities (singers, soccer players, famous leaders, or historic figures) or individuals the young person was in contact with regularly (a schoolteacher, an uncle, etc). Another group of about one-third of the young generation referred to either parent as the role model they looked up to and wanted to be like when they grew up. Adolescent boys and girls are equally likely to identify a parent as a role model (32.7 percent of boys and 36.3 percent of girls), and both are much more likely to name the father than the mother.

All adolescents who identified a role model were asked: "What do you like most about this person?" Table 2 shows the reasons for identifying parents or others as role models and suggests the likelihood of inter-generation convergence among adolescents who identified parents as role models. The majority of this group (86.7 percent) referred to the manners, attitudes, behavior, or strong character of the selected parent as the main attribute they admired. Identifying others (than parents) as a role model was also related to these innate personal characters but to a lesser degree (only 62.9 percent). Social standing and financial ability, which we can assume may have been lacking among their parents, also emerged in the responses of this group.

Table 2

Adolescents Responses Concerning What They Like Most About the Person Identified as Role Model

What they like most	Parents	Other (than a parent)
Manners, behavior, attitudes	57.6	42.3
Strong character	29.1	20.6
Social sptanding	4.0	17.8
Financial ability	0.2	2.5
Sub-total	**90.9**	**83.2**
Other reasons	9.1	16.8
Total	**100.0**	**100.0**

Individual and contextual factors influence boys and girls differently to appreciate parents and relate positively to them as role models (Table A, end of text). Education attainment and region of residence have a strong impact on how boys, but not girls, relate to their parents. Boys continuing in secondary education appreciate their parents almost twice as much as boys who left school before secondary. Also, boys in the urban governorates are 60% more likely to report parents as role model compared with boys in Lower or Upper Egypt. Boys appear to have aspirations that distance them from admiring their parents when residing in small town or rural areas.

Girls' perceptions and appreciation of parents on the other hand seem to be influenced more by the stage of social transformation than by other individual, socio-economic, or cultural factors. Boys are also significantly influenced by this factor, but not so unilaterally. Adolescents from families going through the second stage of transformation (where the adolescent's education attainment is higher than the father's) are the least likely to identify their parents as role models, while those from families which have already reached beyond this stage (where high education is shared by both generations) are the most likely to relate to parents as role models. This is consistent among boys and girls with some exceptions. Girls from families with poor education attainment in both generations, in particular among girls and fathers, are also unlikely to identify parents as role models. This is not the case among boys, who are almost equally and highly likely to look up to their fathers as long as they belong to consistent families on the education variable (early or late stages of transformation).

It is worth mentioning in this respect that boys from Lower Egypt, who are anticipated to be going through the heightened transformation process, are twice as likely as boys from other regions not to have a role model at all. Also, boys and girls who never attended school or did not continue to the secondary stage are significantly more likely not to have a role model at all, compared with those who did continue. Education thus plays an expected role in helping young people to observe and then consider the adult lives and achievements they might aspire to in the future.

Convergence of Views Related to the Parameters of Family Formation and Marriage Relations

Adolescents have the example of their parents' marriage before them as they begin to think and plan for their own new family. We were able to compare the actual situation of parents on several dimensions such as educational differences between the partners, sharing of household tasks, etc, with the parallel attitudes expressed by adolescents. Table 3 contrasts the attitudes of our sampled adolescents with the attitudes or actual experiences of the parents' generation along several dimensions related to marriage[7].

---

[7] Attitudinal data on the parameters of family formation and marriage relations were administered to one-quarter of the original sample. Hence, for the second part of the analysis, the sample size is reduceed to 516 cases.

Table 3

Attitudes of Never Married 16-19 Year-old Adolescents Living with Both Parents and the Attitudes or Actual Corresponding Experience among the Parents' Generation

Percent of adolescents who agree that:	Boys	Girls	Parents' generation experience/ attitudes*
- Both husband & wife should have the same level of education attainment	47.8	66.7	22.4**
- The age difference between husband & wife should be less than or equal to 5 years	94.2	85.9	46.6
- A girl should be circumcised before marriage	76.4	56.8	97.0***
- If a relative proposed and the father accepted, the daughter should comply	26.5	15.8	39.0****
- Both husband & wife should provide for the family	1.7	11.9	14.2
- Both husband & wife are responsible for watching children and playing with them	10.1	25.2	4.2
- Both husband & wife are responsible for helping children do homework	15.6	37.5	5.7
- Household budget should be a shared decision among husband & wife	53.3	74.7	74.8◊
- Wife is justified to file for divorce if husband beats her	73.7	60.4	47.4◊
- Wife is justified to file for divorce if husband ignores her opinions and views	54.1	47.4	24.6◊

* In this column, we report basically the percentages of parents from the ASCE survey whose actual marriage experience agrees with the statement.

** In fact, 40.5% of the parents of adolescents in our sample have equally no education and only 22.4% had ever attended school and acquired the same years of education. Since almost 90% of sampled adolescents have ever attended school, then their inclination toward equal education attainment among the spouses refers to equal years of schooling greater than zero.

*** Data not available from the ASCE survey, however, the EDHS (95) reported that 97% of ever married Egyptian women of reproductive age are circumcised, a rate that varied little with age.
**** Data not available from the ASCE survey, however, the EDHS(95) reported that 39% of ever married Egyptian women over 34 years old were married to a relative.
$^{◊}$ As reported in the EDHS(95).

Ibrahim et al. (1998), in their analysis of the ASCE data, highlighted the high convergence of adolescents and parents, girls and boys, toward traditional gender-segregated expectations concerning who should be responsible for specific household chores. (Gender differences were more pronounced regarding views on appropriate styles of couple decision-making.) Our analysis here indicates gender differences as well, but further finds that adolescents overall show a significant level of divergence from their parents' generation on important aspects related to the formation of a new family and relations within marriage. The younger generation express preferences for marriages that match spousal characteristics like education, and tolerate less traditional characteristics and roles. To a striking degree, attitudes of adolescent girls in our sample diverge from the average experience of their parents' generation (Table 3). The only exceptions are convergence on matters related to family finances and to a lesser degree on justifications to seek divorce. On the other hand, while adolescent boys do not exactly replicate the experiences and attitudes of the older generation, they display an overall higher level of convergence with parents than do adolescent girls. The five dimensions where this was significant include: differences in education attainment, girls' circumcision, marriage to a relative, caring for children, and helping children with schoolwork.

To further test this large gender difference in the inter-generation gap, we conducted a multiple classification analysis where the dependent variable is a continuum reflecting the extent of inter-generation divergence of each group. This composite indicator of a generation gap is based on the differences between the attitudes of adolescents toward the ten aspects of family formation and marriage relations and the average experience of the parent-generation presented in Table 3. Only significant explanatory variables were retained in the final model. Table B displays these results.

The difference between the average score on the constructed index among the two sexes is statistically significant, and reinforces the conclusion that girls have a higher degree of divergence with the parental generation overall than do boys and parents.

Among adolescent girls, continuing to general secondary education and residing in an urban governorate are strong correlates of diverging attitudes and preferences when compared with the parents actual experience in family formation and marriage relations. In other words, this generation of girls prefers and probably aspires to marriage arrangements not typically present in their parents' generation. The two groups (adolescent girls, continuing to general secondary education and residing in an urban governorate) emphasize equal education attainment among spouses, undermine female circumcision and consanguineous marriages, stress sharing, and express a higher degree of rejection of violence toward wives (Table 4).

Among boys, it is not simply their own educational attainment but rather the differences in education among the two generations that appear significant in relation to divergent views. Attaining a low level of education consistent with the father's correlates with even *more* conventional attitudes than the average experience of the older generation. Attainment of high levels of education equivalent to the mother's and residence in an urban governorate are both related to divergence from the experience of the older generation in the direction of a more egalitarian pattern. High socio-economic status contributes to divergence between boys and the parents' generation in a pattern that is on the whole more egalitarian, although not in the areas of women's employment or sharing roles between spouses.

Table 4

Attitudes of Selected Sub-Groups of Adolescents Regarding Parameters of Family Formation and Marriage Relations

% who agree that:	Boys having				Girls in	
	(1)	(2)	(3)	(4)	(5)	(4)
Both husband & wife should have the same level of education attainment	36.9	62.8	50.5	60.5	73.5	77.0
The age difference between husband & wife should be less than or equal to 5 years	100.0	90.2	90.6	94.0	79.9	82.5
A girl should be circumcised before marriage	95.9	58.5	69.3	70.1	25.9	20.5
If a relative proposed and the father accepted, the daughter should comply	64.2	-	21.6	18.3	0.7	1.0
Both husband & wife should provide for the family	-	-	-	-	29.1	29.4
Both husband & wife are responsible for watching children and playing with them	-	-	11.4	23.5	41.7	47.6
Both husband & wife are responsible for helping children do homework	31.0	33.2	20.3	26.0	42.3	45.7
Household budget should be a shared decision among husband & wife	52.6	52.4	48.5	55.9	80.9	87.5
Wife is justified to file for divorce if husband beats her	64.2	80.5	81.4	86.5	71.4	74.0
Wife is justified to file for divorce if husband ignores her opinions and views	56.5	55.8	59.9	66.4	40.8	47.5
Number of cases	21	21	96	72	90	69

(1) Same low education as father
(2) Same high education as mother
(3) High socio-economic status
(4) Urban governrate
(5) General secondary

- Number of cases less than five

Inter-Generational Dynamics: Links Between an Adolescent's Background and the Socialization Style at Home

The previous analysis focused on establishing an inter-generation gap and examined some of its correlates. Here we look more closely at aspects of family dynamics that may lead to the generational differences. In addition to the direct influence, the 'distant' background variables--education level, ages of parents, and family status--are expected to exert an indirect impact on the inter-generation gap through a major intervening variable, the socialization style at home. Socialization style refers to the degree and quality of interaction between adults and the younger generation, whether it involves listening, dialogue, and taking account of young people's views, or is more unidirectional, distant, and authoritarian on the part of parents. The ASCE questionnaire included a battery of questions to capture one or more dimensions of this crucial determinant. In this analysis we restrict ourselves to four measures that were asked of all respondents in the sample.

The first indicator measured the adolescent's report about how dialogue is conducted within his or her family and how parents respond. We have called this dimension "family integration" and divided it into two categories: one if the adolescent says he or she usually voices opinions/ideas/ suggestions that are respected and considered by parents or the other if the adolescent does not voice opinions on family issues or, if s/he does, those opinions are dismissed by parents. The first category is comparable to the concept psychologists term a *democratic socialization style*, although not identical, as we do not have data on how this impacts the way decisions are actually taken; i.e., whether the democratic mode of socialization is followed through or overruled.

The second indicator relates to the level of parent--adolescent communication, classified as either high or low. Adolescents classified into the high communication group reported that they communicate with either parent about their problems with friends and with other family members. The other group communicated one type of problem but not both, or reported no communication with either parent over these problems. We believe that communication with parents about problems with friends is a particularly important variable because it suggests that an adolescent is sharing with the parent issues that are in his/her exclusive domain. Parents will not necessarily know about their son's or daughter's problems with friends unless the young person tells them, since much of the interaction with peers may take place beyond the home at school, work, or leisure.

The third indicator aimed at capturing exposure to socialization channels other than family members through mass media, consisting of books, radio, and television. While not directly controlled by parents, this indicator is probably a reflection of how adolescent activities reflect the value parents place on reading and being exposed to modern mass media. Adolescents in the ASCE survey were asked about all the different activities they had carried out on the day before the interview, including reading non-school related books, listening to the radio, and watching television. Based on this information, we divided the sample into two groups: adolescents exposed to one type of media only or with no exposure at all to the mass media on the day before the interview, and adolescents exposed to at least two media types.

The final indicator was physical mobility beyond the home, which had two categories: adolescents not allowed to meet with friends at all or allowed to exchange home visits only, and adolescents allowed to meet and go out with friends beyond the neighborhood of residence. This indicator is useful in showing the degree of restriction imposed on adolescents by parents and, by extension, how much autonomy adolescents are granted in finding a space of their own in which they can interact with peers. Particularly for girls in Egypt, this also indicates a level of trust and autonomy that is consistent with accepting more cosmopolitanism. We expect that allowing girls more physical mobility will be associated with a later stage of social transformation and/or with parents having fairly high levels of education.

Family integration (style of dialogue in the family) is strongly tied to several of a girl's background characteristics (Table C). Integration for girls increases significantly with higher levels of education attainment, a relationship that is independent from the education of parents. The highest levels of integration are found among girls who have attained general secondary education. It is not clear which direction this influence moves, whether girls who are integrated with their families are able to lobby successfully for longer periods of education, or whether higher comunication/integration comes as a reward to these girls for their personal attributes and scholastic achievement. Interestingly, integration of girls is highest in Lower Egypt, where we hypothesized a faster pace of social change than elsewhere, and also in families with consistent education attainment between the two generations.

For boys, family integration appears to be more influenced by community or cultural norms and to depend less on their personal qualities or achievements (education for example). To some extent, this is also the case among girls, but only in Lower Egypt. For boys, family integration is highest in both the urban governorates and Lower Egypt and lowest in Upper Egypt. This is consistent with more patrriarchal norms guiding communication between elders and youth in Upper Egypt and with greater heterogeneity of family communication styles likely to be found in and near metropolitan areas. Although more difficult to explain, integration of boys also intensifies as the age of the mother increases (Table C).

A high level of communication with parents about adolescent problems is not related to any of the distant variables in the case of boys. Other models will be needed to explain variation among boys. For girls, however, it is significantly linked to belonging to families with high education attainment for both adolescent and father. These are families conforming to our 'post-transition' typology. In these families, girls are almost twice as likely to communicate well with parents compared with girls in either pre-transformation families (having equally low education attainment among the two generations) or those experiencing the height of the transformation process.

Exposure to mass media increased significantly among boys who had access to some education and also with school continuation. It also increased significantly among boys in the urban governorates and Lower Egypt compared with boys in Upper Egypt. Among adolescent girls, exposure to the mass media was only linked to access to education but appeared not to be related to school continuation. Also, it increased significantly only among girls in the urban governorates. A very peculiar finding is the significantly lower exposure to mass media among girls whose mothers have equally high education as their daughters. The only plausible explanation for this unexpected result is the high degree of mobility this particular group of girls is allowed. This probably leads them to spend less time at home reading books, listening to the radio or watching television (Table D).

As expected, mobility is much higher for boys than girls, with large variations in the patterns predicting their mobility levels. In general, the mobility of girls in this age group is highly restricted unless they continue to general secondary education. Their mobility is also significantly enhanced if their mothers acquired a high education level. For boys, mobility is more of a cosmopolitan characteristic, with boys in the urban governorates enjoying significantly higher levels of mobility compared with boys in Lower and Upper Egypt.

Conclusion

This paper has explored possibilities inherent in national survey data to increase understanding of the complex relationship between adolescents and parents in Egypt. Without an earlier baseline for comparison, we cannot know whether the great variablility we found in how the two generations interact and view the world is increasing or not. What is possible with data of this kind is a simultaneous consideration of multiple factors influencing the closeness or gap between the generations. Gender emerges as a crucial determinant of similarity in the views of parents and adolescents, with girls less likely than boys to agree with the parental generation on a number of basic issues related to marriage and couple relations.

Beyond the gender differences, however, we also found a measurable link between intergenerational distance and where families are located along the continuum of social transformation in Egypt. Educational attainment was our marker for that transformation, and gaps in education between the two generations have implications for almost every indicator examined here. Rapid strides in access to basic education during the last decade suggest that the substantial distance we found between parents and adolescents will probably decrease in the future as these better educated young people become parents themselves.

While the transformation process intensifies inter-generational differences, personal background factors are also potent predictors of a gap. Less educated girls are unlikely to have a role model, but when they do it is rarely their parents. These girls may observe the opportunities open to peers in better off households--for education, recreation, or mobility--and feel alienated from their parents who have not been able to secure a share of this change for their offspring.

Social transformation, which we hypothesize is occuring intensely in Lower Egypt and urban centers, may lead to generational gaps but it does not necessarily mean a tumultuous or conflictual family setting. Particularly for girls, the end point of social transformation correlates with a positive family setting in which their views are heard and respected, though only if both generations have equally high education. The middle transitional group, on the other hand, are least likely to identify parents as a role model and are also least likely to voice opinions that are respected and heard. Without more information on how disagreements are handled, we have used the term 'intergenerational differences' rather than 'conflict'.

A positive finding relating to communication with family is that girls in post-transformation households communicate *more* than those in pre- or during-transformation families. Our survey data do not allow for further probing of the meaning behind these levels of communication. Are transitional families places where adolescents are, by necessity, more independent of parents for solving problems, or where the problems are simply going unresolved? Answers to these kinds of questions are important but would require in-depth study techniques.

A final point relates to the importance of a mother's education. The mother's education turned out to be a significant predictor of higher spatial mobility for girls. It is also associated with a more egalitarian outlook among boys. These are trends that may be expected to continue as the proportion of women with higher education levels increases. However, because education levels for women nationwide are lower than those for men, mothers with high education levels are still the exception. This could suggest that there are other unique characteristics of those households today with highly educated mothers. Most probably these mothers have been able to win respect and a 'voice' in family decision making. This would lead boys to view a more equal sharing of roles as normal.

How and why the educational attainment of boys and girls influences each in a different way is not well explained. This difference was seen clearly in attitudes towards gender roles and marriage formation. Added years of education push girls more forcefully toward more egalitarian views of marriage and relationships. This leads to speculation about future relations between these men and women in marriage. As girls achieve higher education levels will they experience more conflict with future spouses, who reach similar levels of schooling but remain closer to parents in their views?

References

Abdalla, Ahmed. 2000. "The Egyptian Generation of 1967: Reaction of the Young to National Defeat" in Roel Meijer, ed., *Alienation or Integration of Arab Youth: Between Family, State and Street*. London: Curzon Press, pp. 71-81.

Abu-Lughod, Lila. 1998. "Television and the Virtues of Education: Upper Egyptian Encounters with State Culture" in Nicholas S. Hopkins and Kirsten Westergaard, eds., *Directions of Change in Rural Egypt*. Cairo: American University in Cairo Press, pp. 147-165.

Berger, P.L., B. Berger, and H. Kellner. 1973. *The Homeless Mind: Modernization and Consciousness*. Harmondsworth: Penguin Books.

Buchholt, Helmut and Ulrich Mai. 1994. *Continuity, Change and Aspirations: Social and Cultural Life in Minahasa, Indonesia*. Singapore: Institute of Southeast Asian Studies.

Davis, Susan S. and Douglas A. Davis. 1989. *Adolescence in a Moroccan Town: Making Social Sense*. New Brunswick: Rutgers University Press.

Ibrahim, Barbara, Barbara Mensch, and Omaima El-Gibaly. 1998. "Transitions to Manhood: Socialization to Gender Roles and Marriage among Egyptian Adolescent Boys." Paper presented at the Seminar on Men, Family Formation and Reproduction, International Union for the Scientific Study of Population (IUSSP), Buenos Aires.

Ibrahim, Barbara and Hind Wassef. 2000. "Caught between two worlds: Youth in the Egyptian hinterland" in Roel Meijer, ed., *Alienation or Integration of Arab Youth: Between Family, State and Street*. London: Curzon Press, pp. 161-185.

Joseph, Suad. 1993. "Connectivity and Patriarchy among Urban Working-Class Arab Families in Lebanon," *Ethos* 21(4):452-479.

Kandiyoti, Deniz. 1991. "Introduction" in *Women, Islam and the State*. London: Macmillan, pp. 1-21.

Kiem, Christian. 1994. "Minahasan festive life in the context of generational change" in Buchholt, Helmut and Ulrich Mai, eds., *Continuity, Change and Aspirations: Social and Cultural Life in Minahasa, Indonesia*. Singapore: Institute of Southeast Asian Studies, pp. 51-67.

Meighan, Roland and Iram Siraj-Blatchford. 1998. *A Sociology of Educating*. New York: Cassell.

Mensch, Barbara, Barbara Ibrahim, Susan Lee, and Omaima El-Gibaly. 2000. "Socialization to Gender Roles and Marriage Among Egyptian Adolescents." New York: Policy Research Division Working Papers, Population Council.

Mitterauer, M. 1986. *Sozialgeschichte der Jugend. Frankfurt, Suhrkamp*. English edition : *A History of Youth*. Oxford: Blackwell, 1992.

Neyzi, Leyla. 2000. "Object or Subject? The Paradox of 'Youth' in Turkey". Cairo: MEAwards Regional Papers, Population Council. No. 45. Reprinted with minor changes as "Object or Subject ? The Paradox of 'Youth" in Turkey" in *International Journal of Middle East Studies* 33(3):411-432 (2001).

Rosenmayr, L and K. Allerbeck, eds. 1979. "Youth and Society," *Current Sociology* 2(3).

Singerman, Diane and Homa Hoodfar. 1996. "The Household as Mediator: Political Economy, Development and Gender in Contemporary Cairo" in *Development, Change and Gender in Cairo*. Indiana University Press, pp. xi-xl.

El-Tawila, Sahar, et. al. 1999. *Transitions to Adulthood: A National Survey of Egyptian Adolescents*. Cairo: The Population Council.

World Bank. 2000. *African Development Indicators*. Washington, D.C.

Young, William C. and Seteney Shami. 1997. "Anthropological Approaches to the Arab Family: An Introduction," *Journal of Comparative Family Studies* 28(2):1-13.

El-Zanaty, F. et al. 1996. *Egypt Demographic and Health Survey 1995*. Cairo: National Population Council and Macro International Inc., Calverton, Maryland USA.

Table A: Odds-Ratios of Reporting Either Parent as a Role Model and Failure to Identify a Role Model at All by Distant Background Variables ◊

	Reporting either parent as a role model		Failure to identify a role model at all	
Background variable	Boys	Girls	Boys	Girls
Education attainment of adolescent				
Never attended school	.29**		13.3***	5.0***
Dropped out before secondary	.53***		3.2***	2.2***
Enrolled/completed vocational secondary	1.3		1.08	0.96
Enrolled/completed general secondary	1.0		1.0	1.0
Inter-generation education difference: father/adolescent				
Same low education	.78	.28***		
Adolescent's education is higher	.43***	.34***		
Same high education	1.0	1.0		
Inter-generation education difference: mother/adolescent				
Same low education				
Adolescent's education is higher				
Same high education				
Age of mother				
Age of father				
Socio-economic level of the household				
Low				
Middle				
High				
Region of residence				
Urban governorates	1.6**		1.42	
Lower Egypt	1.04		1.90***	
Upper Egypt	1.0		1.0	
Total percent	32.7	36.3	22.5	28.5

◊ All distant background variables listed in Table 1 were included in the model. Stepwise logistic regression using likelihood ratio test for retaining significant variables was used.

*: .01<P<.05 , **: .001<P<.01 , ***: P<.001

Table B

Multiple Classification Analysis: Index of Divergence from The Average Experience of the Parent-Generation by Distant Explanatory Variables

Background variable	Boys	Girls
Education attainment of adolescent		
Never attended school		-0.27
Dropped out before secondary		-0.24
Enrolled in/completed vocational secondary		-0.10
Enrolled in/completed general secondary		0.36
Inter-generation education difference: father/adolescent		
Same low education	0.32	
Adolescent's education is higher	-0.02	
Same high education	-0.10	
Inter-generation education difference: mother/adolescent		
Same low education	-0.30	
Adolescent's education is higher	-0.01	
Same high education	0.44	
Mean age of mother		
Mean age of father		
Socio-economic status of the household		
Low	-0.32	
Middle	0.01	
High	0.17	
Region of residence		
Urban governorates	0.26	0.49
Lower Egypt	-0.13	-0.14
Upper Egypt	0.03	-0.22
Average Score on the index	3.64	4.21

Table C

Socialization Style at Home; Odds-Ratios of Family Integration and High-Level Inter-Generation Communication by Distant Background Variables◊

	Family Integration		High-level inter-generation Communication	
Background variables	Boys	Girls	Boys	Girls
Education attainment of adolescent				
Never attended school		.19***		
Dropped out before secondary		.37***		
Enrolled/completed vocational secondary		.64**		
Enrolled/completed general secondary		1.0		
Inter-generation education difference: father/adolescent				
Same low education		0.80		0.50***
Adolescent's education higher		0.48**		0.61**
Same high education		1.0		1.0
Inter-generation education difference: mother/adolescent				
Same low education				
Adolescent's education is higher				
Same high education				
Mean age of mother	1.03**			
Mean age of father				
Socio-economic status of the household				
Low	1.60***	1.3		
Middle	1.68***	1.62***		
High	1.0	1.0		
Region of residence				
Urban governorates				
Lower Egypt				
Upper Egypt				

◊ All distant background variables listed in Table 1 were included in the model. Stepwise logistic regression using likelihood ratio test for retaining significant variables was used.
*: .01<P<.05 , **: .001<P<.01 , ***: P<.001

Table D

Socialization Style at Home; Odds-Ratios of High Exposure To the Mass Media and Less Restricted Mobility by Distant Background Variables◊

Background variables	Exposure to the mass media		Less restricted mobility	
	Boys	Girls	Boys	Girls
Education attainment of adolescent				
Never attended school	.22***	.29**		.42**
Dropped out before secondary	.35***	.66		.37***
Enrolled/completed vocational secondary	.70***	1.07		.48***
Enrolled/completed general secondary	1.0	1.0		1.0
Inter-generation education difference: father/adolescent				
Same low education				
Adolescent's education higher				
Same high education				
Inter-generation education difference: mother/adolescent				
Same low education		3.36***		.34**
Adolescent's education is higher		2.28***		.44**
Same high education		1.0		1.0
Mean age of mother				
Mean age of father				
Socio-economic status of the household				
Low				
Middle				
High				
Region of residence				
Urban governorates	1.62**	1.58**	1.87**	
Lower Egypt	1.53**	1.04	1.43	
Upper Egypt	1.0	1.0	1.0	

◊ All distant background variables listed in Table 1 were initially included in the model. Forward stepwise logistic regression models were applied. Only significant explanatory variables were retained in the final model presented here, based on a likelihood ratio test criterion
*: .01<P<.05 , **: .001<P<.01 , ***: P<.001

TERMINATING MARRIAGE

PHILIPPE FARGUES

Introduction

"The family is the basic unit of society, and marriage is the exclusive framework for the practice of sexuality." We were forcefully reminded of this observation when Cairo was preparing to host the International Conference on Population and Development (1994), a conference whose program of action included among other topics the variety of non-marital forms of union and sexuality that one can meet throughout the world. It proved an occasion collectively to reaffirm the unchangeable character of the institution of marriage for Muslims, an institution essentially regulated by *shari'a* law. While the majority of civil laws are broadly derived from European legislation, family law seems relatively exempt from these external contributions, the reason being that the judicial provisions most clearly stated in the Quran and Sunna precisely relate to matters such as marriage and divorce, inheritance and child custody. The legal norm and the non-law-determined custom which together regulate the matrimonial life of individuals project an image of stability of the family and marriage in Arab-Muslim society.

On the other hand, the statistical norm projects the very different picture of a radical evolution. Over the short period that the registries of marriage and divorce provide for observation--the entire twentieth century in the best cases (Egypt and Algeria)--we can in effect witness the growing but paradoxical influence of globalization. Universal developments, such as the spread of mass education, urbanization, or the dominance of the service sector in the economy, have delayed the age of marriage and thus turned upside down a whole equilibrium which previously depended on early marriage. The impact of the West, initiated by colonial domination then strengthened by the consecration of major international forums dedicated to the promotion of individual rights, and especially women's rights, has brought with it the evolution of legislation pertaining to divorce, polygamy, or child custody, and altered previous practices in these areas. The paradox resides among other things in the fact that the manifest influence of the West has been accompanied by tendencies contrary to those we have witnessed in the West, e.g., by the stabilization of the marriage institution rather than its weakening. Judicial permeability, if we may call so the interference of non-*shari'a* systems in changes affecting personal status, went hand-in-hand with sociological resistance in the form of the rejection of explicit models of the Western family.

Instability of Individual Marriages and Equilibrium of the Traditional Matrimonial System

This first section depicts a model. This is not a purely imaginary model, but the schematization of the situation revealed by the earliest statistics available on marriage and its dissolution, those of Egypt and Algeria at the end of the nineteenth and the beginning of the twentieth centuries. For convenience, we describe this model as the "traditional system", without suggesting that it has existed since the beginnings of Islam. It serves us as a starting point for evaluating the significant changes registered throughout the twentieth century, especially in its second half.

Inspired by the neoclassical economy, the notion of "marriage market" considers marriage as a transaction which involves two persons, presupposes that each person is informed at least of the existence of the other, and is concluded at a price, possibly associated with profit. The fact that each marriage, without exception, associates a man and a woman[1] requires a strict arithmetic constraint: at the moment of marriage, men and women are of equal number. As a social phenomenon, however, eligibility for marriage complies with all sorts of regulations that differentiate between men and women, the result being that, within the population recognized as marriageable, the two sexes are only exceptionally of equal numbers. Each society finds a solution to reconcile the numerical inequality of the sexes within the marriageable population with their numerical equality at the moment of marriage, i.e., in order to balance the market.

---

[1] Including polygamous marriage since a man does not marry two women at once. There is polygamy when a man whose previous marriage stands--he is neither a widow nor divorced--marries anew another woman. This marriage is wrongly described as polygamous; it is in reality the man who is polygamous.

The Arab-Muslim tradition allows for two practices whose association, specific to that tradition, complicates the equilibrium of the matrimonial market. We refer to repudiation and polygamy. The two are well founded in Muslim law. The first, which makes divorce an initiative of the man simply ratified by the *qadi*, has surely been very widely prevalent at various periods, including recent history. The second, which allows the married man to contract a new marriage without the break-up of his first marriage, within the limit of four simultaneous wives, has probably never been as popular a practice among Arabs as it still is in West Africa.[2] Repudiation and polygamy are two legal courses offered for a man to be the husband of several women, either successively when he repudiates a first wife to marry another, or simultaneously in the case of polygamous marriage. They presuppose that women are in excess compared to men within the marriageable population.

What could lead to an excess of marriageable women? Could it be the product of a biological norm specific to the Arab people, which would provide more women at the age of marriage? This fanciful explanation cannot withstand observation: at nearly 20 or 30 years old, and within a similar age group, there would likely be more men than women. Would it be a question then, not of a biological norm but to the contrary a sociological exception, allowing certain privileged groups to reserve for themselves a larger number of women, to the detriment of other groups in which men would thus be more frequently doomed to bachelorhood? The hypothesis is more serious than the previous one. Indeed, polygamy is considered more widespread among rich men than among poor ones; it is also considered more acceptable for a young girl whose initial condition is modest, and who hopes for upward mobility through such a marriage. This second explanation, however, hardly better withstands the test of statistical evidence: almost all men marry, regardless of their social condition; the hypothetical monopoly of women by privileged categories is not attested by a corresponding scarcity among underprivileged categories. Sociological exception is not better than biological regularity in offering a solid explanation for the excess of women to marry, and it is to other specific features of the Arab-Muslim matrimonial market that we must turn.

---

[2] In some West African societies, up to 50% of women are married to polygamous men.

Two seemingly trivial regularities provide an explanation. They are the universality of marriage and the magnitude of the age gap between spouses. The universality of marriage is of a prescriptive character. Every believer has a duty to be married. The social order sees to it that each person executes the religious prescription. There are all sorts of inducements to marriage, the strongest being the capacity to practice one's sexuality, authorized by the Muslim religion only within marriage. There also exists a dissuasion of celibacy: a dissuasion of a judicial character for women, who are subject up to their marriage to the authority of the father or guardian; and a social dissuasion for men, for whom the environment would disapprove in a thousand and one ways a very prolonged celibacy. Marriage alone frees the individual from his/her family of birth and gives access to autonomy. In fact, celibacy becomes an exceptional status beyond a certain age. Demographic censuses in the twentieth century indicate a high frequency of marriage: everywhere more than 95 percent, and sometimes nearly 100 percent of those who are 45 years old or beyond have been or are still married, among men as well as women.

The second regularity, an important age difference between the two spouses, is of a different nature. A man generally marries a woman younger than himself--on average 7 to 10 years younger than he is in the earliest statistics[3]--but this is not prescribed, and is not even explicitly recommended. Indeed, all possible situations can be found: partners of the same age, and even men younger than their wives, are not rare. An older husband within the married couple is simply a much more frequent situation compared with others. Its frequency relates to the strength of social and judicial rules of another kind, those that push numerous men to marry at a

---

[3] In Algeria between 1905 and 1914, the difference was 9 years. In Egypt in 1946, the average age at the first marriage was 18.6 years for women and 26.9 for men, that is a difference of 8.3 years at the end of celibacy. Not all married to single men, young Egyptian girls were married to men aged 27.1 years, i.e., 8.5 years their elders (Fargues 1986a). The history of the West seems to offer few examples of such a large difference. In France between 1720 and 1909 men were married on average at the age of 28.1 to women of 25.5 years old; this slight age difference at the time of the first marriage (2.6 years) was otherwise accompanied by a significant proportion of persons remaining unmarried during their whole life, a more frequent situation for women (12.5 percent) than for men (9.4 percent) (Henry and Houdaille 1978 and 1979).

relatively late age[4]. Such rules will be examined later. For the moment, let us draw the arithmetic consequences of this association of universal marriage with age difference between partners, an association which suffices to produce an excess, at first glance enigmatic, of marriageable young women.

Let us have a look at an age pyramid: at an equal age, men (on the left) and women (on the right) are nearly equal in number. But for each sex, the size grows thinner as age increases.[5] Examining the conditions of mortality and fertility, both high, of Arab populations at the onset of the demographic transition--the beginning of the twentieth century--we find that for every 100 girls aged 15-19 there would be: 102.7 boys of the same age, but 91.4 of 20-24 years old, and 80.1 of 25-29. If the girls were married at the age of 15-19 to boys of 20-24, an age difference of 5 years would produce an excess of 8.6 girls, and a difference of 10 years an excess of 19.9 girls. In order for all young girls to be able to get married, some of them must marry for the first time non-single men, either still married or divorced.[6] What is a first marriage for the woman is then for the man either a polygamous marriage or a re-marriage (after the repudiation of the preceding spouse). The surplus of marriageable women presupposed by polygamy and repudiation is thus the product, indirect but inevitable, of social rules regulating the age at marriage and the frequency of marriage.

Repudiation, because it liberates the man and places him again on the marriage market, and polygamy, because it keeps him on that market despite a previous non-broken marriage, play an identical role of regulator of the matrimonial market: they ensure everyone a chance to marry while

---

[4] For certain women, the habit of marrying men older than themselves finds its justification indirectly in a religious rule, as expressed very well by this 17-year-old female student from a popular quarter in Cairo at the end of the 1980s: "According to our religion, a wife has to obey her husband. But no one can obey someone who is not as wise as she is, and consequently, there would be lots of arguments and the marriage will fall apart, and what would happen to the children? Therefore it is better for a woman to marry someone who is older, more educated, who has much more experience in life than she has, and so it would not be illogical for her to obey him" (Hoodfar 1997:58).
[5] Mortality suffices to produce this reduction. But throughout the whole period of the "demographic transition"--the twentieth century--there is the additional fact that numbers of births are increasing from one year to another, so the generational cohorts are larger and larger.
[6] Or widowers, but widowerhood is rare among young men.

respecting an age inequality between partners[7]. Nevertheless, repudiation makes available not just the man, but also the woman for a new marriage. In order for it to be a regulator of the market, it is necessary either that the repudiated woman has fewer chances for remarriage than the man who has repudiated her, or that the delay of remarriage is longer for her.

Reduction of Gender Inequalities and Stabilization of the Individual Union

This section depicts the evolution of the two institutions that create the inequality of the sexes within marriage: polygamy and divorce. In order to grasp this evolution, we discuss the longest time series data sets. Two countries only have such a series, Algeria and Egypt. The following analyses relate to those two countries and cannot necessarily be extrapolated to all of Arab-Muslim society.

The limits of polygamy. What was the frequency of polygamy in the remote past? It seems polygamy has always had a moderate extension among Arab Muslims[8]. We possess numerous contemporary testimonies according to which it was not very widespread during the nineteenth century. "Polygamy," states Burckhardt (1831:106-7),

> according to the Turkish law, is a privilege of the Bedouins; but the greater number of Arabs content themselves with one wife: very few have two wives, and I never met with any person who could recollect a Bedouin that had four wives at once in his tent.

Lane (1836:185) makes, at the same period, the same observation in another country, Egypt:

> It is not very common for an Egyptian to have more than one wife, or a concubine-slave; though the law allows him *four* wives (as I have

---

[7] There is a kind of paradox underlying this arithmetic: the frequency of divorce (i.e., the end of marriage) determines the conditions of the first marriage; or more, the first marriage depends at each moment on the stability of families formed in the past. In this way, the factors affecting the stability of marriage are (remote) determinants of the first marriage.

[8] Polygamy does not exist among non-Muslim Arabs (Christians), or among Druzes, a community professing a syncretism of Islam and Christianity.

before stated), and, according to common opinion, as many concubine-slaves as he may choose.

These subjective impressions are impossible to translate into numbers. The oldest statistics go back to the period around 1900 and reveal that polygamy was then non-negligible, even if it was far from having the same massive character as in certain societies of Africa south of the Sahara. In Algeria, 15% of married men were polygamous in 1886, and 6 percent in Egypt in 1907. As for women, more than 26 percent were married to a polygamous man in Algeria and more than 11 percent in Egypt.[2]

Polygamy has probably declined in the majority of Arab societies in the course of the twentieth century, but in a way that varies from one society to another, and according to social conditions. Tunisia is the only country in which it has completely disappeared, with the enforcement of a personal status code (1956) that proscribed it. Elsewhere, polygamists constitute 2 percent to 5 percent of married men[10] or, which amounts to the same thing, 4 percent to 10 percent of women. It is only in Algeria and Egypt that we can follow the evolution of this phenomenon over a relatively long period. Algeria records an important reduction of polygamy, the rate declining from 15 percent of men in 1886 to less than 2 percent in 1966, the date of the last census publishing a statement on the question.[11] Other sources provide a

---

[9] If all such marriages involve a man and two women, recording 15 percent of polygamy among men amounts to counting 85 monogamous and 15 polygamous men, having respectively 85 and 30 wives. The corresponding proportion of women living in polygamous union is thus 30/115, or 26 percent. If certain polygamous men live with more than two wives, the corresponding proportion of women in a polygamous situation would then be more than 26 percent.

[10] Except in Sudan, a country in transition towards marriage models specific to Africa South of the Sahara.

[11] Here are the percentages of polygamy among married men in Algeria in different censuses: 1886: 14.8; 1896: 11.9; 1906: 7.3; 1911: 6.4; 1948: 3.0; 1954: 2.0; 1966: 1.8. Subsequent censuses do not address polygamy anymore, but an indirect estimate is provided by reporting the ratio of married women to married men in the resident population of Algeria. We respectively find 1.049 and 1.026 at the censuses of 1987 and 1998, which would correspond to 4.9 and 2.6 percent of polygamists. These numbers, calculated on the basis of the population residing in Algeria, overestimate polygamy because a certain number of married women are without their husbands, the reason being that the latter have emigrated and currently reside in another country. On this country, see Kateb (1998). The same indicator yielded a figure of 1.095 at the census of 1994 in Morocco.

slightly higher rate, such as the 1992 survey on fertility[12] where we find 5.5 percent of married women living in polygamous unions, corresponding to a male polygamy rate of 2.8 percent.

In Egypt, the diminution is less evident and we even witness a rise in polygamy during the last quarter of the 20th century.[13] This rise was initiated during the *infitah* ("economic opening") period. *Infitah* was marked in Egypt by an afflux of resources of foreign origin as well as the emigration of several million Egyptians to the oil countries of the Arabian Peninsula and Libya. On the one hand, it allowed for the blooming of a new property-owning class and offered a increase of material comfort to a sizeable middle strata. On the other hand, it diffused models of existence imported from the Gulf, in particular those that affect the condition of women and which had hardly penetrated Egypt under the regime of President Nasser. The resumption of polygamy could be an aspect of the new behavior patterns favored by the political turn Egypt took during the 1970s[14].

The arithmetic of polygamy reveals another aspect of the sociology of that practice in Arab-Muslim societies. Indeed, one can measure polygamy either within the population, by the proportion of current polygamists among married men, or at the moment of marriage, by the frequency of polygamous unions. We would expect the two measures to give equivalent results. For instance, where 5 percent of married men are polygamous (corresponding to 105 spouses for 100 men, or 10 spouses living in a polygamous situation in a total of 105), we would expect marriages, in

---

[12] The inquiry "Papchild" conducted by the Arab League in 10 countries, including Algeria, in the 1990s.

[13] For 100 married men, 105.8 married women were registered in 1907: allowing for counting errors, 5.8 percent of married men were polygamous then. At the following censuses, we find: 1917: 104.6; 1927: 104.4; 1937: 102.4; 1947: 103.4; 1960: 103.0; 1976: 101.2; 1986: 101.6; 1996: 106.9. The increase in the last decade is the product of two effects: a possible resumption of polygamy and the emigration of married men leaving their spouses in Egypt--emigration towards Saudi Arabia in particular, during the years that followed the Gulf War and the return of numerous Egyptian families who had emigrated to Iraq.

[14] The resumption of polygamy equally takes the form of the increase of customary marriage *(zawaj 'urfi)*, which often hides a polygamous situation (Botiveau, 1993). In Egypt, after the 1979 law, every marriage which is not legally registered is actually considered to be *'urfi*. While it does not conform to *fiqh*, since the latter requires that a marriage be public, *'urfi* marriage allows people to circumvent the measures restraining polygamy since it escapes the tribunals charged with the application of such measures.

which a man is already married, to represent 5 percent of all marriages. This is not the case. In Egypt, where the two types of calculation are possible, we record a much higher rate of polygamy at the moment of marriage than within the population. In 1947, for example, there were 103.1 wives for every 100 married men: assuming that cases of unions with 3 or 4 wives simultaneously were negligible in number, polygamous men would then represent 3.1 percent of married men. In the same year, however, 9.6 percent of concluded marriages were of a polygamous character.

Whatever the period under consideration, polygamy measured by the frequency of polygamous marriages appears clearly higher than polygamy measured by the frequency of polygamous men. This characteristic of polygamy is not specific to Egypt. One finds it, for instance, in Jordan, where 3.8 percent of polygamists were counted among men in the census of 1979 compared to 8.2 percent of polygamous unions among marriages concluded in 1975-79. The difference between these two measures is explained by a feature of Arab-Muslim polygamy, namely that a little after a polygamous marriage, the man frequently divorces his first spouse. In Egypt nearly 7 polygamous marriages out of 10 are thus followed by a rapid divorce of the first spouse, a stable proportion over all the period covered by marriage statistics (that is, since 1935). Given that polygamous marriages are in the vast majority of cases of a bigamous type[15] and that by divorcing one of their spouses the men will keep only one, the proportion of polygamists who regain their previous monogamous status is 7 out of 10. Divorce almost always transforms those men whose last marriage was polygamous into monogamous men.

This arithmetic shows that polygamy and divorce are not just two institutions that work together to ensure the equilibrium of the matrimonial market, but they are frequently associated one with the other for the same individual. Fatima Mernissi (1985) has emphasized that they respond each in its way to the sexual instincts of men: polygamy to the intensity of their desire, and repudiation to their whims. Both aiming at the maintenance of sexuality within marriage, they guard society from the dangers it would incur by authorizing extra-marital sexuality. Paradoxically, the instability of

---

[15] 92.7 percent of polygamous marriages in the periods 1936-37 and 1946-47 were concluded by a man already married to a woman, 6.7 percent to two women, and 0.6 percent to three women. In 1991, 97 percent of polygamous unions were only bigamous.

the marital union, easily undone by polygamy and divorce, has as a counterpart the stability of the family institution and, beyond that, that of the social order as a whole.

The decline of divorce. Often associated for the same individual, polygamy and divorce are the two complementary facets of the same process of regulating marriage. While the first has commonly been viewed as a relatively marginal phenomenon, the second has generally been seen as a very common practice at all times. This is the situation observed by Burckhardt in Arabia at the dawn of modern times. "Most Arabs are contented with a single wife," he writes,

> but for this monogamy they make amends, by indulging in variety. They frequently change their wives, according to a custom founded on the Turkish law of divorce, which, however, has been much abused among the Arabs [...] I have seen Arabs about forty-five years of age who were known to have had above fifty different wives. (Burckhardt 1831:110-1)

In Egypt, during the period of Muhammad Ali, Lane (1836:185) also reveals the ease of divorce:

> But, though a man restrict himself to a single wife, he may change as often as he desires; and there are certainly not many persons in Cairo who have not divorced one wife, if they have been long married.

One hundred years later, the situation has hardly changed in Egypt. Affecting half of marriages at the beginning of the 1930s, divorce was then an almost ordinary step in life. "All social classes make good usage of it. It substitutes for polygamy among the poor," noted an Egyptian academic (Mboria 1938). To annotate the first statistics on marriage to which he just had access--in 1931-1936, 49.4 divorces were recorded for each 100 marriages in the country as a whole (and up to 53.2 percent in Cairo!), but hardly 10 to 11 percent of polygamous marriages[16]--he relies on the comment of a woman, who didn't hesitate to attribute to her sisters the extreme fragility of the marital union:

---

[16] Statistics unpublished in the yearbooks, provided by Mboria (1938).

They easily move from one husband to another with extraordinary detachment and easy forgetfulness; in exchange for a frugal meal and a modest home, they gladly offer their bodies. It is a more or less durable transaction, subject to the man's wish.....[17]

One marriage out of two broken by divorce--such a frequency of divorce is not exceptional in the Arab world at that period. In Algeria, 42.8 divorces for each 100 marriages are recorded in 1880 (Richoux 1881); in Morocco, 49 percent among the generations 1895 to 1915 (Vanessa Maher 1974). In Morocco, the rate of divorce is higher in villages (52 percent) than in cities (38 percent).

Divorce in Arab-Muslim societies presents some very particular traits, which do not seem to be directly related to its high frequency since we also find them where it is more rare. Divorce appears very early within marriage, on average just two years after its conclusion, and the union that it has just broken is still sterile in three out four cases. These characteristics appear at all times--we find them in Egypt since the existence of divorce statistics: from 1931-36 to 1991-96, the proportion of divorces pronounced prior to the fifth wedding anniversary is nearly invariably 8 out of 10--and all places-- during the 1980s and 1990s, according to available data, the proportion of marriages without children among those that end in divorce is 74 percent in Egypt, 67 percent in Jordan and 68 percent in Syria. Divorce appears here as a sanction for a particular form of failure of the marriage: its infertility. Shall we see in the seeking of fertility and the clan's concern to increase its reproductive potential one of the ancestral concerns behind the ease of repudiation that we observe in Arab-Muslim societies? The matrimonial turnover produced by divorce and remarriage effectively reduces the risk of infertility, since the sterility of a couple is not necessarily that of the two partners at the same time.[18] This is how in any case experience has molded common sense: numerous are the women who feel the threat of repudiation so long as they have not given birth to a child as a testimony for their fertility, and especially to a boy to guarantee the continuity of the line.

---

[17] Mboria (1938) cites Niya Salima, "Harems et Musulmanes d'Egypte."
[18] The sterility of a couple can result from the sterility of the man, that of the woman, or the genetic incompatibility between a man and a woman who are both fecund.

The ease of repudiation goes hand in hand with that of remarriage. Hence the scarcity of divorced people in the population, despite the frequency of acts of divorce. People do not remain divorced for a long time, since they remarry quickly. In Egypt, the proportion of divorced among non-single persons is between 1.5 and 2 percent for men, and 2.5 and 4 percent for women, according to censuses. This is the same at the beginning of the twentieth century, when divorce represented almost 50 percent of marriages, and at its end, when divorce was less common. The fact that the state of being divorced is met a little more frequently among women is simply explained by a longer delay between divorce and remarriage among them compared with men. The latter is, as we have seen, a condition if divorce is to exercise a regulatory function on the matrimonial market.

The twentieth century witnessed a radical change with the continued regression of divorce (Table 1). In Algeria, the proportion of marriages broken by divorce falls from more than 40 percent at the end of the nineteenth century to less than 10 percent after independence; in Egypt, from about 50 percent at the beginning of the 1930s to 17.8 percent in 1991-95; and in Syria, from 15 percent in 1945-49 to 9 percent in 1991-95. In all Arab countries where we can establish time series, we observe a stabilization of the marital union, at a time when the family in the west is, to the contrary, destabilized by the increase in divorce[19]. A rapid interpretation of this exchange of places in terms of divorce rates would be that, by abandoning a custom adopted by the West, Arab societies demonstrate the irreducibility of cultures and somehow affirm their refusal to let globalization enter the domain of values and private behavior. In opposition to this reading, we note that the reduction of the frequency of divorce accompanies the evolution of Arab legislation on family matters under the influence of European codes, and that it thus matches a certain form of globalization, that affecting the regulation of the rights and duties of individuals.

While statistics reveal the decline of divorce over the century, people feel that it is becoming more noticeable. To the truth of figures is opposed that of experiences. Why do the man on the street or the sociologist note that divorce is more and more present in daily life, especially that of city-dwellers, while numerical evidence shows it to be in decline? This gap

---

[19] And because marriage itself is getting rarer.

between the facts and the representations might well put us on the track of a major cause for the decline of divorce.[20] If divorce is more visible in society while it takes place more rarely, it is perhaps because it is more and more consequential for each of the individuals concerned. The reasons that make it increasingly tangible, restrictive legislation and a substantial cost for the man demanding divorce, have actually exercised a dissuasive effect on the phenomenon itself. The legal norm is somehow altering the statistical norm.

Legal Norm and Statistical Norm. Egypt and Syria were the first Arab countries to reform the legal framework of marriage and its dissolution. In Egypt, the judicial apparatus first tried to improve the condition of divorced women, transformed by urbanization into a social question. Two laws, those of 1920 and 1929, sought to reduce the threat of divorce and the insecurity in which it puts women by codifying three points on which schools of Islamic jurisprudence provide contradictory rules: the modalities of divorce, the alimony due by the husband, and child custody. The institution of judicial divorce (1920), which gives the judge the power to intervene in order to favor the continuation of marital life, breaks with the formula of repudiation in which justice would practically never participate. By entitling the repudiated women to the right to ask for a procedure of judicial divorce, the law of 1920 established a first restriction on repudiation, one that was reinforced by the law of 1929, which invalidated cases of repudiation involving flaws from the standpoint of *fiqh*.[21] The second dissuasive measure is the transformation of *nafaqa*, the alimony due to the divorced woman by her ex-husband, into an indefeasible and enforceable claim on his wealth. The third measure, which simply specifies the rule of *fiqh* according to which the child belongs to the father while his education pertains to the mother, attributes the custody of the children to their mother up to the age of 7 for boys and 9 for girls.[22]

---

[20] The continuous decline of divorce in several Arab societies is shown by several demographers. It is not convincingly explained by any of them.
[21] Conditional repudiations, repudiations pronounced in a state of frenzy or under coercion, repudiations pronounced just once while *fiqh* only recognizes 'triple' repudiations, etc.
[22] The mother loses her right of custody if she marries a man unrelated to the child.

Syria, whose provinces remained under the direct authority of the Ottoman Empire until its collapse in the aftermath of World War One, benefited from all the modernizing reforms of the Empire, in particular the Ottoman code of 1917 which remained in force until the end of the French mandate in 1945. The existence of a detailed text gives individuals access to a precise knowledge of their rights and duties. Moreover, the legality of marriage was for the first time conditional on the registration of the contract by the *shari'a* tribunal, which means that all demands to dissolve the marriage automatically become issues for the courts:

> The legislator has moved from the notion of *talaq* (repudiation or the generic form of divorce) to that of separation (*tafriq* decided by a judge), or, in other words, from *fiqh* to positive law. (Botiveau 1993:205)

The transformation of every divorce into a judicial act by the Syrian administration could well explain why divorce was twice as rare in this country as in Egypt in the 1940s.

In the course of the twentieth century, the context of divorce evolved under the effect of the great transformations of the social and economic order such as urbanization, the diffusion of formal education, the introduction of the monetary economy, the transformation of workers into wage-earners, and also the appearance of female work outside of the domestic unit. The needs of divorced persons, for themselves as well as for the children that they care for, are affected by all these transformations, as are the patterns of solidarity enabling them to cope with such needs: the family of birth, from now on dispersed by migrations is insufficiently supported by neighbors or by the enterprise to provide for the needs of the women left alone and their children. At the same time, the political context of legislation on personal status changed with the collapse of the Ottoman Empire, the end of colonial or mandatory periods, and the birth of new nations. At various times, the States elaborated legislation on the family that brought different solutions to a general question posed by divorce, that of the security of women and children.

In Egypt, the law of 1979, known by the name of its instigator, Jihan Al-Sadat, which was rejected by the Supreme Constitutional Court then amended in 1985, put an end to the purely consensual character of marriage by imposing a written contract, registered obligatorily at the *ma'zoun*, the official in charge of questions of marriage and divorce (Fahmi 1986). The public registration of the contract, including the notation of the matrimonial history and social situation of the man, provides the woman with written elements enabling her to exercise her rights in case of divorce. Diverse provisions strengthen the obligatory character of the alimonies that the man is required to pay to the divorced wife and to his children; others stipulate penal sanctions when procedures are not respected. The law also introduces criteria adapted to the new situations created by the emigration of numerous Egyptians to the Gulf since the 1970s. Thus the notion of abandoning the marital domicile is not applied to the wife who cannot accompany her migrant husband. In its initial form (1979), the law finally granted to women the right to ask for a divorce in the case of polygamous remarriage of her husband. This provision, representing the main innovation of the law of Jihan al-Sadat, came under attack from religious circles however, and was abandoned in the revision of 1985, according to which the woman must prove the reality of a material or moral harm she suffered as a result of her husband's polygamy in order to ask for a divorce. A subsequent revision, coming into force in March 2000, established the capacity of a woman to ask for divorce, without limiting it, as the Jihan law had done, to cases of polygamous marriage by the husband: the formula of *khul'* enables her to obtain divorce without the consent of the husband, on condition that she renounces her financial rights[23]. By granting women equal rights to men regarding divorce, Egypt has joined Tunisia, which was until then the only Arab country to have established the equality of the sexes on that matter. Hardly a month later, a small feminist revolution was announced on the judicial terrain: for the first time in the country's history, a woman lawyer applied to become a *ma'zoun* in a district in the suburbs of Cairo[24].

In Syria, it is above all polygamy that has been restricted by the law of 1975, by enabling the judge to require from the husband a strong cause--for example the sterility of his wife--to accept a polygamous marriage. In Tunisia, the personal status code of 1956, a text of a secular look in which there is no mention of Islam, makes polygamy a penal offence and abolishes repudiation, establishing judicial divorce upon the request of any one of the

---

[23] On the debates stirred by that new law, see Tadros (2000).
[24] See Shahine (2000).

two spouses. On the contrary, the Moroccan *Mudawwana* (compilation) of 1957-58, which maintains repudiation, and the Algerian family code of 1984 which stipulates (art. 48) that

> divorce [...] takes place through the will of the husband, by mutual consent between the two spouses, or upon the request of the wife within the limit of the cases provided for in articles 53 and 54 [articles stating certain exceptions]

are very conservative. What all these developments of the law have in common is to subject divorce and its consequences to heavier judicial procedures. In this, they are all likely to have curbed the frequency of divorce.

Imbalance of the Matrimonial System and the Birth of Female Celibacy

Throughout the twentieth century, the duration of marital life has been subjected to two opposite influences: the decline of divorce, which tends to lengthen the duration of the union, and the delay of the age at first marriage, which tends to shorten it. These two phenomena do not respond to the same transformations of society, but they are related in part. The reduction of the rate of divorce produces a paradoxical effect. When individual married families are taken into consideration, it rather provides stability by gradually averting a mode of dissolution that previously constituted a major threat. But once we are interested in the equilibrium of the marriage market, it rather brings more instability. Reducing the frequency of divorces actually amounts to enlarging the non-reabsorbed part of the excess of marriageable women. Given that the other form of regulation, through polygamy, has itself diminished, we must expect that the mechanisms which have produced that excess respond: either because the age difference between spouses is reduced, or because not all women enter the competition for marriage.

The age of women at the time of the first marriage has increased everywhere during the second half of the twentieth century, in particular under the influence of the schooling of girls. In Egypt, the American economist W. Cleland noted as early as 1936 that the proportion of girls below 18 years old who were married[25] had been regularly diminishing from one census to the other--from 484 out of 1000 in 1907, they fell to 393 in 1917 and 348 in 1927. He attributed this to the 1923 law that fixed a legal age of marriage of 16 for girls and 18 for boys. The legislator, he argued, took into account the dangers of early marriage, while the birth of industrial and commercial employment of young women did the rest (Cleland 1936). Cleland overestimated the effect of the law. It may reflect the change in the values of the legislator, or changing external influences on him, but it does not therefore change the practices of the population, especially when no serious penalty accompanies it. At the beginning of the 1950s, an Egyptian researcher addressed again the village habit of marrying girls at the age of 12 or 13, an age at which "they can't have any say as to the determination of their proper destiny" (Ammar 1954).

Sixty years after the law came into effect, the population continues to get round it on a large scale. "In the Governorate of Fayoum and certain regions of Upper-Egypt," the official report presented by Egypt to the Cairo Conference on Population and Development (1994) indicates,

> the proportion of women marrying prior to the legal age is alarming and exceeds 30%; in other parts of Upper-Egypt and in the Governorate of Damietta, it still reaches 20-25%. In 1980-84, 21% of women were less than 16 years old when first married. While this number is high, it represents a significant progress compared to the years 1960-64 when it was 48.3%.[26]

The ministry in charge of population and family welfare, which published these figures on the occasion of an international conference, does not seek to conceal that social progress is still to be accomplished in the country, since in this way it justifies the maintenance of an international support. The civil services of the state which daily collect announcements of marriage and then set up the annual statistics answer to a different logic. Marriages concluded below the legal age, and which either benefit from an exemption or are subject to false declaration of age, do not appear any longer in the publications of those services. Giving the impression of a unanimous

---

[25] Approximated by the proportion of non-single women in the age group 15-19.
[26] National Population Council, Egypt (1993). These figures do not correspond to those of an survey on adolescence conducted in 1998, which gives a much lower percentage of marriage below the legal age (5.8 percent) (Ibrahim & al. 1999).

respect for the law, the first distinguished category, that of people below 20, is named "16-19" for girls and "18-19" for boys. The sheer size of this age group in the marriage statistic (39 percent of all female marriages) indicates that marriages contracted below the legal age are included within it. The marriages concluded at less than 20 years of age, including those below the legal age, are distributed in a very distinctive way in Egypt: they are rare in urban governorates, more frequent in the provinces of the Nile Delta, and they remain the norm in the statistical sense of the most frequent situation in all the provinces of Upper-Egypt (Table 2). Early marriages trace in effect the geography of the shortcomings of public policies--on issues like education and social welfare--and of the barriers to the control of the state and the legal norms which the family opposes.

Between the 1930s and the 1990s, the average age of first marriage had nevertheless increased in Egypt, moving from 18.7 to 21.9 years old for women, and from 25.7 to 28.4 for men.[27] The age difference between the sexes at the first marriage seemed, however, to have hardly diminished: from 7 years in the 1930s it only declined by half a year in 60 years and was still 6.5 years[28] in the 1990s, a norm that seems to transcend social diversity. With a declining divorce rate but an unchanged age difference between spouses, will the market be regulated by the appearance, for the first time, of a substantial number of women never getting married? The last generations for whom this indicator is known, those who are born right after World War Two, show no trace of that: of those born in 1942-1951,[29] 98.8 percent of men and 98.7 percent of women have been married at least once in the course of their lives. This shift should only by evident in subsequent generations, those born in the 1970s, At the beginning of the 1990s, the "total nuptiality rate" (TNR), or the final proportion of persons ever-married in a generation that would be subject throughout its life to the conditions observed over a single year, reached 90.2 percent for men, but only 78.7 percent for women[30]. In other words, if the tendencies observed during the

---

[27] First marriages according to the age of the spouses, see Egypt (1935, 1991).
[28] Taking into account dissolutions of unions and remarriages which take place later in the life of a man than a woman, the age difference between spouses is a little higher than at the moment of the first marriage: it reached 7.5 years in 1995 (National Population Council, Egypt 1996).
[29] Individuals aged 45-54 in the census of 1996.
[30] Indexes calculated on the basis of the marriage statistics of 1991, last available year.

1990s were maintained, there would be 21.3 percent of women who would never marry. This would represent an unprecedented departure from family traditions.

This will probably not happen, for the TNR confounds two developments: a simple delay of the first marriage and a reduction of its final frequency. The first development means that the new generations will be the first to move towards the equality of the sexes in terms of age at marriage, while the second prefigures the appearance of a category of population hitherto unknown in Arab societies: that of women who will never marry. Egypt is less advanced than other countries in this double development[31]. It is late compared with countries such as Kuwait, UAE, Tunisia, and Lebanon, where the tendency of men to marry women of their own age reflects a rapid diminution of the age difference between spouses. It is also late compared with Morocco, where the age of women at the moment of the first marriage approached 28 in cities and reached 25 in villages in 1998/99, while less than a generation ago it didn't exceed 17 years of age[32]. Libya presents the most singular experience. In this country, the publication in 1998 of the first demographic data since a quarter of a century before[33], reported a surprising result for all those who, from the outside, underestimated the social transformations taking place under the regime of President Qadhafi. With just 5 percent of women married by the age of 20 and an average age at first marriage of 29.1, the timing of the first female marriage in Libya has become one of the latest. In the 1965 generation, more than 40% of Libyan women were not yet married at the age of 30. Has the mentality of men changed enough to leave intact their chances to find a husband? Or would these single women rather be facing the results of an incomplete fulfillment of their equality to men: equality before public institutions from which springs in part the delaying of marriage, but not

---

[31] Interviewed in 1998 on what they thought would be the ideal age of marriage (Ibrahim & al. 1999), adolescents (10-19) of the two sexes shared the view that men should be older than women. According to them, 20 years old for women and 25 for men are the ideal ages for the first marriage. The parents of these adolescents express nearly the same opinion (19 and 25).

[32] In 1998 in Morocco, the average ages of the first marriage were 27.9 and 25.0 for women, in urban and rural areas respectively, compared with 17.3 and 17.2 in 1960 (CERED, 1998), and to 32.5 and 29.3 for men (Royaume du Maroc, 2000).

[33] In 1998, the Arab League published the volume on Libya in the "Papchild" survey conducted in ten Arab countries. The last demographic data on the country dated back to the census of 1973.

within the family? In this case, many of these women who are still single at the age of 30 would be at risk of having passed beyond the age at which they might find an available man.

Conclusion

This paper has explored three aspects of marriage, which hide as many paradoxes. The first aspect (section 1), is the statistical interdependence between first marriage, subsequent marriages (polygamous or not) and the rupture of marriage by divorce. The paradox resides here in the fact that the combination of four characteristics of marriage in Arab-Muslim societies-- universality of first marriage, age difference between spouses, existence of polygamy, and frequency of divorce--tended somehow, in the recent past, to tie the stability of the global matrimonial system to the instability of the conjugal union. A single marriage, between two given individuals, depends on all other marriages and on the stability of all of them. Each individual is married within a small circle, that of the persons he/she knows. But the sum of all these marriages is subject to a perfect equilibrium between the sexes in the total marriageable population: this law, an arithmetic one, is opaque for individuals; they are unaware of it. The correspondence between individual choices and this requirement, hidden from the population, is the product of the ensemble of rules, legal or just social, which command marriage and are specific to a given society, or to one or another of its parts. This is the local dimension of marriage.

The second aspect is the growing tendency to reduce the two practices allowing a man to marry several women: polygamy and divorce. While the decline of polygamy is attested by empirical data and confirmed by ordinary discourse, the evolution of divorce is subject to two contradictory evaluations: that of the book-keeping of the civil service, showing its decline, and that of the members of society, who perceive it as growing. The explanation of the paradox probably lies in the effects of divorce, which is getting more and more restrictive for men. The intervention of exogenous elements in judicial provisions and practices, especially under the effect of a growing activism on the part of the international community in different domains touching the situation of women, might have contributed to increasing the consequences of divorce. Together with other factors that equally affected the age of marriage, from the spread of schooling to the transformations of the national economies, this is the global dimension of marriage.

The third aspect is the rise of female celibacy. We usually interpret this through its sociological determinants, such as the increasing duration of schooling for girls, the more widespread practice of a remunerative economic activity before marriage, urbanization with its accompanied increase in housing cost, migration extends the circles of preferential marriage, and the growing expenses of marriage. We can also interpret female celibacy as a corollary of the two previous specificities: the surplus of women to marry, produced by an important age interval between spouses, added to a declining capacity of divorce and polygamy to reabsorb that surplus. The essential question is to know which of the two rules will bend first: that which establishes the universality of marriage, in which case for the first time it is women who will remain single during their lifetime, or that which favors the age difference between spouses, in which case the conjugal union will move towards more equality between spouses, with regard to age at least. In either scenario, we can foresee a sociological change.

References

Ammar, Hamed. 1954. *Growing Up in an Egyptian Village*. London: Routledge & Kegan Paul.

Botiveau, Bernard. 1993. *Loi islamique et droit dans les sociétés arabes*. Paris-Aix-en-Provence: Karthala-Iremam.

Burckhardt, John Lewis. 1831. *Notes on the Bedouins and Wahabys. Collected during His Travels in the East*. 2 volumes. London: Henry Colburn and Richard Bentley.

CERED, Royaume du Maroc, Centre d'Études et de recherches démographiques. 1988. *Situation démographique régionale au Maroc*. Rabat.

Chamie, Joseph. 1986. "Polygyny among Arabs," *Population Studies* 40(1):55-66.

Cleland, Wendell. 1936. *The Population Problem in Egypt: A Study of Population Trends and Conditions in Modern Egypt*. Lancaster PA: Science Press Print Co.

Egypt. 1935. *Statistical Yearbook*.

--------------. 1991. *Statistics of Marriage and Divorce* (Arabic text). Cairo: CAPMAS.

Fargues, Philippe. 1986. "Un siècle de transition démographique en Afrique méditerranéenne: 1885-1985," *Population* 41/2:205-232.

Fahmi, Hoda. 1986. *Divorcer en Égypte. Étude de l'application des lois du statut personnel*. Cairo: Dossier du CEDEJ, n°3.

L. Henry and J. Houdaille. 1978-79. "Célibat et âge au mariage aux XVIIe et XIXe siècles en France," *Population* 33(1):43-84 and 34(2):403-442.

Hoodfar, Homa. 1997. *Between Marriage and the Market. Intimate Politics and Survival in Cairo*. Berkeley: The University of California Press.

Ibrahim, Barbara, Sahar El Tawila et al. 1999. *Transitions to Adulthood. A National Survey of Egyptian Adolescents*. New York and Cairo: The Population Council.

Kateb, Kamel. 1998. "Histoire Statistique des populations de l'Algérie pendant la période coloniale (1830-1962)." Paris: Thèse de doctorat, EHESS.

Lane, Edward William. 1836 [1963]. *Manners and Custom of the Modern Egyptians*. London: Dent, London, and New York: Dutton (Everyman's Library).

Maher, Vanessa. 1974. *Women and Property in Morocco*. Cambridge Studies in Social Anthropology n°10. Cambridge: Cambridge University Press.

Mboria, Lefter. 1938. *La population de l'Egypte*. Paris: Faculté de droit.

Mernissi, Fatima. 1985. *Sexe, idéologie, Islam*. Rabat: Editions Maghrébines.

Mernissi, Salima 1992. "Quelques aspects de la codification du statut personnel marocain" in Jean-Yves Carlier, ed., *Le statut personnel des Musulmans*. Bruxelles: Bruylant.

National Population Council, Egypt. 1993. "Egypt National Report on Population," submitted to the ICPD 1994. Cairo.

---------------. 1996. *Demographic and Health Survey 1995*.

Royaume du Maroc, Ministère de la Prévision Économique et du Plan, Direction de la Statistique. 2000. *Enquête nationale sur les niveaux de vie des ménages 1998/99.*

Shahine, Gihan. 2000. "A Turban--and Heels," *al-Ahram Weekly*, 13 April, No. 477 (http://www.ahram.org.eg/weekly).

Tadros, Mariz. 2000. "The Beginning or the End?" *al-Ahram Weekly*, 9 March, No. 472 (http://www.ahram.org.eg/weekly).

Table 1
Reduction of Divorce and Polygyny Rates in Egypt and Algeria

Egypt	Divorces per hundred marriages	Polygynous marriages per cent
1936-40	26.2	11.4
1941-45	32.4	10.0
1946-50	27.7	9.6
1951-55	26.1	8.4
1956-60	26.6	8.0
1961-65	24.3	7.0
1966-70	22.7	7.4
1971-75	22.0	7.1
1976-80	19.9	6.9
1981-85	18.0	6.5
1986-90	18.2	6.0
1991-95	17.8	5.6

Algeria	Divorces per hundred marriages
1888-90	40.2
1903-04	32.7
1905-09	34.5
1910-14	29.8
1915-19	30.1
1920-24	30.4
1925-29	32.1
1930-34	28.8
1935-39	28.2
1940-44	23.8
1945-49	22.7
1950-54	10.1
1955-59	12.6

Sources: Egypt: annual issues of CAPMAS, *Statistical Yearbook* (before 1954: Statistique Générale de l'Égypte, Annuaire statistique)
Algeria: Gouvernement Général de l'Algérie, Service Central de statistique, *Annuaire Statistique de l'Algérie* (1892 and all years from 1904)

Table 2

Regional Patterns of Nuptiality in Egypt in 1935 and 1991

Governorate	Marriages per 1000 Inhabitants 1935	Marriages per 1000 Inhabitants 1991	Mean Age at First Marriage in 1991 Males	Mean Age at First Marriage in 1991 Females	Early Female Marriages in 1991(%)*	Divorces per 100 Marriages 1935	Divorces per 100 Marriages 1991
Cairo	13.9	7.4	30.3	24.1	20.5	47.2	24.8
Alexandria	12.4	6.2	31.2	24.8	19.0	40.4	23.6
Port Said	17.2	8.0	30.0	24.2	21.7	38.6	28.5
Suez	12.5	9.6	28.9	22.6	29.9	47.0	27.3
Dumyat	11.2	9.8	28.1	21.5	38.2	28.4	17.6
Daqahliya	14.5	9.1	28.2	21.5	39.1	24.5	13.5
Sharqiyya	16.2	8.2	27.8	21.6	37.9	29.0	11.9
Qalyubiya	14.1	7.5	28.0	21.6	38.9	30.1	18.5
Kafr al-Shaykh		7.6	28.1	21.9	35.0		9.8
Gharbiya	15.3	7.9	28.9	22.4	31.9	23.9	14.0
Minufiya	15.0	8.5	28.3	21.7	35.6	25.5	9.8
Buhayra	13.7	6.8	28.2	21.9	38.6	16.8	10.8
Isma'iliya	17.2	9.6	28.9	22.6	31.2	38.6	20.4
Giza	12.9	4.5	27.9	21.7	46.2	31.7	25.7
Bani Suwayf	12.5	8.1	26.6	20.0	58.1	26.4	12.4

Fayum	15.4	8.1	26.3	19.9	59.5	28.7	14.8
Minya	12.7	7.4	26.4	20.3	55.9	19.1	11.4
Asyut	12.5	6.0	27.6	20.9	48.8	19.0	8.9
Suhag	12.2	7.1	27.8	20.8	50.8	17.1	12.2
Qina	12.6	7.1	28.1	20.6	57.4	25.9	16.3
Aswan	10.6	5.8	29.2	21.7	46.9	31.8	20.3
Red Sea	18.7	8.3	29.3	23.1	27.0	36.4	7.7
Wadi al-Gadid	-	8.4	27.4	22.0	30.5	-	21.4
Matruh	-	4.0	36.1	29.2	21.3	-	24.2
North Sinai	-	6.8	30.6	25.3	26.9	-	33.4
South Sinai	-	7.2	36.5	29.1	15.2	-	13.8
Urban Egypt			29.5	23.2	27.4		
Rural Egypt			27.6	21.0	47.0		
Egypt	13.8	7.3	28.4	21.9	39.0	26.9	16.0

* Women aged less than 20 at marriage

Sources: For 1935, Département de la Statistique Générale de l'Etat, *Annuaire Statistique 1935*. Le Caire

For 1991, CAPMAS, *Statistics of Marriages and Divorces 1991*. CAPMAS, 1996 (in Arabic)

ABOUT THE CONTRIBUTORS

Dr. Josette Abdalla is Associate Professor of Psychology, The American University in Cairo (AUC).

Dr. Soraya Altorki is Professor of Anthropology, AUC.

Dr. Philippe Fargues is Director of International Migrations and Minorities Unit, National Institute of Demographic Studies, Paris.

Dr. Nicholas Hopkins is Dean of the School of Humanities and Social Sciences, AUC.

Dr. Barbara Ibrahim is Regional Director, Population Council, Cairo.

Dr. Suad Joseph is Professor of Anthropology, University of California, Davis.

Dr. Zeinab Khedr is Associate Research Professor, Social Research Center, AUC.

Dr. Lilia Labidi is Professor of Clinical Psychology and Anthropology, Faculty of Social and Human Studies, University of Tunis.

Dr. Magued Osman is Research Professor, Social Research Center, AUC.

Dr. Hoda Rashad is Director, Social Research Center, AUC.

Ms. Laila S. Shahd is Research Assistant, Social Research Center, AUC.

Dr. Hania Sholkamy is Visiting Scholar at the Institute for Gender and Women's Studies/Forced Migration and Refugees Studies, AUC.

Dr. Diane Singerman is Associate Professor of Political Science, American University, Washington DC.

Dr. Carol B. Stack is Professor of Anthropology, Graduate School of Education, University of California, Berkeley.

Dr. Sahar El Tawila is Associate Professor, Faculty of Economics and Political Science, Cairo University

Ms. Hind Wassef is researcher on women's issues, youth, and education.

Dr. Laila El Zeini is Associate Research Professor, Social Research Center, AUC.

CAIRO PAPERS IN SOCIAL SCIENCE
بحوث القاهرة فى العلوم الإجتماعية

VOLUME ONE 1977-1978
1 *WOMEN, HEALTH AND DEVELOPMENT, Cynthia Nelson, ed.
2 *DEMOCRACY IN EGYPT, Ali E. Hillal Dessouki, ed.
3 MASS COMMUNICATIONS AND THE OCTOBER WAR, Olfat Hassan Agha
4 *RURAL RESETTLEMENT IN EGYPT, Helmy Tadros
5 *SAUDI ARABIAN BEDOUIN, Saad E. Ibrahim and Donald P. Cole

VOLUME TWO 1978-1979
1 *COPING WITH POVERTY IN A CAIRO COMMUNITY, Andrea B. Rugh
2 *MODERNIZATION OF LABOR IN THE ARAB GULF, Enid Hill
3 STUDIES IN EGYPTIAN POLITICAL ECONOMY, Herbert M. Thompson
4 *LAW AND SOCIAL CHANGE IN CONTEMPORARY EGYPT, Cynthia Nelson and Klaus Friedrich Koch, eds.
5 THE BRAIN DRAIN IN EGYPT, Saneya Saleh

VOLUME THREE 1979-1980
1 *PARTY AND PEASANT IN SYRIA, Raymond Hinnebusch
2 *CHILD DEVELOPMENT IN EGYPT, Nicholas V. Ciaccio
3 *LIVING WITHOUT WATER, Asaad Nadim et. al.
4 EXPORT OF EGYPTIAN SCHOOL TEACHERS, Suzanne A. Messiha
5 *POPULATION AND URBANIZATION IN MOROCCO, Saad E.Ibrahim

VOLUME FOUR 1980-1981
1 *CAIRO'S NUBIAN FAMILIES, Peter Geiser
2&3 *SYMPOSIUM ON SOCIAL RESEARCH FOR DEVELOPMENT: PROCEEDINGS, Social Research Center
4 *WOMEN AND WORK IN THE ARAB WORLD, Earl L. Sullivan and Karima Korayem

VOLUME FIVE 1982
1 GHAGAR OF SETT GUIRANHA: A STUDY OF A GYPSY COMMUNITY IN EGYPT, Nabil Sobhi Hanna
2 *DISTRIBUTION OF DISPOSAL INCOME AND THE IMPACT OF ELIMINATING FOOD SUBSIDIES IN EGYPT, Karima Korayem
3 *INCOME DISTRIBUTION AND BASIC NEEDS IN URBAN EGYPT, Amr Mohie El-Din

VOLUME SIX 1983
1 *THE POLITICAL ECONOMY OF REVOLUTIONARY IRAN, Mihssen Kadhim
2 *URBAN RESEARCH STRATEGIES IN EGYPT, Richard A. Lobban, ed.
3 *NON-ALIGNMENT IN A CHANGING WORLD, Mohammed El-Sayed Selim, ed.
4 *THE NATIONALIZATION OF ARABIC AND ISLAMIC EDUCATION IN EGYPT: DAR AL-ALUM AND AL-AZHAR, Lois A. Arioan

VOLUME SEVEN 1984
1 *SOCIAL SECURITY AND THE FAMILY IN EGYPT, Helmi Tadros
2 *BASIC NEEDS, INFLATION AND THE POOR OF EGYPT, Myrette El-Sokkary
3 *THE IMPACT OF DEVELOPMENT ASSISTANCE ON EGYPT, Earl L. Sullivan, ed.
4 *IRRIGATION AND SOCIETY IN RURAL EGYPT, Sohair Mehanna, Richard Huntington and Rachad Antonius

VOLUME EIGHT 1985
1&2 ANALYTIC INDEX OF SURVEY RESEARCH IN EGYPT, Madiha El-Safty, Monte Palmer and Mark Kennedy

VOLUME NINE 1986
1 *PHILOSOPHY, ETHICS AND VIRTUOUS RULE, Charles E. Butterworth
2 THE 'JIHAD': AN ISLAMIC ALTERNATIVE IN EGYPT, Nemat Guenena

3   *THE INSTITUTIONALIZATION OF PALESTINIAN IDENTITY IN EGYPT, Maha A. Dajani
4   *SOCIAL IDENTITY AND CLASS IN A CAIRO NEIGHBORHOOD, Nadia A. Taher

VOLUME TEN 1987
1   *AL-SANHURI AND ISLAMIC LAW, Enid Hill
2   *GONE FOR GOOD, Ralph Sell
3   *THE CHANGING IMAGE OF WOMEN IN RURAL EGYPT, Mona Abaza
4   *INFORMAL COMMUNITIES IN CAIRO: THE BASIS OF A TYPOLOGY, Linda Oldham, Haguer El Hadidi, Hussein Tamaa

VOLUME ELEVEN 1988
1   *PARTICIPATION AND COMMUNITY IN EGYPTIAN NEW LANDS: THE CASE OF SOUTH TAHRIR, Nicholas Hopkins et. al.
2   PALESTINIAN UNIVERSITIES UNDER OCCUPATION, Antony T. Sullivan
3   LEGISLATING *INFITAH* : INVESTMENT, FOREIGN TRADE AND CURRENCY LAWS, Khaled M. Fahmy
4   SOCIAL HISTORY OF AN AGRARIAN REFORM COMMUNITY IN EGYPT, Reem Saad

VOLUME TWELVE 1989
1   *CAIRO'S LEAP FORWARD: PEOPLE, HOUSEHOLDS AND DWELLING SPACE, Fredric Shorter
2   *WOMEN, WATER AND SANITATION: HOUSEHOLD WATER USE IN TWO EGYPTIAN VILLAGES, Samiha El-Katsha et. al
3   PALESTINIAN LABOR IN A DEPENDENT ECONOMY: WOMEN WORKERS IN THE WEST BANK CLOTHING INDUSTRY, Randa Siniora
4   THE OIL QUESTION IN EGYPTIAN-ISRAELI RELATIONS, 1967-1979: A STUDY IN INTERNATIONAL LAW AND RESOURCE POLITICS, Karim Wissa

VOLUME THIRTEEN 1990
1   *SQUATTER MARKETS IN CAIRO, Helmi R. Tadros, Mohamed Feteeha, Allen Hibbard
2   *THE SUB-CULTURE OF HASHISH USERS IN EGYPT: A DESCRIPTIVE ANALYTIC STUDY, Nashaat Hassan Hussein
3   *SOCIAL BACKGROUND AND BUREAUCRATIC BEHAVIOR IN EGYPT, Earl L. Sullivan, El Sayed Yassin, Ali Leila, Monte Palmer
4   *PRIVATIZATION: THE EGYPTIAN DEBATE, Mostafa Kamel El-Sayyid

VOLUME FOURTEEN 1991
1   *PERSPECTIVES ON THE GULF CRISIS, Dan Tschirgi and Bassam Tibi
2   *EXPERIENCE AND EXPRESSION: LIFE AMONG BEDOUIN WOMEN IN SOUTH SINAI, Deborah Wickering
3   IMPACT OF TEMPORARY INTERNATIONAL MIGRATION ON RURAL EGYPT, Atef Hanna Nada
4   *INFORMAL SECTOR IN EGYPT, Nicholas S. Hopkins ed.

VOLUME FIFTEEN, 1992
1   *SCENES OF SCHOOLING: INSIDE A GIRLS' SCHOOL IN CAIRO, Linda Herrera
2   URBAN REFUGEES: ETHIOPIANS AND ERITREANS IN CAIRO, Dereck Cooper
3   INVSTORS AND WORKERS IN THE WESTERN DESERT OF EGYPT: AN EXPLORATORY SURVEY, Naeim Sherbiny, Donald Cole, Nadia Makary
4   *ENVIRONMENTAL CHALLENGES IN EGYPT AND THE WORLD, Nicholas S. Hopkins, ed.

VOLUME SIXTEEN, 1993
1   *THE SOCIALIST LABOR PARTY: A CASE STUDY OF A CONTEMPORARY EGYPTIAN OPPOSITION PARTY, Hanaa Fikry Singer
2   *THE EMPOWERMENT OF WOMEN: WATER AND SANITATION INIATIVES IN RURAL EGYPT, Samiha el Katsha, Susan Watts
3   THE ECONOMICS AND POLITICS OF STRUCTURAL ADJUSTMENT IN EGYPT: THIRD ANNUAL SYMPOSIUM

4 *EXPERIMENTS IN COMMUNITY DEVELOPMENT IN A *ZABBALEEN* SETTLEMENT, Marie Assaad and Nadra Garas

VOLUME SEVENTEEN, 1994

1 DEMOCRATIZATION IN RURAL EGYPT: A STUDY OF THE VILLAGE LOCAL POPULAR COUNCIL, Hanan Hamdy Radwan
2 FARMERS AND MERCHANTS: BACKGROUND FOR STRUCTURAL ADJUSTMENT IN EGYPT, Sohair Mehanna, Nicholas S. Hopkins and Bahgat Abdelmaksoud
3 HUMAN RIGHTS: EGYPT AND THE ARAB WORLD, FOURTH ANNUAL SYMPOSIUM
4 ENVIRONMENTAL THREATS IN EGYPT: PERCEPTIONS AND ACTIONS, Salwa S. Gomaa, ed.

VOLUME EIGHTEEN, 1995

1 SOCIAL POLICY IN THE ARAB WORLD, Jacqueline Ismael & Tareq Y. Ismael
2 WORKERS, TRADE UNION AND THE STATE IN EGYPT: 1984-1989, Omar El-Shafie
3 THE DEVELOPMENT OF SOCIAL SCIENCE IN EGYPT: ECONOMICS, HISTORY AND SOCIOLOGY; FIFTH ANNUAL SYMPOSIUM
4 STRUCTURAL ADJUSTMENT, STABILIZATION POLICIES AND THE POOR IN EGYPT, Karima Korayem

VOLUME NINETEEN, 1996

1 NILOPOLITICS: A HYDROLOGICAL REGIME, 1870-1990, Mohamed Hatem el-Atawy
2 *IMAGES OF THE OTHER: EUROPE AND THE MUSLIM WORLD BEFORE 1700, David R. Blanks et al.
3 *GRASS ROOTS PARTICIPATION IN THE DEVELOPMENT OF EGYPT, Saad Eddin Ibrahim et al
4 THE ZABBALIN COMMUNITY OF MUQATTAM, Elena Volpi and Doaa Abdel Motaal

VOLUME TWENTY, 1997

1 CLASS, FAMILY AND POWER IN AN EGYPTIAN VILLAGE, Samer el-Karanshawy
2 THE MIDDLE EAST AND DEVELOPMENT IN A CHANGING WORLD, Donald Heisel, ed.
3 ARAB REGIONAL WOMEN'S STUDIES WORKSHOP, Cynthia Nelson and Soraya Altorki, eds.
4 "JUST A GAZE": FEMALE CLIENTELE OF DIET CLINICS IN CAIRO:AN ETHNOMEDICAL STUDY, Iman Farid Bassyouny

VOLUME TWENTY-ONE, 1998

1 TURKISH FOREIGN POLICY DURING THE GULF WAR OF 1990-1991, Mostafa Aydin
2 STAE AND INDUSTRIAL CAPITALISM IN EGYPT, Samer Soliman
3 TWENTY YEARS OF DEVELOPMENT IN EGYPT (1977-1997): PART I, Mark C. Kennedy
4 TWENTY YEARS OF DEVELOPMENT IN EGYPT (1977-1997): PART II, Mark C. Kennedy

VOLUME TWENTY-TWO, 1999

1 POVERTY AND POVERTY ALLEVIATION STRATEGIES IN EGYPT, Ragui Assaad and Malak Rouchdy
2 BETWEEN FIELD AND TEXT: EMERGING VOICES IN EGYPTIAN SOCIAL SCIENE, Seteney Shami and Linda Hererra, eds.
3 MASTERS OF THE TRADE: CRAFTS AND CRAFTSPEOPLE IN CAIRO, 1750-1850, Pascale Ghazaleh
4 DISCOURES IN CONTEMPORARY EGYPT: POLITICS AND SOCIAL ISSUES, Enid Hill, ed.

VOLUME TWENTY-THREE, 2000
1. FISCAL POLICY MEASURES IN EGYPT: PUBLIC DEBT AND FOOD SUBSIDY, Gouda Abdel-Khalek and Karima Korayem
2. NEW FRONTIERS IN THE SOCIAL HISTORY OF THE MIDDLE EAST, Enid Hill, ed.
3. EGYPTIAN ENCOUNTERS, Jason Thompson, ed.
4. WOMEN'S PERCEPTION OF ENVIRONMENTAL CHANGE IN EGYPT, Eman El Ramly

* currently out of print

ملخص

في الآونة الاخيرة ، تراجعت دراسة الأسرة في العلوم الاجتماعية لصالح دراسات النوع على الرغم من التغيرات التي تشهدها الأسرة والتي تؤثر بدورها على المجتمع ككل. من هنا اختارت **مجلة القاهرة في البحوث الاجتماعية** ان تكون الأسرة العربية الجديدة موضوع ندوتها التاسعة التي عقدت في مايو ٢٠٠٠ بالإشتراك مع مركز البحوث الاجتماعية بالجامعة الامريكية بالقاهرة ومجلس السكان والتي خصص هذا العدد لنشر أوراقها.

وقد قامت فكرة الندوة على الجمع بين منهجين مختلفين لدراسة الأسرة ، هما المنهج الديموجرافي و المنهج الاجتماعي والانثروبولوجي الأشمل . وعلى الرغم من التركيز على مصر ، الا ان جانب من هذه الاوراق قام بتقديم دراسات حالة من تونس ولبنان والسعودية ناهيك عن تلك التي اعتمدت على بيانات ديموجرافية من مختلف انحاء العالم العربي. أما من ناحية الموضوع ، فقد تعرضت هذه الأوراق لمختلف القضايا المتعلقة بالأسرة العربية خاصة فيما يتعلق بأمور الزواج والطلاق -- مثل ارتفاع سن الزواج و العنوسة والجوانب الإقتصادية للزواج -- و العلاقات بين الأخوة وأمور الميراث. كما تناولت بعض الدراسات ظاهرة التحول البطئ من الاسرة الممتدة الى الاسرة النووية؛ ومن الزواج كعلاقة تسلطية الى علاقة ندية. وأخيراً كان دور الاسرة في اعادة انتاج النظم الاجتماعية والثقافية في المجتمع ضمن النقاط الرئيسية التي اشتملت عليها ابحاث الندوة.

وبشكل عام يمكن القول ان خلاصة هذه الابحاث تقوم على فرضية ان التغيرات الاقتصادية والتعليمية قد اثرت على سلوك الناس داخل الاسرة والاسرة المعيشية وبين الزوجين. فهناك الآن انماط جديدة من الاسر والاسر المعيشية أو على الاقل هناك تغير في درجة شيوع الانماط التقليدية السائدة ، الامر الذي أدى بدوره الى حدوث تحول آخر في اشكال العلاقات الاخوية. وفي النهاية ، تساهم هذه القيم والمفاهيم والسلوكيات في خلق مجتمع جديد يفرز بدوره مزيد من التحولات في العلاقات الاسرية والزوجية.

حقوق النشر محفوظة لقسم النشر بالجامعة الامريكية بالقاهرة
١١٣ شارع قصر العينى ، القاهرة - مصر.
طبعة أولى: ٢٠٠٣
جميع الحقوق محفوظة. ممنوع اعادة طبع أى جزء من الكتاب أو حفظه بعد تصحيحه أو نقله فى أى صورة و بأى واسطة الكترونية أو ميكانيكية أو تصويرية أو تسجيلية أو غير ذلك بدون التصريح المسبق من صاحب حق النشر.

رقم دار الكتب: ٢/١١٦٧١.
الترقيم الدولي: ٩ ٧٦٣ ٤٢٤ ٩٧٧

بحوث القاهرة في العلوم الاجتماعية

مجلد ٢٤   عدد ١/٢   ربيع/صيف ٢٠٠١

الأسرة العربية الجديدة

تحرير

نيكولاس هوبكنز

قسم النشر بالجامعة الامريكية بالقاهرة
القاهرة   نيويورك